LABOR AND THE SHERMAN ACT

LABOR

AND THE SHERMAN ACT

BY

EDWARD BERMAN, Ph.D.

ASSISTANT PROFESSOR OF ECONOMICS

UNIVERSITY OF ILLINOIS

HARPER & BROTHERS PUBLISHERS

NEW YORK AND LONDON

1930

LABOR AND THE SHERMAN ACT

Copyright, 1930, by Harper & Brothers

Printed in the U. S. A.

First Edition

L-E

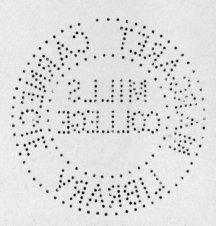

TO

D

.

COMRADE
AND
CO-WORKER

CONTENTS

PART III: ANALYSIS AND CONCLUSIONS

INTRODUCTION

It is evident from the recent rejection, by the Senate of the United States, of the President's nomination to the Supreme Court of Justice Parker, mainly on account of his opinion in the Red Jacket case, that public opinion, or at least political opinion, is attacking the Supreme Court on account of its interpretation of the Sherman and Clayton Acts. When the time is thus reached that the Supreme Court is treated as the highest legislative body of the land instead of merely a judicial body, and when the economic theories of the court are becoming tests of the eligibility of justices, it is a matter of national importance to discover how it came about that the Supreme Court became a supreme legislature.

Mr. Berman's minute investigation is not only a contribution to the subject of conflicts between organized capital and organized labor—it goes to the foundations of the historical supremacy of the Supreme Court in the constitutional system of the American Commonwealth. It is a third chapter in that history, comparable to the former chapters on the slavery and greenback opinions of the court.

Like every issue in economics and politics the same words may be given opposite meanings according to the leanings of the interpreter towards one side or the other of the conflict. Mr. Berman has rightly directed his attention to the meanings of words.

JOHN R. COMMONS

University of Wisconsin

FOREWORD

THE Sherman Law has now been on the statute books for forty years. Probably no law ever passed by Congress sought to regulate more powerful forces. Through the Sherman Law, Congress attempted to canalize the economic processes of the United States within the social policy underlying the prohibition of "restraint of trade or commerce among the several states, or with foreign nations." Obviously aimed to curb the menacing power of concentrated capital, no single factor is more significant in the national economy of the United States since the enactment of the Sherman Law than the steady increase in the growth of industrial combinations.

Superficially, there is ground for the feeling that the thoroughness of condemnation of combinations by the Sherman Law is exceeded only by the extent of its disregard. Whether this impotence is due to the inaptness of law to cope with the forces that underlie modern economic organization, or whether, here again, the seeming impotence of law is really ineffectiveness in administration, is, in the present state of our ignorance, not susceptible of answer. Nor will it do to say that the Sherman Law has in fact been futile, that without it the economic scene would be the same. Because of it, certainly some forms of industrial combination and conduct have not been pursued and the exercise of economic power to some extent has been limited. While such combinations as the United Shoe Machinery Company and the United States Steel Corporation were found by the Supreme Court not within its reading of the Sherman Law, the Court, strangely enough, has condemned certain business arrangements, like price maintenance and trade association activities, for which there appear sound social justifications. That the Sherman Law is not wholly a dead letter to the desires and ambitions of industrial leaders is evinced by the recurring attacks against its pricks. Especially when business goes wrong, the Sherman Law is dressed up to look like a scapegoat. In some quarters, the depression of 1930 is partly at least charged to the Anti-trust Act. In sum, so far as it applies to industrial combinations, both the good of the Sherman Law and its evil have become the football of unillumined speculation. Nor have we scientific data on the deeper question of the effectiveness of law to regulate economic forces.

But in one field of its operations the Sherman law has had clear results. There can be no doubt of its potency as a restraint upon the activities of organized labor. Here again, one must avoid attributing to law the consequences of economic forces and charging to court decrees the inadequacies of labor leadership. But when all discounts are made, it is common ground among students of the Sherman Law, as well as among industrial and labor leaders, that it has been one of the strongest influences counteracting trade unionism in the United States. Yet labor consistently denies that its activities are even subject to the Sherman Law. Though it has been judicially settled since 1908 that labor is amenable to the Sherman Law, the question is not closed for historians and it is wide open in the minds of labor. If moral assent to the authority of a law is of vital importance to the reign of law in a democracy, it can never be too late or too academic to examine the grounds on which rest even so well settled a doctrine as that the Sherman Law governs the activities of labor organizations. And the scope of its applicability, in any event, will continue to present issues of policy for the judgment of courts.

These old questions Professor Berman treats with new thoroughness. The evidence which he marshals will help to inform the reader's judgment. It will also help to shed light upon the legislative process, particularly when it resolves sharp and social economic conflicts by ambiguities which embroil courts, because of their duty of interpretation, in political and social controversies. Professor Berman gives us not only the events and debates which led to the enactment of the Sherman Law. He tells, with a scholar's soberness, the long story by which the judiciary, like a silkworm spinning its own cocoon, has given meaning to the meaningless language of the Sherman Law. The story is deeply important because labor passionately believes that the courts' meaning is unduly restrictive of labor's right of association, if labor is to serve as a just counterpoise to the immunized activities of industrial combinations.

Professor Berman's book deals with one phase of what are perhaps the most contentious issues of modern society. He thus enters a domain in which feelings are intense. The credentials he brings are disinterestedness, long study, and a frank avowal of his own social bias.

FELIX FRANKFURTER

Harvard Law School

PREFACE

The Supreme Court decision in the Bedford Stone case, which was rendered in 1927, was the immediate inducement to the undertaking of this study. The author is convinced that many of our outstanding economic problems are so affected by legal principles, legal traditions, and legal habits of thought, that they can be adequately studied only if one subjects the economic situations produced by the courts and the legislatures to a fundamental social-economic analysis. The present study is a special attempt to make such an analysis.

The author is greatly indebted to a large number of persons who read the manuscript and made many helpful criticisms and suggestions. Those who examined the entire manuscript were as follows: Professor John R. Commons, of the University of Wisconsin; Professor Felix Frankfurter, of Harvard University; Professor H. A. Millis, of the University of Chicago; Dr. E. E. Witte, Chief of the Wisconsin State Legislative Reference Library; Dr. Benjamin M. Squires, impartial chairman in the Chicago Clothing Industry; Professor Selig Perlman, of the University of Wisconsin; Professor Clarence A. Berdahl, of the University of Illinois; Mr. Frederick N. MacMillin, Secretary of the Wisconsin League of Municipalities; and Mrs. Elizabeth Brandeis Raushenbush, of the University of Wisconsin.

The following persons read and made helpful suggestions with respect to parts of the manuscript: Professor Francis S. Philbrick, of the University of Pennsylvania; Professor Jay

Finley Christ and Professor Arthur H. Kent, of the University of Chicago; and Mr. Stanley A. Katcher, of the New York Bar.

The publication of this study is due in part to the generosity of the Committee on Grants-in-Aid, of the Social Science Research Council.

The author wishes to take this opportunity to express his gratitude to Professor Gordon S. Watkins, of the University of California at Los Angeles, and to Dr. Abram Leon Sachar, Director of the Hillel Foundation at the University of Illinois. Their friendship has been a source of inspiration and encouragement for many years.

EDWARD BERMAN.

Urbana, Illinois
September, 1930

PART I

THE INTENT OF CONGRESS

CHAPTER I

THE CONTROVERSY

Introductory.—The Sherman Anti-trust Act of 1890[1] was passed in order to eliminate the evils of trusts and monopolies. That this was the primary purpose of Congress has been recognized by practically all writers who have discussed the law. The second instance in which the act was successfully invoked, however, was in connection with a strike of draymen in New Orleans.[2] From 1890 until the Supreme Court, on March 22, 1897, rendered its first decision under the statute against a business combination,[3] the lower federal courts had held in only one case that such a combination had violated the law.[4] On the other hand they had, during the same period, declared certain activities of labor unions to be violations of the act on twelve different occasions.[5]

---

[1] 26 Stat. 209.
[2] U. S. v. Amalgamated Council, 54 Fed. 994, March 25, 1893. The first instance was in the case of U. S. v. Jellico Mountain Coal Co., 46 Fed. 432, June 4, 1891.
[3] U. S. v. Trans-Missouri Freight Association, 166 U. S. 290.
[4] U. S. v. Jellico Mountain Coal Co.
[5] Only those instances in which the courts rendered opinions which found their way into the official reporters are here considered. The 12 are as follows: U. S. v. Amalgamated Council, 54 Fed. 994 (1893), 57 Fed. 85 (1893); Waterhouse v. Comer, 55 Fed. 149 (1893); U. S. v. Elliott, 62 Fed. 801 (1894), 64 Fed. 27 (1894); Thomas v. Cincinnati, 62 Fed. 803 (1894); U. S. v. Agler, 62 Fed. 824 (1894); In re Grand Jury, 62 Fed. 828

This use against labor of a law intended to restrain business monopolies has continued to the present day. Approximately eighteen per cent of all the cases which have arisen under the Sherman Act have been brought against trade unions or their members.[6] From 1890 to December 10, 1928, labor was the defendant in a total of 83 cases of which record could be found.[7] Labor activities were finally held to have been in violation of the statute in 51 of these cases. (This count does not, of course, include cases which have never been reported, officially or otherwise. The number of such cases is unknown.) The courts have so extended the application of the law that it has been used to prohibit a number of important union activities which were generally considered legal at the time of its passage.[8] Its use has by this time so many precedents, among them numerous ones laid down by the highest court in the land, that nothing short of its substantial amendment or a marked change in the attitude of the courts is likely to free organized labor from its restrictions.

(1894); In re Grand Jury, 62 Fed. 834 (1894); In re Grand Jury, 62 Fed. 840 (1894); U. S. v. Debs, 64 Fed. 724 (1894); U. S. v. Cassidy, 67 Fed. 698 (1895). All but the first two of these cases arose out of the Pullman strike of 1894.

[6] In a recent report of the National Industrial Conference Board on *Mergers and the Law*, 1929, p. 140, a total of 436 suits was said to have been brought under the act up to June 30, 1927. As a result of the present study it appears that 79 suits have been brought against labor during the same period. These figures are probably approximately correct.

[7] See Appendix C.

[8] See below, the Amalgamated Council case, p. 59; the Pullman strike cases, p. 64; the coal cases, pp. 130, 132; the Leather Workers' case, p. 154; and the Brims case, p. 161.

The purpose of this study is to describe the application of the act to labor organizations, to analyze its effects, to evaluate these effects from an economic and social viewpoint, and to suggest to what extent and in what direction the present situation might profitably be changed.

The Controversy.—The present study would lack completeness unless it were preceded by a thoroughgoing inquiry to determine whether or not Congress intended that the Sherman Act should be applied to labor unions. Before proceeding to examine the evidence available in the pages of the Congressional Record it will be of advantage to consider the opinions of persons interested in this question.

In 1910 Samuel Gompers, for many years president of the American Federation of Labor, made the following statement:

We know the Sherman law was intended by Congress to punish illegal trusts and not the labor unions, for we had various conferences with members of Congress while the Sherman Act was pending, and remember clearly that such a determination was stated again and again.[9]

Commissioner Lennon, of the United States Commission on Industrial Relations, a labor leader of long service, in answer to the assertion that the Sherman Act was intended to apply to labor unions, said,

I had the pleasure of interviewing Sen. Sherman and Sen. Plumb and a large number of gentlemen in the Senate at the time, and they did not look upon it in that way.[10]

[9] Gompers, "The Sherman Law. Amend It or End It." *American Federationist.* Vol. 17, No. 3, March, 1910, pp. 197, 202.
[10] *Report of the United States Commission on Industrial Relations,* Washington, 1916, Vol. XI, p. 10654.

Judges and lawyers, however, have held very different views from those of Messrs. Gompers and Lennon. Of all the members of the Fifty-first Congress, which enacted the Sherman Law, the one who was most responsible for its wording was Senator George F. Edmunds.[11] The senator's opinion as to the intent of Congress is therefore important. In November, 1892, he was interviewed in Chicago by a reporter for the Chicago *Inter-Ocean*. The newspaper was especially interested in the senator's opinion as to whether the Sherman Act could be used against the alleged monopolistic activities of the Philadelphia and Reading Coal Company. Mr. Edmunds, in the course of the interview, said that the act was "intended and I think will cover every form of combination that seeks to in any way interfere or restrain free competition, whether it be capital in the form of trusts, combinations, railroad pools or agreements, or labor through the form of boycotting organizations that say a man shall not earn his bread unless he joins this or that society. Both are wrong. Both are crimes, and indictable under the anti-trust law."[12] Also indicative of the senator's attitude is the statement he made on the same occasion, that "it is only a question of time until between tyranny of capital on one side and labor on the other there will be no liberty for the people worth the name." It will

[11] Conclusive evidence that the senator wrote the words of most of the act (he was chairman of the Senate Judiciary Committee which finally reported the measure as it now stands) is presented by the editor of the *North American Review* in a foreword accompanying an article written for that periodical by Mr. Edmunds in 1911. "The Interstate Trust and Commerce Act of 1890," *North American Review*, December, 1911, Vol. 194, No. 673, p. 801.

[12] Chicago *Inter-Ocean*, November 21, 1892, p. 1, col. 1.

be observed that these opinions were expressed before any attempt to invoke the act against labor took place.[13]

The Sherman Act was first applied to labor combinations in the case of United States v. Workingmen's Amalgamated Council of New Orleans, decided by Judge Billings, of the Circuit Court for the Eastern District of Louisiana in March, 1893.[14] The court had to determine whether a strike of draymen which threatened to tie up commerce passing through New Orleans was an illegal restraint of interstate commerce. The decision was an affirmative one, and for the first time an injunction was issued against strikers under the Sherman Act. The court said:

I think the congressional debates show that the statute had its origin in the evils of massed capital; but when the congress came to formulating the prohibition which is the yardstick for measuring the complainants' right to the injunction . . . [the] subject had so broadened in the minds of the legislators that the source of evil was not regarded as material, and the evil in its entirety is dealt with. They made the interdiction include combinations of labor, as well as of capital . . .[15]

In one of the contempt cases arising in connection with the Pullman Strike, that of United States v. Debs, decided by Judge Wood in December, 1894, the court entered into a lengthy consideration, based on the congressional debates, of the intent of Congress. It pointed out that though specific provisos exempting labor from the operation of the act had been discussed at length in the Senate, the bill as finally

[13] The first case recorded in the Federal Reports of an attempt to apply the terms of the act against labor unions was Blindell v. Hagan, 54 Fed. 40, February 9, 1893.
[14] 54 Fed. 994, March 25, 1893.
[15] 54 Fed. 994, 996.

passed contained no such proviso. It seemed clear, therefore, that Congress did not intend to exempt labor.[16]

It was not until February 3, 1908, that the United States Supreme Court, in the case of Loewe v. Lawlor,[17] decided whether the Anti-trust Act was meant to apply to labor. In holding that the secondary boycott conducted by the Hatters' Union violated the act the court made the following statement:

The act made no distinction between classes. It provided that "every" contract, combination or conspiracy in restraint of trade was illegal. The records of Congress show that several efforts were made to exempt, by legislation, organizations of farmers and laborers from the operation of the act and that all these efforts failed, so that the act remained as we have it before us.[18]

The above-mentioned decisions are the precedents upon which federal judges in large part later based their conclusions as to the applicability of the Sherman Act to labor combinations. After the Supreme Court decision in Loewe v. Lawlor one finds almost no discussion on the part of the courts as to the general intent of Congress. It is assumed as a matter of course that labor as well as capital combinations are embraced by the act, and the considerations of the courts are confined to determining whether some particular labor activity is a violation.

Organized labor, however, had objected strenuously to such an assumption, and after the Supreme Court decision in the Hatters' case, it devoted considerable attention to a campaign to secure its exemption from the operations of the statute. As a result of this campaign public discussion

[16] 64 Fed. 724, 744-745.
[17] 208 U. S. 274.
[18] 208 U. S. 274, 301.

during the period frequently centered on the old question of the intent of Congress. In answer to labor's claims numerous authorities defended the conclusions of the Supreme Court. Their opinions are well represented by the statement of Senator Borah on the floor of the Senate on May 5, 1913. He spoke as follows:

There were senators who entertained the view, especially in the first part of the debate, that the bill did not include labor organizations, but I think anyone must come to agree in reading the debate in full that the Senate finally came to the conclusion that its purpose was to prohibit restraint of trade and not to inquire who were the authors of the restraint. While in the first instance it had in view alone the question of industrial combinations, there can be no doubt, it seems to me, but what as they finally came to pass upon it they thought it unsafe to except any class of people from interfering with interstate trade.[19]

[19] *Congressional Record*, Vol. 50, p. 1108. The following references are cited as further examples of this general position: *Report of the United States Commission on Industrial Relations,* 1916, Vol. XI, p. 10654, Testimony of Daniel Davenport; Emery, "Labor Organizations and the Sherman Law," *Journal of Political Economy,* June, 1912, Vol. 20, No. 6, p. 599; Thornton, *A Treatise on the Sherman Anti-Trust Act,* Cincinnati, 1913, Chap. 1; Joyce, *A Treatise on Monopolies and Unlawful Combinations or Restraints,* New York, 1911, p. 175. Both Emery (p. 606) and Thornton (note, p. 679) base their conclusions not only on the congressional debates, but upon the above-mentioned interview of Senator Edmunds in the Chicago *Inter-Ocean* of November 21, 1892. In the course of the debates in the Senate on the Clayton bill Senator Pomerene stated the conclusion, based upon a study of the debates of 1890, that there was clearly no intention on the part of Congress to exempt labor. *Congressional Record,* Vol. 63, pp. 13907-13908, August 18, 1914. A lengthy discussion of the intent of Congress may be found in Mason, *Organized Labor and the Law,* Durham, 1925,

In view of the fact that the weight of judicial authority is clearly on the side of those who believe that the Sherman Act was levelled at labor as well as capital combinations, and in view of the additional fact that since 1893 some of the courts have based their decisions on that belief, it may appear unnecessary to proceed with an examination of the debates in Congress. If such an examination were to result in a corroboration of the above-mentioned belief it would be true that, apart from the historical value of the inquiry, it would add little of importance to the present study. It is believed, however, that a careful examination of all the available evidence gives very slight support to the position that Congress intended to restrain labor unions when it passed the Act of 1890.

Chaps. VII and VIII. On the basis of a study of the congressional debates and the common law Mason concludes that Congress intended that the statute should embrace labor combinations.

CHAPTER II

THE CONGRESSIONAL DEBATES ON THE ANTI-TRUST BILLS

An Earlier Measure.—Prior to the passage of the Act of 1890 numerous unsuccessful bills against trusts had been offered in both houses of Congress. One of the first of these was introduced by Senator Sherman of Ohio on August 14, 1888.[1] It was entitled, "A bill to declare unlawful trusts and combinations in restraint of trade and production." The first section declared that "all arrangements between persons or corporations made with a view, or which tend, to prevent full and free competition . . . or which tend to advance the cost to the consumer of . . . articles, are hereby declared to be against public policy, unlawful, and void." The bill was referred to the Committee on Finance, and was reported out in amended form by Senator Sherman on September 11, 1888.[2]

On February 4, 1889, the bill was debated in the Senate. It was especially criticized by Senator George, who feared it would prevent innocent and necessary combinations of workers and farmers. He declared:

[This] bill not only prevents combinations between farmers to raise the price of their products, but it would (though not so intended by the framers) embrace combinations among work-

---

[1] *Bills and Debates Relating to Trusts,* No. 147, Senate Documents, Vol. 14, 57th Congress, 2nd Session, pp. 11-13, hereafter referred to as *Bills and Debates.*
[2] *Bills and Debates,* pp. 11-13.

ingmen to increase the amount of their wages. For an increase
in their wages would tend to increase the price of the product
to the consumer, and thus would come within the express terms
of the bill.[3]

It should be noted at this point that Senator George was
desirous that labor and farmers' organizations should not be
affected by an attempt to restrain monopolies, and that he
feared that such organizations would be affected by a measure which declared unlawful combinations tending to raise
prices to consumers.

Most of the anti-trust measures introduced prior to the
passage of the Sherman Act, and several introduced thereafter for the purpose of making the restraints upon trusts
more effective, declared against combinations the tendency
of which would be to raise prices. It is significant that nearly
all of these bills directed against price fixing combinations
contained provisos exempting labor and farmers' organizations from their operation. Bills of this kind were introduced on January 30, 1888, by Representative Rayner, on
December 4, 1889, by Senator George, and on December 18,
1889, by Representatives McRae, Blanchard, Anderson, Stewart, Lane, and Perkins. After the passage of the Sherman
Act bills with the same provisions as to price raising combinations and the exemption of labor and farmer organizations were introduced by Senator George and Representatives
Lane, Blanchard, McRae and Tucker in 1892, and by Representative Little in 1898.[4]

The Sherman Bill and the Reagan Amendment.—The
first bill introduced in the Senate on the assembling of the

[3] *Congressional Record,* 50th Congress, 2nd Session, Vol. 20, p. 1459.
[4] *Bills and Debates,* pp. 411, 417, 431, 433, 437, 441, 449, 451, 465,
469, 473, 477, 481, and 581.

Fifty-first Congress was presented by Senator Sherman on December 4, 1889. It was entitled, "A bill to declare unlawful trusts and combinations in restraint of trade and production." It was read twice and referred to the Committee on Finance of which Senator Sherman was chairman. Twice thereafter, on January 14 and on March 18, 1890, Senator Sherman reported amendments to the measure from the Finance Committee.[5]

The most important part of the bill as reported on the latter date was as follows:

Section 1. That all arrangements, contracts, agreements, trusts, or combinations between two or more citizens or corporations . . . of different States, or . . . of the United States and foreign states, . . . made with a view or which tend to prevent full and free competition in the importation, transportation, or sale of articles imported into the United States, or with a view or which tend to prevent full and free competition in articles of growth, production, or manufacture of any State or Territory, . . . or in the transportation or sale of like articles, . . . ; and all arrangements, trusts, or combinations between such citizens or corporations, made with a view or which tend to advance the cost to the consumer of any such articles, are hereby declared to be against public policy, unlawful, and void. And the circuit courts of the United States shall have original jurisdiction of all suits of a civil nature at common law or in equity arising under this section, and to issue all remedial processes, orders, or writs proper and necessary to enforce its provisions. . . .[6]

[5] *Bills and Debates*, pp. 69, 71, 89.
[6] The rest of Section 1 empowered the United States attorneys to prosecute violations of the law. Section 2 provided for suits to recover double damages and costs. The provisions of the bill in its earlier form providing fines or imprisonment in case of violation were now absent.

On March 21, 1890, the bill was extensively debated in the Senate.[7] Senator Sherman made a speech devoted to a defense of the measure as a means of preventing the activities of trusts.[8] There is no evidence in his remarks of an intent to reach any combinations other than those of a business nature, and there is no indication that he believed the proposed bill would reach labor unions.[9]

Senator Hiscock believed the bill to be unconstitutional because it interfered with the jurisdiction of the states. He also pointed out that the bill would affect labor unions. "I hope I shall be told in the progress of this discussion," he asserted, "if there is a labor organization in the United States that is not affected by it. Every organization which attempts to take control of the labor that it puts into the market to advance its price is interdicted by this bill. . . . Will it be said that [labor] combinations are not made with a view of advancing costs and regulating the sale of property? Will it be argued that they do not directly do it?"[10]

On March 24 the Senate again debated the bill.[11] Three days earlier Senator Reagan had offered a substitute.[12] He now suggested that this be added to the Sherman bill. In

[7] *Congressional Record,* Vol. 21, pp. 2455-2474.

[8] *ibid.,* p. 2456.

[9] In the account of the congressional debates which follows no attempt will be made to cover any phase unrelated to the question of the intent of Congress in passing the act. The discussion, therefore, will deal almost entirely with the question as to whether the proposed bill would apply to labor organizations. Actually, this matter occupied but a small part of the debates. Much attention was devoted to a discussion of penalties, whether placing goods competing with those produced by trusts on the free list was not the best remedy, and many similar matters.

[10] *Congressional Record,* pp. 2467-2468.

[11] *ibid.,* pp. 2556-2572.

[12] *ibid.,* p. 2456.

this proposed form Section 3 of that measure provided that anyone engaging in the activities of a "trust" was to be deemed guilty of a high misdemeanor and punishable by fine or imprisonment or both. Section 4 declared that "a trust is a combination of capital, skill, or acts by two or more persons, firms, or associations of persons, or any two or more of them, for either, any, or all of the following purposes": (1) to carry out restrictions of trade, (2) to limit production or to increase or reduce the price of commodities, (3) to prevent competition in manufacture, purchase, sale, or transportation of commodities, (4) to fix a standard or figure for the purpose of controlling prices, (5) to create a monopoly in manufacture, purchase, sale, or transportation, and (6) to enter into a contract of any kind for the purpose of restricting competition, setting prices, etc.[13]

The Views of Senators Teller and George.—Senator Teller discussed the proposed Reagan amendment at length. The following remarks are especially significant:

[There] has recently been organized all over this country what is called the Farmers' Alliance. What is the object and what is the purpose of it? The very purpose of it is to increase the price of farm products, and that I regard as a thing most desirable to be done, and I regard it as absolutely essential to the prosperity of this country . . . Shall it be said that these organizations are forbidden by law? Is it possible that we are putting it in the power of some men to coerce and force the farmers to abandon these organizations? Does anybody believe that these organizations are inimical and hostile to the public welfare?

Senator George interrupted and asked whether the objection which Senator Teller was making to the Reagan amend-

[13] *ibid.,* p. 2560.

ment did not also apply to the Sherman bill as reported from the Committee on Finance. Senator Teller agreed, except that whereas the latter bill provided only for civil proceedings, the Reagan amendment provided criminal penalties.

Senator George asserted that under the bill as reported by the committee "every farmer belonging to one of these alliances would be liable to a civil action and to the recovery of double damages against him for being a member of that organization, the tendency of which is to increase the price of his farm products."

Senator Teller agreed with this and continued his address as follows:

While I am extremely anxious to take hold of and control these great trusts, these combinations of capital which are disturbing the commerce of the country and are disturbing legitimate trade, I do not want to go to the extent of interfering with organizations which I think are absolutely justifiable by the remarkable condition of things now existing in this country.

I believe this bill will go further than that. I believe it will interfere with the Knights of Labor as an organization. While I have never been very much in love with the Knights of Labor, because of some of their methods, yet their right to combine for their mutual protection and for their advancement can not be denied. While in many instances I think they have gone beyond what was legitimate and proper, yet on the whole we can not deny to the laborers of the country the opportunity to combine either for the purpose of putting up the price of their labor or securing to themselves a better position in the world, provided always, of course, that they use lawful means. I do not believe the mere fact of combining to secure to themselves a half dollar a day more wages or greater influence and power in the country can be said to be an unlawful combination.

Senator George interjected another question. Pointing out that the object of the Knights of Labor, as he understood it, was to increase the wages of its members, and that such an increase had the tendency to increase the price of the product of their labor, he asked whether they would not also be included in Senator Sherman's bill, as well as in the Reagan amendment.

Senator Teller answered that in his judgment they were included in both. "I do not believe," he continued, "that anybody in the Senate proposes to go to that extent. It is suggested to me by a Senator near me that the Typographical Union would come in in the same way." At this point Senator Hiscock remarked, "And it would practically include all the trades unions." Senator Teller agreed with this statement.

Senator Reagan defended his amendment and suggested that the Farmers' Alliance and the Knights of Labor would not come under it; "but if they did the way to prevent all such organizations is to strike down first the organizations which give rise and necessity to this local labor association."

Senator Teller continued his address:

I know that nobody here proposes to interfere with the class of men I have mentioned. Nobody here intends that by any of these provisions, either in the original bill or in any amendment; and I have only called attention to it to see if the effort of those who have undertaken to manage this subject can not in some way confine the bill to dealing with trusts which we all admit are offensive to good morals. . . . Therefore, I suggest that the Senators who have this subject in charge give it special attention, and by a little modification it may be possible to relieve the bill of any doubt on this point.

Senator Sherman's View.—When Senator Teller had concluded his remarks Senator Sherman rose to explain the purpose of his bill. He said:

It does not interfere in the slightest degree with voluntary associations made to affect public opinion to advance the interests of a particular trade or occupation. It does not interfere with the Farmers' Alliance at all, because that is an association of farmers to advance their interests and to improve the growth and manner of production of their crops and to secure intelligent growth and to introduce new methods. . . . [Such organizations] are not business combinations. They do not deal with contracts, agreements, etc. They have no connection with them. And so the combinations of workingmen to promote their interests, promote their welfare, and increase their pay if you please, to get their fair share in the division of production, are not affected in the slightest degree, nor can they be included in the words or intent of the bill as now reported.[14]

This assurance did not satisfy the senators who had previously criticized the bill, however. Senator Stewart asked "If you say there shall be no combination the tendency of which shall put up prices, how far would that reach?" In answer to his own question he declared:

[It] would reach to nearly every transaction in life and would be particularly oppressive upon the struggling masses who are making combinations to resist accumulated wealth . . . It is not the intention of anybody here to make that construction of it; we are trying to remedy the evil; but it is very probable that if this bill were passed the very first prosecution would be against combinations of producers and laborers whose combinations tend to put up the cost of commodities to consumers.[15]

[14] *ibid.*, pp. 2560-2562.
[15] *ibid.*, p. 2565.

Senator Teller expressed the belief that the Sherman bill could not destroy the Standard Oil trust. "I do not know— I am not absolutely certain—" he declared, "that under this bill the Knights of Labor, the Alliance, the Wheel, the National League, could be attacked, but it strikes me there is a great deal more probability of their being attacked than there is of these great, strong corporations being."[16]

On the next day, March 25, 1890, the Senate resumed the debates on the anti-trust proposals. Senator George reviewed the history of such proposals since 1888, and denounced the Sherman bill now before the Senate as a sham.[17] A long discussion, participated in by many senators, ensued. The bill was attacked and defended. Throughout the debate the question at issue was whether the proposed bill was satisfactory as a measure to restrain the trusts. There is no trace in the debates of that day or in any of the discussions preceding, which indicates that any senator desired to see a measure passed the effect of which would be to hinder labor unions.

Senator Stewart reiterated his opposition to the Sherman bill. He declared that only by permitting the right of association could monopoly be fought and competition be maintained. "Suppose . . . ," he asserted, "there should be a combination among laborers which would increase the cost of production and increase the cost of all articles consumed. Suppose there should be a combination among the laborers to protect themselves from grasping monopolies; they would all be criminals for doing it."[18]

The Proposal to Refer to the Judiciary Committee.— Much of the debate was concerned with the desirability of referring the Sherman bill to the Committee on the Judiciary.

[16] *ibid.*, p. 2571.
[17] *ibid.*, p. 2598-2601.
[18] *ibid.*, p. 2606.

The proposition was favored by some senators because they desired the advice of that committee as to the constitutionality of the bill and of the amendments which had been offered to it. A number of senators had attacked the measures as being unconstitutional. Considerable objection to Senator George's motion to refer to the committee was made by those who feared that that body was averse to anti-trust legislation and would kill the bill.[19] In order to meet this objection Senator Morgan moved an amendment to Senator George's motion that the committee be instructed to report the bill back to the Senate in twenty days.[20]

Speaking in favor of the proposal that the bill be referred to the Committee, Senator Morgan called attention to the fact that the wording of the Sherman bill was applicable to labor and farmers' organizations. "I do not know," he declared, "of anything that has a greater or more direct impression upon our foreign commerce and our interstate commerce than the price of labor." He continued:

If we pass a law here to punish men for entering into combination and conspiracy to raise the price of labor, what is the reason why we are not within the purview of the powers of Congress in respect to international commerce? Who can answer the proposition as a matter of law?

There is great danger in any direction you look in respect of such a measure as this, and I am afraid to take ground on it until that committee of this body which is charged with the consideration of judicial questions have had an opportunity to report a bill, or, if it can not agree upon a bill, to report that it can not agree.

In spite of this plea the Senate turned down the motion to refer the bill to the committee by a vote of 28 to 15.

[19] *ibid.*, pp. 2600-2611.
[20] *ibid.*, p. 2600.

Immediately afterwards, acting as in Committee of the Whole, it adopted the Reagan amendment[21] as an addition to the Finance Committee bill reported by Senator Sherman. The vote was 34 to 12.[22]

The Labor Exemption Provisos.—At this point Senator Sherman offered a proviso exempting labor and farmers' organizations from the operation of the bill. He declared, "I do not think it necessary, but at the same time to avoid any confusion, I submit it to come in at the end of the first section."[23] As approved in the Committee of the Whole, the proviso was as follows:

Provided. That this act shall not be construed to apply to any arrangements, agreements, or combinations between laborers, made with the view of lessening the number of hours of their labor or of increasing their wages; nor to any arrangements, agreements, associations, or combinations among persons engaged in horticulture or agriculture, made with a view of enhancing the price of their own agricultural or horticultural products.

This amendment was adopted without the formality of a roll call.[24]

The Senate then considered other amendments to the Sherman bill. It adopted one offered by Senator Ingalls which imposed taxes on dealing in futures.[25]

On March 26, the senators, still in Committee of the Whole, continued their consideration of the Sherman bill. Senator Stewart expressed his approval of the proviso ex-

[21] See above, pp. 14-15.
[22] *Congressional Record,* Vol. 21, p. 2611.
[23] The proviso as first presented was taken from S. 6, a measure introduced by Senator George on December 4, 1889, and referred to the Finance Committee. *Bills and Debates,* p. 411.
[24] *Congressional Record,* Vol. 21, pp. 2611, 2612.
[25] *ibid.,* p. 2613.

empting labor and farmers' organizations. Though he considered the bill greatly improved in this respect he criticized that portion of it added by the Reagan amendment because he feared its vagueness might result in putting "everyone in the penitentiary."[26]

Senator Aldrich offered an additional proviso for the purpose of exempting labor. This proviso, to be added after the first section, was likewise adopted without a roll call. It was as follows:

Provided further, That this act shall not be construed to apply to or declare unlawful combinations or associations made with a view or which tend, by means other than by a reduction of the wages of labor, to lessen the cost of production, or to reduce the price of any of the necessaries of life, nor to combinations or associations made with a view or which tend to increase the earnings of persons engaged in any useful employment.[27]

The Encumbering Amendments.—By the time the second proviso was adopted the Senate showed that it did not desire to consider the matter further in serious fashion. It adopted additions to the Ingalls amendment taxing dealing in futures. Amid laughter and joking it passed proposals designed to prevent gambling in stocks and bonds, cotton prints, steel rails, salt, boots and shoes, lead, woolen goods, "whisky and all kinds of intoxicating liquors."

This humorous interlude ended when Senator Gorman declared that though he had opposed referring the bill to the Judiciary Committee the day before, he thought it had been so amended as to make it inoperative and ineffectual, "worse than a sham and a delusion." He urged that the measure be committed to the Judiciary Committee and that it report within twenty days. Senator Sherman asserted that the

[26] *ibid.*, p. 2643.
[27] *ibid.*, pp. 2654-2655.

amendments of the preceding few minutes had been intended to bring the bill into contempt and to defeat it.[28] After further discussion the bill was declared reported to the Senate from the Committee of the Whole.[29]

Believing that the measure as it stood, burdened with so many amendments which were not pertinent, would not be constitutional, Senator Cullom proposed that it be recommitted to the Finance Committee. Senator Sherman, however, objected to the delay which recommitment to his committee would involve. Senator Hawley expressed the opinion that the bill ought to go to the Judiciary Committee, which was capable of straightening it out, and he made a motion to that effect. This motion was opposed by Senator Edmunds, who believed that it was a matter for the Finance Committee to work out.

Thereupon the Senate refused to commit the bill to the Finance Committee by a vote of 31 to 17. It also voted down the proposal to refer to the Judiciary Committee by a vote of 29 to 24.[30]

The Views of Senator Edmunds.—On the next day, March 27, 1890, consideration of the anti-trust bill was resumed. After some discussion as to procedure it was decided to consider one by one the amendments which had been adopted in Committee of the Whole. This procedure was uninterrupted until the proviso offered by Senator Sherman, exempting labor and farmers' organizations, was reached. The Senate then heard the first and only statement against the exemption of labor unions made in all the debates on the bill. Senator Edmunds spoke at length to this effect. The following excerpts are representative of his position:

[28] *ibid.,* p. 2655.
[29] *ibid.,* p. 2657.
[30] *ibid.,* pp. 2659-2661.

We can not shut our eyes, Mr. President, to the fact that if capital combines, if great industrial establishments combine, . . . if the people who own the capital and the plant combine to regulate the price of the wages of laborers, . . . labor is compelled to combine to defend itself; and so the country has been turned and other countries have been turned in the last forty years into great social camps of enemies when they ought to be one great camp of cooperative friends. . . .

But if capital and plants and manufacturing industries organize to regulate and so to repress and diminish, if you please, below what it ought to be, the price of all the labor everywhere that is engaged in that kind of business, labor must organize to defend itself on the other side. . . . However, the whole thing is wrong, as it appears to me; and so I think the amendment is wrong in the same way, which says that while the capital and the plant in any enterprise shall not combine to defend and protect itself, to increase the price of the product of that capital and plant, the labor which is essential to the production of that plant may combine to increase the price of the work that is to be done to make the production of that enterprise.

Senator George asked Senator Edmunds, "Can not the manufacturers of iron practically put up the price, each for himself, according to the cost that it may be to him to manufacture, without combinations?"

To this Senator Edmunds answered, "So he can undoubtedly, and so can the laborer put up the price in any particular mill of his labor in making that iron. They stand in a perfect equality before the law and in morals. . . ."

Having in mind, presumably, the worker's relative weakness in bargaining power, Senator George then asked, "If the capitalists, the manufacturers, are allowed to combine, they having the means to live and support their families during a shut down of the work, what good will a combination of the laborers do when they would starve for want of their daily wages to feed themselves and their wives and children?"

Senator Edmunds answered this question as follows:

It will not do any good at all; and if, on the other hand, the laborers combine and say, "We will not do this thing anywhere in the United States of America unless you give us all there is in it, and you shall not arrange among yourselves not to destroy each other and sell your things by common consent at a higher price than you did before, unless you go to the penitentiary" (for that is prohibited) what good will that do except to break down the whole interests of society and destroy everybody?

The fact is that this matter of capital . . . and of labor is an equation, and you can not disturb one side of the equation without disturbing the other. . . . If we are to have equality, as we ought to have, if the combination on the one side is to be prohibited, the combination of the other side must be prohibited or there will be certain destruction in the end.

The senator then considered the bill from the constitutional point of view. He agreed that monopolies ought to be curbed, but he considered the Ingalls amendment taxing dealing in futures an unconstitutional interference with the police power of the states, and declared that he could not support the bill as it then stood.[31]

On the conclusion of Senator Edmunds' address Senator Hoar spoke in defense of the proviso exempting labor. He said:

I hold . . . that as legislators we may constitutionally, properly, and wisely allow laborers to make associations, combinations, contracts, agreements for the sake of maintaining and advancing their wages, in regard to which, as a rule, their contracts are to

[31] *ibid.*, pp. 2727-2728.

be made with large corporations who are themselves but an association or combination or aggregation of capital on the other side. When we are permitting and even encouraging that, we are permitting and encouraging what is not only lawful, wise, and profitable, but absolutely essential to the existence of the commonwealth itself.

When, on the other hand, we are dealing with one of the other classes, the combinations aimed at chiefly by this bill, we are dealing with a transaction the only purpose of which is to extort from the community, monopolize, segregate, and apply to individual use for the purposes of individual greed, wealth which ought properly and lawfully and for the public interest to be generally diffused over the whole community.

Senator Edmunds responded by reiterating his position as already set forth. "On the one side," he said, "you say that it is a crime and on the other side you say that it is a valuable and proper undertaking. That will not do." If one side is to be authorized to combine the other must have the same right. Otherwise there would be "universal bankruptcy." "Then the laborer, whose interests and welfare we are all so really desirous to promote, will turn around and justly say to the Senate of the United States, 'Why did you go to such legislation as that? . . . When you allowed us to combine and to regulate our wages, why did you not allow the products that our hands produced to be raised in price by an arrangement, so that everybody that bought them might pay the increased price, and everybody that was making them all around for whom we were working could live also?' "

Senator Hoar declared that his remarks were intended neither as an attack upon nor a defense of the bill, but only to point out what he thought Senator Edmunds "failed to appreciate thoroughly, the distinction between the associations of laborers and this class of cases at which this bill aims."

Reference to the Judiciary Committee.—Senator Platt criticized the bill in general and asserted that much of it was probably unconstitutional. He continued as follows:

I am sorry, Mr. President, that we have not had a bill which had been carefully prepared, which had been honestly prepared, which had been thoughtfully prepared, to meet the object which we all desire to meet. The conduct of this Senate for the past three days—and I make no personal allusions—has not been in the line of the honest preparation of a bill to prohibit and punish trusts. It has been in the line of getting some bill with that title that we might go to the country with. . . .

. . . Every effort to refer this bill to any committee that would give it careful and honest consideration has been voted down in the Senate, and it is better to vote the bill down than it is to go to the people with a measure which shall resemble the apples which grow in the region of the fated plain on which once stood the city of Sodom.

Immediately after Senator Platt had finished, Senator Walthall moved to refer the bill and the amendments to the Committee on the Judiciary with instructions to report within twenty days. The motion was at once put to the Senate, and a roll call showed it adopted by a vote of 31 to 28, 23 members being absent. With the bill thus committed the debates ended.[32]

The Judiciary Committee Bill.—The Judiciary Committee used only a fraction of the time given it by the Senate. On April 2, 1890, the chairman, Senator Edmunds, reported the Sherman bill with the recommendation that everything after the enacting clause be stricken out and that the measure formulated by the committee be substituted. As thus re-

[32] *ibid.*, pp. 2728-2731.

ported the bill was identical with the so-called Sherman Act as it now stands. The most important sections of the measure were as follows:[33]

Section 1. Every contract, combination in the form of trust or otherwise, or conspiracy, in restraint of trade or commerce among the several States, or with foreign nations, is hereby declared to be illegal. Every person who shall make any such contract or engage in any such combination or conspiracy, shall be deemed guilty of a misdemeanor, and, on conviction thereof, shall be punished by fine not exceeding five thousand dollars, or by imprisonment not exceeding one year, or by both said punishments, in the discretion of the court.

Section 2. Every person who shall monopolize, or attempt to monopolize, or combine or conspire with any other person or persons, to monopolize any part of the trade or commerce among the several States, or with foreign nations, shall be deemed guilty of a misdemeanor, and, on conviction thereof, shall be punished by fine not exceeding five thousand dollars, or by imprisonment not exceeding one year, or by both such punishments, in the discretion of the court.

Section 4. The several circuit courts of the United States are hereby invested with jurisdiction to prevent and restrain violations of this act; and it shall be the duty of the several district attorneys of the United States, in their respective districts, under the direction of the Attorney-General, to institute proceedings in equity to prevent and restrain such violations. . . .

Section 7. Any person who shall be injured in his business or property by any other person or corporation by reason of anything forbidden or declared to be unlawful by this act, may sue therefor in any circuit court of the United States in the district in which the defendant resides or is found, without respect to the amount in controversy, and shall recover threefold the dam-

[33] See Appendix A for the complete copy.

ages by him sustained, and the costs of suit, including a reasonable attorney's fee.

The Sherman bill had been entitled, "A bill to declare unlawful trusts and combinations in restraint of trade and production." The Judiciary Committee proposed the following title instead, "A bill to protect trade and commerce against restraints and monopolies."

Senator Edmunds as well as other members of the committee asserted their general approval of the bill, though each would have preferred some changes or additions here and there.[34]

On April 8 the Senate, acting in Committee of the Whole, took up the consideration of the Judiciary Committee substitute. Senator Sherman made the following statement:

I do not intend to open any debate on the subject, but I wish to state that, after having fairly and fully considered the amendment proposed by the Committee on the Judiciary, I shall vote for it, not as being precisely what I want, but as the best under all the circumstances that the Senate is prepared to give in this direction. Therefore, without enlarging or entering into debate, I shall vote for the proposition of the Judiciary Committee as it stands.

The substitute bill was then agreed to in the Committee of the Whole and reported to the Senate.[35]

In the course of the general discussion Senator Hoar, who was a member of the Judiciary Committee, made the following remarks:

The complaint which has come from all parts and all classes of the country of these great monopolies, which are becoming not only in some cases an actual injury to the comfort of ordinary

[34] *Congressional Record,* Vol. 21, p. 2901.
[35] *ibid.,* p. 3145.

life, but are a menace to republican institutions themselves, has induced Congress to take the matter up. I suppose no member of this body who remembers the history of the processes by which this bill reached the shape in which it went to the Judiciary Committee will doubt that the opinion of Senators, themselves, of able and learned and experienced lawyers, were exceedingly crude in this matter.

Now the Judiciary Committee has carefully and as thoroughly as it could agreed upon what we believe will be a very efficient measure, under which one long forward step will be taken in suppressing this evil. We have affirmed the old doctrine of the common law in regard to all interstate and international commercial transactions, and have clothed the United States courts with authority to enforce that doctrine by injunction.[36]

In the belief that small farmers and others injured by the trusts might thus more easily get relief, Senator Reagan offered an amendment to Section 7, providing that suit for recovery of damages might be brought in "any State court of competent jurisdiction as well as in the federal circuit courts," without respect to the amount in controversy.[37]

Senator Hoar believed this amendment would be unconstitutional. Nevertheless Senator George, who was also a member of the Judiciary Committee, defended the Reagan proposal and offered an amendment of his own providing that plaintiffs with small interests might combine to bring a united suit for damages.[38] An active debate ensued with respect to these proposals, opposition to them being led by Senators Edmunds and Morgan. Senator George defended them and declared his belief that unless they were adopted "not one suit [would] ever be brought under this seventh section by any person who is simply damaged in his char-

[36] ibid., p. 3147.
[37] ibid., pp. 3146, 3150.
[38] ibid., pp. 3147-3148.

acter as consumer." Though he felt the bill would be weak without his amendment and that of Senator Reagan, he did "not mean to say that this bill ought not to pass." "I believe it ought to pass," he said, "whether amended as proposed by the Senator from Texas [Reagan] and myself or not."

When the Reagan and George amendments were put to a vote of the Senate they were both rejected.[39] Several further amendments were offered but were also rejected.

The Judiciary Committee measure was then read for the third time and was finally passed by the Senate. The vote was 52 for and one against the bill, 29 members being absent.[40]

It should be noted that absolutely no mention was made in the Senate debates, after the Judiciary Committee had reported, of the applicability of the bill to labor and farmers' organizations. The entire attention of the senators appeared to be directed to a single question, "Was or was not the measure well suited to restrain the undesirable activities of business combinations?" In view of the fact that the applicability of the original Sherman bill and of the Reagan amendment to labor and farmers' organizations was much in the foreground in the debates on those measures, the silence concerning this matter in the debates on the Judiciary Committee substitute should be considered pertinent. Its relation to the question of whether Congress intended the Anti-trust Act to apply to labor will receive the necessary consideration in the following chapter.

The Bill in the House of Representatives.—The debates on the anti-trust bill which took place in the House had

[39] *ibid.,* pp. 3148-3151.

[40] The only vote cast against the bill was that of Senator Blodgett, who had taken no active part in the anti-trust debates. *Congressional Record,* Vol. 21, p. 3152.

nothing to do with the possible application of the measure to labor and farmers' organizations. This is not surprising, in view of the fact that the measure before the House was that reported by the Senate Judiciary Committee, rather than the Sherman bill as reported from the Senate Finance Committee. The former bill, as passed in the Senate on April 8, was read and debated in the House on May 1, 1890.

Although much discussion ensued, a considerable part of it critical of the Senate measure, the House accepted only one amendment. This was offered by Representative Bland. Its purpose was to add to the bill a section outlawing every contract or agreement for the purpose of preventing competition in goods shipped in interstate commerce, or of preventing competition in interstate transportation. Having adopted this proposal the House, on May 1, 1890, passed the Senate bill as amended, without the formality of a roll call.[41]

The amended bill was thereafter considered by a conference committee of both houses, and was the subject of further debate on the floors of Congress. After considerable delay the House agreed with certain senators who believed that the House amendment was unnecessary, since its objects could be secured by the enforcement of the provisions of the Senate bill directed against restraints of trade and commerce and against monopolies. As a result the bill was finally passed in the form in which it first came from the Senate. The date of passage in the House was June 20. The bill became law on being signed by the President on July 2, 1890.[42]

[41] *ibid.*, pp. 4088-4104.

[42] The later debates in the House and Senate antecedent to the final adoption of the Judiciary Committee bill are reported in the

It has already been pointed out that there was no discussion in the House of Representatives as to whether the Senate bill applied to farmers' and labor unions. Such organizations were mentioned, however. Representative Stewart, in the debates of June 11, 1890, criticized the Bland amendment because he thought it would prevent all agreements between railroads. He expressed the opinion, since widely accepted, that unrestricted competition among the railroads was harmful to all classes. In the course of his argument he made the following remarks:

Why do the laborers organize and combine to put up the price of labor, and so enhance the cost of everything to the consumer? Because of excessive competition. Yet my friend from Missouri [Rep. Bland] does not propose to apply any remedy in that direction. Nothing more largely affects the cost of articles to every consumer . . . than the combinations of labor. Who complains of it? I do not. I think the laborer is justified, where competition is excessive . . . in entering into combinations for self protection . . .

I understand that the Farmers' Alliance—and I think they were right, they were wise in it—entered into a sort of combination to withhold their products from the markets and enhance their prices. . . .

But what leads the farmers of Kansas and everywhere else to make a combination? . . . They were driven to it by competition.[43]

A careful examination of the House debates fails to produce any other extended references to labor and farmers' organizations. It appears significant that the foregoing discussion by Representative Stewart assumed as a matter of

Congressional Record, Vol. 21, pp. 4123-4124, 4559-4560, 4598-4599, 4735, 5950-5961, 5981-5983, 6116-6117, and 6312-6314.
[43] ibid., p. 5956.

course that the Judiciary Committee bill did not extend to such organizations, and that Mr. Stewart, who represented the House on the conference committee which negotiated the final agreement as to the adoption of the Anti-trust Act, declared that he had no objection to labor and farmers' organizations.

CHAPTER III

THE INTENT OF CONGRESS

It is now essential to give thorough consideration to the Senate debates in order to test the conclusions of judges and other legal writers that the Sherman Act was intended to reach labor organizations. It should be clear by this time that the "intent of Congress" resolves itself into the "intent of the Senate"; since the deliberations which finally resulted in the wording of the bill as it became law and all consideration as to whether the proposed Sherman bill applied to labor and farmers' unions were confined to that body.[1]

The Significance of the Omission of the Provisos.—Of all the reasons for the belief that Congress intended the Sherman Act to apply to labor organizations, the most important and most frequently mentioned one is that when the Senate passed the measure with the labor provisos eliminated it did so because it had concluded that labor should not be exempted.[2] To what extent is this contention a valid one? In order to answer this question the nature of the bill to which the provisos were attached must be noted.

[1] See above, pp. 31-34.

[2] For statements of this argument see Loewe v. Lawlor, 208 U. S. 274, 301; Emery, "Labor Organizations and the Sherman Law," *Journal of Political Economy,* Vol. 20, No. 6, p. 599; Joyce, *A Treatise on Monopolies and Unlawful Combinations or Restraints,* New York, 1911, p. 175; Senator Pomerene, in the *Congressional Record,* Vol. 63, pp. 13907-13908, August 18, 1914; Mason, *Organized Labor and the Law,* Durham, 1925, pp. 122-127.

The Sherman bill as it was reported from the Finance Committee, and the Reagan amendment to that bill, prohibited all combinations the effect of which was to increase the prices of commodities to consumers.[3] It was this provision against price raising which the senators who feared the effect of the proposals on labor and farmers' organizations had in mind. Criticism on this ground was expressed by Senators Hiscock, Teller, George, Stewart, and Morgan. Each of these senators pointed out that such organizations tended to increase prices, and hence would be unlawful.[4]

On March 25, Senator Sherman, though he thought it unnecessary, offered a proviso exempting labor and farmers' organizations. This was adopted in the Committee of the Whole without a roll call.[5] It was so worded as to meet the objection that the anti-price raising provisions would embrace labor and farmers' unions. A similar purpose was in the mind of Senator Aldrich, when, on March 26, he proposed a further proviso, one of the clauses of which exempted "combinations or associations made with a view or which tend to increase the earnings of persons engaged in any useful employment." This proviso was also adopted without a roll call in the Committee of the Whole.[6]

When Senator Edmunds, on March 27, made his remarks against the inclusion of the Sherman proviso, he likewise directed his attention to the effect of labor organizations upon prices. As will be recalled, he objected to a bill which permitted labor to combine to raise wages and thus costs,

[3] See pp. 12-15 above; *Bills and Debates,* p. 89; *Congressional Record,* Vol. 21, p. 2560.
[4] See Chapter II.
[5] *Congressional Record,* Vol. 21, pp. 2611-2612.
[6] *ibid.,* pp. 2654-2655.

but which at the same time, in his belief, forbade the combination of employers to pass these costs to the consumers.[7]

Thus, almost every mention of the applicability of the Sherman bill to labor and farmers' organizations dealt with the anti-price raising prohibition and its effect upon such organizations.

When the Judiciary Committee reported the final bill to the Senate there were no provisos exempting labor and farmers' unions. Is it not likely that they were not reported because they were thought unnecessary? The final bill declared unlawful combinations in restraint of interstate trade and commerce, and monopolies in or attempts to monopolize such trade and commerce. It said nothing about combinations to increase prices. The labor provisos exempted certain combinations whose tendency it was to increase prices. Why should such provisos be included in the new bill?

It may be said that any combination which raised the prices of goods in interstate trade was intended to be considered a combination in restraint of interstate trade; and that since labor organizations having this effect were not specifically exempted in the final bill, it was intended that they should be included. It is, of course, conceivable that the Judiciary Committee may have reasoned to this effect, though there is no evidence to prove it.

The Position of the Senators Who Supported Labor Exemption.—The foregoing conclusion is further supported by other considerations. The Senate, after the final bill was reported from the Judiciary Committee, was the scene of extended debates. Many speeches were made in favor of the bill and some in opposition to it, but the question of its applicability to labor and farmers' organizations was not mentioned, though it had been extensively discussed in the

[7] *ibid.*, pp. 2727-2728.

earlier debates on the Sherman bill. This is significant if one considers the attitude of those senators who objected to the earlier measure because they thought it would include labor unions.

Senator George, who desired to amend the final bill to facilitate the bringing of minor suits, and who was probably the most outstanding critic of the Sherman bill because of its applicability to labor, declared that he would support the Judiciary Committee bill.[8] Senator Hoar, who had eloquently defended the Sherman proviso against Senator Edmunds' criticism, actively supported the final measure.[9] Senator Sherman, who had not wished his own bill to reach labor, also declared his support of the new bill.[10]

None of the senators who had supported labor criticized the bill for its applicability to labor unions, nor did they speak a word which implied that they thought unions would be affected. None of them cast a vote against it. Senators Teller, Stewart, Hoar and Sherman voted in favor of it. Senators George, Hiscock and Aldrich were absent when the roll was called.[11] It should be noted, further, that Senators George and Hoar, determined supporters of labor unions, were members of the Judiciary Committee which drew up the final bill, were present at its deliberations, and supported the bill on the floor of the Senate.

What significance do these facts have with respect to the intent of Congress? If one adopts the conclusion that the elimination of the provisos meant that the Senate intended to have the final bill apply to labor one must assume a complete change of mind on the part of five senators be-

[8] ibid., pp. 3148-3151.
[9] ibid., p. 3147.
[10] ibid., p. 3145.
[11] ibid., p. 3152.

tween the time the Sherman bill was referred to the Judiciary Committee and the time that committee reported its own measure. (Since Senators Hiscock and Aldrich took no active part in the debate on the final bill and were absent when it was voted on, they are not included.) If these senators did change their minds there is no evidence to indicate it.

Senator Edmunds' Position.—Some of those who insist that the elimination of the labor provisos showed an intention to include labor combinations lay much stress on the fact that Senator Edmunds objected to the exemption of unions on the floor of the Senate, that he was chairman of the Judiciary Committee and actually the author of most of the final bill,[12] and that on November 21, 1892, in a public interview, and before the bill was applied by the courts to labor unions, he had declared that the act would extend to them.[13]

This contention proves at the utmost only that Senator Edmunds desired that the final bill should apply to labor organizations; it does not prove that the Senate as a whole desired this. The senator was the only member of either house of Congress who expressed an objection to the exemption of labor unions. Opposed to his view was that of eight other senators (including Senator Morgan) expressed on the floors of Congress. If he was a member of the Judiciary Committee which framed the final bill so also were Senators Hoar and George, who actively supported labor unions, and who expressed disagreement with Senator Edmunds'

---

[12] *North American Review,* December, 1911, p. 801.
[13] Chicago *Inter-Ocean,* November 21, 1892. James A. Emery emphasizes the above-mentioned interview as evidence of the fact that Congress intended the Anti-trust Act to apply to labor. *Journal of Political Economy,* June 1912, pp. 599, 606.

position as soon as he stated it.[14] As a matter of fact there is no direct proof that Senator Edmunds, at the time he wrote most of the final bill, thought that he was wording it so that labor would be included. His own criticism of the labor proviso was exclusively concerned with the matter of price raising. The bill which he reported to the Senate made no mention of price raising. Finally, supposing it to be true that the senator really did intend that his bill should extend to labor unions, it is surely significant, as Dr. E. E. Witte has said, that "he most scrupulously kept this view to himself and did not bring it to the attention of the Senate."[15]

Why was the Bill Referred to the Judiciary Committee? —It may be asserted that when the Senate, after listening to a vigorous attack by Senator Edmunds against the proviso exempting labor from the terms of the Sherman bill, decided, on March 27, 1890, to refer that bill to the committee of which the senator was chairman, there was implied a belief that the Edmunds argument was well made.

Reference to the Judiciary Committee came after the debates had shown that the Sherman bill was encumbered with many amendments which were not pertinent or were probably unconstitutional. The adoption of the Reagan and Ingalls amendments, and such other provisions as those pro-

[14] *Congressional Record,* Vol. 21, p. 2727 et seq.
[15] The author desires to acknowledge the debt owed to Dr. E. E. Witte, of Madison, Wisconsin. In 1914 Dr. Witte was asked by the United States Commission on Industrial Relations to write a report on the question, "Was the Sherman Anti-trust Act intended by its framers to apply to organized labor?" This report is the most satisfactory treatment of the question which has been found. Unfortunately it has not been published. The writer is grateful for the opportunity granted him to consult the report. It has yielded him several significant suggestions, and its conclusions are identical with those here reached.

hibiting gambling in articles ranging from salt to "whisky and all kinds of intoxicating liquors,"[16] so greatly confused matters that reference to some committee seemed essential. What committee was better fitted to straighten out such a tangled measure and to consider its constitutionality than the Judiciary Committee?

Two of the staunchest defenders of labor unions, Senators George and Hoar, were members of the Judiciary Committee. The fact that Senator Edmunds was its chairman is no stronger evidence that the Senate desired the committee to produce a bill embracing labor unions than is the fact that Senators George and Hoar were members of it evidence that the Senate desired the opposite.

Senators George and Teller, who did not wish the Sherman bill to embrace labor, voted in favor of referring to the Judiciary Committee. On the other hand, Senators Sherman and Hoar, who were also supporters of labor, voted against the motion to refer. Senator Edmunds opposed reference to his own committee.[17] This distribution of votes indicates that reference to the committee had no relation to Senator Edmunds' opinion as to whether the bill should embrace labor.[18]

The Difference Between "Restraint of Trade" and "Restraint of Competition."—Professor Alpheus T. Mason,[19] in an effort to show that the Anti-trust Act was intended to embrace trade unions, places great emphasis upon the fact that the final bill declared against "restraints

[16] *Congressional Record*, Vol. 21, p. 2655.

[17] *ibid.*, p. 2731.

[18] Senators Hiscock, Stewart and Aldrich, who had also supported labor exemption, were absent when the Senate voted to refer to the Judiciary Committee.

[19] *Organized Labor and the Law*, Chaps. 7 and 8.

of trade," rather than against agreements preventing "full and free competition." The latter phrase, but not the former, appeared in the Sherman bill as it came from the Finance Committee. Professor Mason asserts that if the final bill had been limited to a prohibition of restraints on competition it would have clearly indicated the intention of the Senate to confine the operations of the measure to business combinations.

The term "competition," he explains, has to do with relationships on a single economic plane. The term "trade," however, embraces relationships between persons on a single, but also on different, economic planes. "Restraint of trade" is thus much more inclusive than "restraint of competition." For example, if a group of manufacturers combined and effected a monopoly there would exist a "restraint of competition." If a combination of workers carried out a secondary boycott, which necessarily embraced several economic planes, since it affected the sale of the manufacturers' products, there would exist a "restraint of trade" rather than a "restraint of competition." "Restraint of trade," being inclusive in meaning, would apply to both of the combinations above described.

According to Professor Mason, the Sherman bill, condemning as it did agreements to prevent "full and free competition," showed that Senator Sherman had no intention of including labor unions. It was the Judiciary Committee bill which passed the Senate, and that bill declared against "restraint of trade," thus indicating an intention to embrace labor organizations as well as business combinations. Furthermore, the bill as passed condemned "conspiracies in restraint of trade," and labor unions had been condemned as such under the common law for many years. Since the difference between "restraint of trade" and "restraint of competition" was well known, and since there were such excellent lawyers in Congress, the intention to include labor appears very clear, according to Professor Mason.[20]

He puts the matter as follows:

Had it been the intention of the framers to confine [the operation of the act] to the eradication of the trust evil, what an easy matter that would have been! That object could have been admirably achieved by the use of the phrase "restraint of competition" rather than "restraint of trade." The fact that the framers preferred to use the one phrase rather than the other cannot be dismissed lightly as an aberration, for so to do is to impute to them less knowledge of the common law than a reading of the congressional debates would warrant.[21]

This argument of Professor Mason's is not convincing. If he limited himself exclusively to a demonstration that the Anti-trust Act contained phraseology which the courts, paying no attention to the purpose of Congress, might interpret to embrace labor unions, there would be little quarrel with him. The doctrine of "conspiracy in restraint of trade" had truly long enough been used against labor unions. But when he assumes that the use of that term was proof that the framers of the Anti-trust Act desired it to embrace labor, he comes to a conclusion which does not seem warranted by the facts.

The title of the Sherman bill, which condemned so-called "restraints of competition," was "A bill to declare unlawful trusts and combinations in restraint of trade and production." It had this title from the time it was introduced by Senator Sherman on December 4, 1889, until it was referred to the Judiciary Committee on March 27, 1890. This was its title, therefore, during all the discussions on whether the bill

[20] *ibid.,* Chap. 8.
[21] *ibid.,* p. 142.

would apply to labor. If the Senate, when it passed the final bill containing a denunciation of "restraint of trade," meant, by including such a denunciation, to have the bill embrace the acts of labor unions, it is fair to assume that Senator Sherman meant the same thing when he entitled his bill one to declare unlawful "combinations in restraint of trade and production." Yet, as he expressly declared on the floor of the Senate, he did not believe that it embraced labor unions.[22]

If, as Professor Mason asserts, the Sherman bill with its declaration against agreements to prevent "full and free competition" did not "militate in the slightest degree against the activities of organized labor,"[23] and if, furthermore, it would be unwarranted to impute to the framers of the act ignorance as to the difference between "restraint of trade" and "restraint of competition,"[24] how can one explain the frequently expressed belief of numerous senators that the original bill would embrace labor unions? It is already sufficiently clear both from the present chapter and the preceding one that these senators, despite the declaration against restraints of competition, feared that the bill's provisions against price raising extended to labor unions, and that only a specific exemption of such organizations would safeguard them in their attempts to increase wages. If the Senate had known about the meaning of "restraint of competition" as Professor Mason explains it, it would have realized that all fear that the Sherman bill would reach labor unions was groundless. If it had known this, it would certainly not have gone to the extent of accepting provisos the purpose of which was to exempt labor.

The Senate debates show clearly that both Senators George

[22] See above, p. 18.
[23] Mason, op. cit., p. 121.
[24] ibid., p. 142.

and Hoar were regarded by their colleagues as legal authorities. They were both members of the Judiciary Committee. They were both staunch supporters of labor unions. They both criticized the Sherman bill, despite the fact that it was directed against restraints of competition, and thus, in Professor Mason's view, did not embrace labor unions. They both supported and voted for the final bill, despite the fact that it was directed against restraints of trade, and thus, in Professor Mason's view, did embrace labor unions.

In view of the foregoing considerations it is difficult to see how any support can be given to the view that the choice of the term "restraint of trade" indicates a purpose on the part of its framers to extend the act to labor unions.

Professor Mason makes an unjustifiable assertion that Senator George was of the opinion that the Judiciary Committee bill would embrace labor combinations. This assertion is given full consideration in a footnote.[25]

[25] On p. 129 of *Organized Labor and the Law* Professor Mason writes that "it is doubtless true that when the members of the Senate judiciary committee wrote into the first section of the bill the language which appears in the Sherman Act today, they did so after deliberation and with full consciousness that they were employing words broad enough to embrace combinations of both capital and labor." He declares that Senator George was clearly of the same opinion. As proof of this assertion the Senator's remarks on the floor of the Senate are quoted (p. 130). Let us compare this quotation with the portion of the *Congressional Record* from which it is presumably taken. In order to facilitate comparison the two items are given in parallel columns, the direct quotation from the *Congressional Record* on the left, the quotation as reported by Professor Mason on the right.

Cong. Rec., Vol. 21, p. 3150	Mason, footnote, p. 130.
It is very well to talk about the symmetry of the work of the	It is very well to talk about the symmetry of the work of the

Judiciary Committee, but when you pass a bill by which you throw the poor unlettered and unskilled American farmer and American mechanic and American laborer, who are the great sufferers by these trusts and combinations, unaided, single-handed, against these large corporations, you just simply pass a bill that will amount to nothing, and I predict—and I put it on the record now as my deliberate judgment—that not one suit will ever be brought under this seventh section by any person who is simply damaged in his character as consumer. I repeat it. I do not propose silently to sit here and be a silent partner, an assenting partner, to the enactment of what I know to be, so far as a remedy to the real parties injured by these trusts is concerned, a sham, a snare, and a delusion.

Judiciary Committee, but when you pass a bill by which you throw the poor unlettered and unskilled American farmer, and American mechanic and American laborer, who are sufferers by these trusts and combinations, unaided, single handed, against large corporations, you simply pass a bill which will amount to nothing. . . .

I do not propose silently to sit here and be a silent partner to the enactment of what I know to be, so far as a remedy to the real parties injured by these trusts is concerned, a sham, a snare, and a delusion.

The excerpt contained in the column on the right is the complete quotation as it is given by Professor Mason. The whole excerpt is run together by him except for the space marked by four dots after the phrase "will amount to nothing."

Immediately after the remarks quoted in the column on the left Senator George continued as follows:

I do not mean by that to say that there are not other classes of the community that will be benefited by this bill. I do not mean by that to say that this bill ought not to pass. I believe it ought to pass. I believe it ought to pass whether amended as proposed by the Senator from Texas and myself or not. There is enough of good in it to justify the American Senate and the American Congress in putting it in the shape of a law; but when we are performing this operation, when we are legislating for the benefit of the people of this country, I do not think that, out of any

Did Congress Intend to Enact the Common Law of Labor?—Mr. James A. Emery,[26] in an effort to show that Congress had intended that the Anti-trust Law should embrace labor unions, points out that a short time before the passage of the law the United States Supreme Court, in the

---

mere sentiment or out of any mere objection to taking a little pains and care in perfecting this bill, we ought to leave out the essential matters contained in the amendment of the Senator from Texas and in the amendment offered by myself. I should like some Senator to get up and show by a specific statement, not by general allegations, in what respect the amendment offered by me would interfere with the beneficial operation of this bill.

Suppose twenty consumers combine in a suit. They have bought cotton bagging; they have been robbed of the amount of five, twenty, fifty, or one hundred dollars each, according to the amount of cotton bagging they have bought. They have all been injured by the same combination, by the same conspiracy. This combination—this conspiracy—controls millions of dollars. The parties injured separately are poor men. Why not allow them to combine in a suit to enforce from this great combination proper redress for the wrongs they have suffered? . . .

There is no justification for concluding, on the basis of these remarks of Senator George, that he believed the words of the Judiciary Committee bill embraced labor unions. He was making a plea, in words as clear as possible, for the adoption of his own and Senator Reagan's amendments to the bill. The purpose of his own amendment is apparent from the last paragraph above quoted. The purpose of Senator Reagan's amendment, as explained in the previous chapter (above, p. 30), was to permit suits to be brought in state as well as federal courts without regard to the amount in controversy. In view of these facts, easily ascertainable from an examination of p. 3150, Vol. 21, of the *Congressional Record*, Professor Mason is not warranted in his statement concerning Senator George's belief, nor in supporting his opinion by an incomplete and misleading quotation.

[26] "Labor Organizations and the Sherman Law," *Journal of Political Economy,* June, 1912, pp. 599, 605.

case of Callan v. Wilson,[27] had declared a boycott carried on by a trade union to be an illegal conspiracy under the common law. According to Mr. Emery this decision "was familiar to every lawyer in Congress, and what more natural than that the grave offense condemned by the Supreme Court should have been included within the prohibitions of the act?"

The first answer to this suggestion is that the debates in Congress are devoid of any reference to the decision in Callan v. Wilson. If any of the lawyers in Congress knew about it they kept the knowledge to themselves. There is no mention made in all these debates about trade union boycotts, and there is no evidence in them to show that members of Congress thought boycotts should be prohibited. The absence of any discussion of the matter is fair presumptive evidence that Congress had no such thought.

Secondary boycotts were in 1890 and are now considered illegal under the common law. If Congress thought the statute should reach secondary boycotts it probably believed that other acts of unions which were illegal under the common law should be reached, to the extent that these acts related to interstate commerce. If it is to be assumed that Congress had labor in mind, the following statement made by Senator Hoar in explaining the bill as passed would support the above position: "We have affirmed the old doctrine of the common law in regard to all interstate and international commercial transactions. . . ."[28]

If the examination stops at this point it might well be argued that the Senate passed a measure intended, among other things, to prevent secondary boycotts, picketing involving intimidation or violence, refusal to work on non-union

[27] 127 U. S. 540 (1888).
[28] *Congressional Record,* Vol. 21, p. 3147.

material, and any other union acts illegal under the common law, so long as they were directly related to interstate commerce.[29]

What is wrong with this position? In the first place, and most important, it must assume that Congress intended to pass a law affecting labor unions, an assumption which appears, in view of the preceding discussion, to be unwarranted. Secondly, it must assume that Senator Hoar, a staunch defender of unions and of their exemption from the Sherman bill, believed that his statement about the common law referred both to labor and to capital transactions. A reference to the complete statement, which is reproduced on pp. 29-30 above, shows that he was concerned, as far as one can tell from what he says, only with the common law as affecting business combinations. Thirdly, considered in connection with the debates on the exemption of labor, it must assume that senators defending or attacking labor exemption were concerned with such acts of labor as were illegal under the common law.

The evidence in the Congressional Record is exhaustive with respect to this last point. Seven senators spoke in favor of exempting unions from the operations of the Sherman bill. One senator spoke in opposition. Twice the Senate, in Committee of the Whole, adopted provisos having the effect of exempting labor. What were the acts of unions upon which the provisos and the debates centered? Were the senators concerned with secondary boycotts, closed shop strikes, and such other activities? The activities of unions which it was feared might be illegal if the Sherman bill were passed

[29] A brief statement of the status of union activities under the common law may be found in Commons and Andrews, *Principles of Labor Legislation,* Revised Edition, New York, 1927, pp. 101-122.

were those which had the effect of increasing prices—as for example collective bargaining and strikes to increase wages and reduce hours. There is no mention in the debates of such activities as secondary boycotts. Except for one brief mention of the injustice of the closed shop in the Government Printing Office, Senator Edmunds himself, who was the only one to speak against the labor provisos, did not refer to any activities of labor unions except their combination to increase wages, and thus to increase prices. The provisos were concerned only with the matters of income raising and price raising.

If the debates are to be accepted as evidence, extension of the common law of labor activities to interstate commerce appears not even to have occurred to the members of the Senate.[30] The common law opposed such activities as secondary boycotts. No mention was made of them in the congressional debates. The common law did not oppose combinations to raise wages. The debates on labor centered about and were practically confined to such activities. If the elimination of the labor provisos meant that the act was intended to reach labor unions, Congress in 1890 must have desired to make unlawful combinations to raise wages which affected interstate commerce. It is certainly only by a great stretch of the imagination that one can reach such a conclusion. It seems clear enough that if Congress desired to apply the common law to transactions affecting interstate commerce, it had in mind only the acts of business combinations, not those of labor unions.

[30] Not for decades had American courts declared that a combination to raise wages was illegal under the common law. In People v. Fisher, 14 Wendell 9 (1835), it was declared that a combination to raise wages was illegal.

The Significance of the House Debates.—So far discussion has been concerned with the intent of the Senate. What about the intent of the House of Representatives? As has already been shown, there is no word in the extensive debates in the House to indicate that its members desired to do more than pass a bill against trusts. The only pertinent mention of labor and farmers' organizations was made by Representative Stewart. He was a member of the conference committee which discussed the bill with the representatives of the Senate. If the bill was intended by the Senate to reach labor he was in an exceptionally good position to find it out. Yet his remarks in the House indicated beyond doubt that he did not believe the bill applied to labor. There is, furthermore, evidence that he thought no one desired that it should do so.[31]

A Summary of the Argument.—On the basis of the congressional debates described in the preceding chapter and the analysis to which they have been subjected in the present one, it is believed that no valid evidence can be found in the records of the legislative proceedings that Congress intended the Anti-trust Act to apply to labor organizations.

Let us summarize briefly the more important considerations upon which this conclusion is based.

(1) The absence of the provisos exempting labor unions from the Judiciary Committee bill does not prove that the Senate intended the bill to reach such organizations. The bill to which the provisos had been attached denounced combinations tending to raise prices. The final bill did not do this, and hence presumably required no such provisos.

(2) This contention receives further support from the fact that there is no reference in the extensive debates on the Judiciary Committee bill to the question of whether it ap-

[31] *Congressional Record,* Vol. 21, p. 5956.

plied to labor. The original Sherman measure, on the other hand, gave rise to much argument devoted to the matter.

(3) None of the senators who had desired to exempt labor from the operations of the Sherman bill opposed the passage of the Judiciary Committee bill. Several of them spoke in favor of it and all of them present at the time voted for it on its final passage.

(4) There is no evidence available in the records of the debates to show that the senators above mentioned believed that the new bill would apply to labor; nor is there evidence to indicate that they had changed their views between the time they had favored labor exemption and the time they supported the final measure.

(5) The fact that the final bill denounced "restraint of trade" does not prove that it was intended to reach labor. The Senators frequently used that term in the same sense as they used "restraint of competition." The supporters of labor exemption considered it necessary to attach a proviso to a bill denouncing "restraint of competition" though that is said not to include labor activities. They spoke and voted for a bill denouncing "restraint of trade," which, it is claimed, embraced unions. In other words, these terms are not significant as indicating the intent to include the acts of labor.

(6) There is no evidence that the Anti-trust Act was intended to apply the common law of labor activities to transactions in interstate commerce. No mention occurs in the debates of labor activities illegal under the common law.

(7) No remark in the debates in the House of Representatives can be found to support the view that Congress desired to reach labor unions. The only reference to such organizations assumes that no one desired a bill which would hinder them.

It thus appears that the courts, in deciding that Congress intended that the Anti-trust Law should reach labor unions, came to a conclusion which cannot be supported by a careful and thoroughgoing examination of the most substantial evidence available, the Congressional Record. The act was intended to be an act against trusts and not against trade unions.

The courts, had they confined themselves exclusively to the meaning of the term "restraint of trade," might justifiably have concluded that the statute embraced labor unions. Congress might then have properly received more of the blame for the application of the act to labor, since it chose a phraseology which did not accurately convey its purpose. The courts which laid down the precedent for so applying the act did not, however, confine their attention exclusively to its terminology. The meaning of that terminology evidently seemed sufficiently uncertain to them to require that some attention be given to the congressional debates. Thus, the lower courts, in the Amalgamated Council case[32] and in one of the Debs cases,[33] and the Supreme Court in Loewe v. Lawlor[34] indicated by their decisions that they had taken the debates into account in reaching the conclusion that the act was meant to embrace labor organizations. It is difficult to see how, had they made a searching examination of the Congressional Record, they could have reached such a conclusion. The courts would have been legally justified in not going behind the terminology of the act. They did go behind it, however, and having done so, they are to be criticized for having reached untenable conclusions as to the intent of Congress. It appears, therefore, that the blame for

[32] 54 Fed. 994, 996.
[33] 64 Fed. 724, 744.
[34] 208 U. S. 274, 301.

the application of the Sherman Act to labor must be shared by Congress, because it chose an inaccurate terminology, and by the courts, because, having taken the congressional debates into consideration, they failed to examine them adequately.

PART II

AN HISTORICAL SURVEY

CHAPTER IV

THE EARLY YEARS: 1890-1908

It is the purpose of this and the succeeding five chapters to present a history of the application of the Sherman Act to labor activities.[1] Attention will be given only to those cases and those events which bear closely on the development of the application of the law to labor, or are of significance in themselves. Accordingly the present section will not present an exhaustive discussion of every case. Its purpose is merely to present the high lights of the development.

The Provisions of the Act.—It is well to set forth again the important provisions of the Sherman Act. It provided:

(1) That "every contract, combination in the form of trust or otherwise, or conspiracy, in restraint of trade or commerce" among the states or with foreign nations, was illegal. (Section 1.)

(2) That every attempt to monopolize such trade or commerce, or every actual monopoly of it, was illegal. (Section 2.)

(3) That every person guilty of these illegal acts, was, on

---

[1] A brief description of every case arising under the Sherman Act in which labor was a defendant, concerning which any information could be secured, appears in Appendix C. It is believed that every case reported in the Federal Reports and practically every case in which the government secured an indictment or injunction, is included. There may be numerous instances in which private parties brought suit for injunction which are not included, especially if the decision of the court was not officially reported.

conviction, liable to a fine not exceeding five thousand
dollars, or to imprisonment not exceeding one year,
or to both of these punishments. (Sections 1 and 2.)

(4) That the district attorneys of the United States, under
the direction of the Attorney-General, might institute
proceedings in equity to restrain violations of the law.
(Section 4.)

(5) That any person injured in his business or property
by any action forbidden under the act might sue for
and recover threefold the damages sustained, plus the
costs of the suit, including a reasonable attorney's fee.
(Section 7.)

Two sets of acts are thus declared to be criminal offenses;
and three types of proceedings are possible under the act
against its alleged violators: (1) the federal government may
seek the return by a grand jury of a criminal indictment
leading to trial; (2) it may sue in equity for an injunction
restraining violations of the law; (3) injured private parties
may sue for damages. All these proceedings, of course, must
be brought in the federal courts.

The First Cases.—The Sherman Act became law on July
2, 1890. On October 13 of the same year the government
instituted the first proceedings under it. It sought an injunction in the Circuit Court at Nashville, Tenn., against the
members of a coal combination which, it was alleged, was
in restraint of interstate commerce. The Circuit Court, feeling its way through new legal territory, denied the petition
until after a hearing. On June 4, 1891, it granted the injunction desired by the government.[2]

The Sherman Act was thus first invoked against a business combination. The second attempt to bring it into play

[2] U. S. v. Jellico Mountain Coke and Coal Co. et al., 43 Fed. 898
(October 13, 1890); 46 Fed. 432 (June 4, 1891).

involved the activities of a group of workers. In December, 1892, the crew of the British steamer, *Violante*, having some complaint against conditions on board, walked off the ship just before it was scheduled to leave port. An injunction suit was brought in the Circuit Court of the Eastern District of Louisiana by the persons in charge of the ship. It was claimed that the crew was guilty of a conspiracy to restrain commerce in violation of the Sherman Act. It was also asserted that an injunction was necessary to prevent irreparable injury to property. The court, in a decision rendered February 9, 1893, ruled that there was no basis for issuing an injunction to a private party under the act, since only the federal government was therein authorized to sue in equity. On the general equity ground, however, that the firm, in the absence of an injunction, was threatened with irreparable injury, and in order to prevent a multiplicity of suits, it issued an order against the defendants. The court did not discuss the question as to whether or not the Sherman Act had actually been violated by the ship's crew.[3]

Almost at the beginning of the history of the law it was thus made clear that the injunction remedy was not available to a private party under its terms. Despite this decision, however, similar suits were brought in later years. It was not until the passage of the Clayton Act, in 1914, that the situation was changed. It is significant, as will appear later, that the Clayton Act, which was hailed at first by trade unionists as "Labor's Magna Charta," actually resulted by this change in greatly increasing the extent to which labor was hampered by the Sherman Act.

At the time of the episode of the British steamer other events were occurring in New Orleans which resulted in the first use of the Sherman Act against labor. In November,

[3] Blindell et al. v. Hagan et al., 54 Fed. 40 (1893).

1892, the draymen's union of the city went on strike. Soon many other unions called their men out on a sympathetic strike intended to aid the draymen. As a consequence the business of the city was tied up and the transportation of goods being conveyed through it in interstate and foreign commerce was "totally interrupted." Federal attorneys brought suit for an injunction, charging that the Sherman Act was being violated. The defendants urged that the act prohibited only combinations of capitalists, not of laborers.

In a decision rendered on March 25, 1893, Judge Billings, of the Circuit Court, asserted that the congressional debates showed that the statute had its origin in the evils of "massed capital," but when the legislators came to formulate the terms of the act the subject had so broadened in their minds "that the source of the evil was not regarded as material." "They made the interdiction include combinations of labor, as well as of capital; in fact, all combinations in restraint of · commerce, without reference to the character of the persons who entered into them."[4] The same court which refused an injunction under the act to a private party in February, thereupon granted one to the government in March. The decision in this case established the precedent which was generally referred to when later courts applied the Sherman Act to labor unions.

United States v. Patterson.—The foregoing interpretation of the Sherman Act differed greatly from one set forth less than a month previously, in the Circuit Court in Massachusetts. Government attorneys had secured indictments charging Patterson and others, manufacturers of cash registers, with violation of the Act of 1890. The court had before

[4] U. S. v. Workingmen's Amalgamated Council et al., 54 Fed. 994. Affirmed by the Circuit Court of Appeals, 57 Fed. 85 (June 13, 1893).

it the question of quashing the various charges in the indictment. These charges not only alleged a combination to monopolize the trade in cash registers, but also a purpose to drive certain competitors out of the field by violence, annoyance, and intimidation. Judge Putnam was primarily concerned, in his decision of February 28, 1893,[5] with the following question: Were the prohibitions of the Sherman Act limited to those activities comprised under the word "monopoly," or did they extend to all interferences with interstate trade whether or not monopoly or the attempt to monopolize appeared?

The attorneys appearing for the government, among whom was Elihu Root, asserted that the term "restraint of trade" referred to unfair interferences with the business of another, and that such interferences had been considered unlawful prior to the passage of the Sherman Act. Many decisions applying this principle to the activities of labor unions were cited. The government position was thus that the statute operated against all combinations to restrain interstate commerce.

The court took the contrary position. It declared that the whole statute must be taken together. "The second section is limited by its terms to monopolies, and evidently has as its basis the engrossing or controlling of the market. The first section [which prohibits contracts, combinations and conspiracies in restraint of trade] is undoubtedly *in pari materia*, and so has as its basis the engrossing or controlling of the market, or of lines of trade."

The following excerpt from Judge Putnam's decision is worth reproducing at length:

Careless or inapt construction of the statute as bearing on this case, while it may seem to create but a small divergence here,

[5] U. S. v. Patterson, 55 Fed. 605.

will, if followed out logically, extend into very large fields; because, if the proposition made by the United States is taken with its full force, the inevitable result will be that the federal courts will be compelled to apply this statute to all attempts to restrain commerce among the states, or commerce with foreign nations, by strikes or boycotts, and by every method of interference by way of violence or intimidation. It is not to be presumed that Congress intended thus to extend the jurisdiction of the courts of the United States without very clear language. Such language I do not find in the statute. Therefore I conclude that there must be alleged in the indictment that there was a purpose to restrain trade as implied in the common-law expression, "contract in restraint of trade" analogous to the word monopolize in the second section. I think this is the basis of the statute. It must appear somewhere in the indictment that there was a conspiracy in restraint of trade by engrossing or monopolizing or grasping the market, and it is not sufficient simply to allege a purpose to drive certain competitors out of the field by violence, annoyance, intimidation, or otherwise.

Something has been said in this connection touching the debates in congress. It is apparently settled law that we cannot take the views or purposes expressed in debate as supplying the construction of statutes . . . But this does not at all touch the question whether or not one can gather from the debates in congress, as he can from any other source, the history of the evil which the legislation was intended to remedy. The debates on this point are very instructive: but they fail to point out precisely what incidents or details of the great evil under consideration were to be reached by the legislation.[6]

The court accordingly sustained those counts in the indictment charging a combination to engross and monopolize interstate trade in cash registers, but it rejected those alleging an intention to destroy certain competitors.

[6] U. S. v. Patterson, 55 Fed. 605, 641.

It seems clear that if later courts had followed the interpretation of Judge Putnam in United States v. Patterson, the act would have been confined to the operations of business combinations. Actually, of course, it was the interpretation of Judge Billings in United States v. Amalgamated Council which was generally accepted.

Waterhouse v. Comer.—A further instance of the readiness of the courts to assume that the Sherman Act extended to unions appears in the case of Waterhouse v. Comer, decided by a federal Circuit Court in Georgia on April 8, 1893.[7] Labor was not here a defendant. On the contrary, it was labor, represented by a committee of the Brotherhood of Locomotive Engineers, which asked the court to order Comer, the receiver of a small Georgian railroad which the court controlled, to renew a trade agreement with the union. The receiver explained his refusal to renew the agreement by calling attention to a rule of the Brotherhood which might result in strikes by the engineers even though they had no grievance against the road on which they were employed.

Judge Speer, considering this rule, declared, "It [was] plainly a rule or agreement in restraint of trade or commerce" and a violation of the first section of the Sherman Act as well as of certain sections of the Interstate Commerce Acts of 1887 and 1889. "Now," he continued, "it is true that in any conceivable strike upon the transportation lines of this country, whether main lines or branch roads, there will be interference with and restraint of interstate or foreign commerce. This will be true also of strikes upon telegraph lines, for the exchange of telegraphic messages between people of different states in interstate commerce. In the presence of these statutes . . . it will be practically im-

[7] 55 Fed. 149.

possible hereafter for a body of men to combine to hinder and delay the work of the transportation company without becoming amenable to the provisions of these statutes." Having concluded that the rule of which Comer complained was unlawful, and assuming that the engineers would therefore ignore it, the court ordered a renewal of the trade agreement.

Thus in March, 1893, a court held that a strike tying up traffic intended for interstate commerce violated the Sherman Act.[8] And a month later another court suggested that any railroad strike would be contrary to the law.[9] The precedents were indeed at hand for what was one of the most thoroughgoing applications of the act to labor on record, its use in the great Pullman strike of 1894.

The Pullman Strike Cases.—There is no space here for an intensive discussion of the Pullman strike, despite the fact that it is probably among the three or four most important labor disputes in our history.[10] It must suffice to explain the occasion of the dispute, the use of the Sherman Act in connection with it, and the views of the courts as to the reasons for such use.

In the winter of 1893-1894 the employees of the Pullman Palace Car Company, working in Pullman, a suburb of Chicago, were greatly disturbed because of a wage reduction. In March, 1894, they joined the new American Railway Union, an industrial union attempting to organize all workers connected with the railways. Early in May, as a result of the failure of attempts to secure concessions from the com-

[8] U. S. v. Amalgamated Council, 54 Fed. 994.
[9] Waterhouse et al. v. Comer, 55 Fed. 149.
[10] A brief account of the various proceedings against the strikers under the Sherman Act may be found in Appendix C, Cases 2, 3, 4, 11, and 12.

pany, most of the employees went on strike. The American Railway Union held its regular convention in Chicago from June 9 to June 26. It attempted to get the Pullman Company to submit to arbitration, but the company declined to receive its communication. On June 21 the convention voted unanimously that members of the union should stop handling Pullman cars on the railroads on June 26, unless the company would consent to arbitration by that time. The company refused to consider arbitration and the boycott went into effect on the 26th. The railroad companies at once decided to fight the union, and refused to detach Pullman cars from their trains. As a result the boycott became a railway strike, which in a few days spread all over the roads in central and western United States.[11]

Several days after the strike began complaints came to the Postoffice Department that the carriage of the mails was being obstructed and that the strike was frequently accompanied by violence. Attorney-General Olney named one of the railway attorneys as special attorney in charge of conducting the government's case against the strikers in the courts, and directed him and the United States Attorney at Chicago to secure an injunction based on the Anti-trust Act and on the law prohibiting obstruction of the mails.[12]

On July 2 Judges Wood and Grosscup, in the Circuit Court in Chicago, in response to the petition of the federal attorneys, granted one of the most sweeping injunctions on record. Eugene V. Debs, the president of the American

[11] *Report of the United States Strike Commission,* Senate Executive Document, No. 7, 3rd Session, 53rd Congress, pp. XXXIII-XXXIX, XLII.

[12] *Appendix to the Report of the Attorney General,* 1896, pp. 59, 60, 61, and 63; Cleveland, *The Government in the Chicago Strike of 1894,* Princeton, 1913, pp. 10-15.

Railway Union, its other officers, and "all other persons whomsoever," were ordered absolutely to refrain

"from in any way or manner interfering with, hindering, obstructing, or stopping" any of the business of the railroads entering Chicago, or any trains carrying United States mails or engaged in interstate commerce;

from interfering with or injuring the property of said railroads;

from trespassing on such property for the purpose of said obstructions;

from injuring signals, switches, etc.;

"from compelling or inducing or attempting to compel or induce, by threats, intimidation, persuasion, force or violence, any of the employees of any of the said railways to refuse or fail to perform any of their duties as employees" in carrying mail or in interstate commerce;

"from compelling or inducing or attempting to compel or induce, by threats, intimidation, force, or violence, any of the employees" to leave the service of the railroads or not to enter their service;

"from doing any act whatever in furtherance of any conspiracy or combination to restrain either of said railway companies or receivers in the free and unhindered control and handling of interstate commerce over the lines of said railroads, and of transportation of persons and freight between or among the states";

"and from ordering, directing, aiding, assisting or abetting in any manner whatever any person or persons to commit any or either of the acts aforesaid."[13]

Similar injunctions were obtained by federal attorneys in districts throughout the West and Central West.[14] Indictments charging Debs and others with violations of the Sherman Act were secured, but they were not tried. Debs

[13] U. S. v. Debs et al., 64 Fed. 724, 726.

[14] *Report of the Attorney General*, 1894, p. XXXIV.

and various other leaders, however, were charged with contempt for violating the injunctions, and were later sentenced to jail.[15] As a result of the various injunctions, indictments, arrests, and the activities of federal troops which reached Chicago following directions from President Cleveland, the strike and the consequent violence were practically at an end by the middle of July.

Numerous cases arising out of the Pullman strike came before the federal courts and found their way into the official reports.[16] The reports have to do with decisions granting injunctions, with cases of contempt for violating these injunctions, and with charges delivered by the courts to grand juries. In many of the instances reported the courts declared the strike to be a violation of the law against restraints of interstate commerce, though the Sherman Act was not in every case specifically mentioned. Frequently the further charge of obstructing the mails was alleged. Some of the judges, as for example Judge Wood, in United States v.

[15] Appendix C, Case 2.

[16] For the reported cases arising out of the Pullman strike and involving the Sherman Act see the following: (1) on issuance of injunctions: U. S. v. Elliott et al., 62 Fed. 801 (July 6, 1894); U. S. v. Elliott et al., 67 Fed. 27, (October 24, 1894); In re Debs, 158 U. S. 564 (May 27, 1895); (2) contempt proceedings: U. S. v. Agler, 62 Fed. 824 (July 12, 1894); U. S. v. Debs et al., 64 Fed. 724 (December 14, 1894); Thomas v. Cincinnati Railway—In re Phelan, 62 Fed. 803 (July 13, 1894) (though the injunction here was not based on the Sherman Act, the contempt case arose out of the strike, which the court held to be in violation of the statute); (3) charges to grand juries: In re Charge to Grand Jury, 62 Fed. 828 (July 10, 1894); U. S. v. Debs et al., 63 Fed. 436 (July 14, 1894) (supplemental to preceding charge); In re Grand Jury, 62 Fed. 834 (June 29, July 2, July 3, and July 11, 1894); U. S. v. Cassidy et al., 67 Fed. 698 (April 1 and 2, 1895).

Debs,[17] and Judge Baker, in United States v. Agler,[18] concluded that not only did the terms of the Sherman Act apply to such an activity as a railroad strike, but that Congress had probably intended that it should be applied to the acts of labor. Others, such as Judge Philips, in United States v. Elliott,[19] and Judge Morrow, in United States v. Cassidy,[20] asserted that though the primary object of the statute was to restrain business combinations, its provisions were broad enough to reach a labor combination which interrupted interstate transportation.

Several brief excerpts from the decisions will illustrate the attitude of the courts.

A combination whose professed object is to arrest the operation of railroads whose lines extend from a great city into adjoining states, until such roads accede to certain demands made upon them, whether such demands are in themselves reasonable or unreasonable, just or unjust, is certainly an unlawful conspiracy in restraint of commerce among the states.[21]

[On] July 2, 1890, congress enacted a law that enlarged the jurisdiction of the federal courts and authorized them to apply the restraining power of the law for the purpose of checking and arresting all lawless interference with . . . the peaceable and orderly conduct of railroad business between the states.[22]

It may be conceded that the controlling, objective point, in the mind of congress, in enacting this statute, was to suppress what are known as "trusts" and "monopolies." But, like a great many other enactments, the statute is made so comprehensive

[17] 64 Fed. 724.
[18] 62 Fed. 824.
[19] 64 Fed. 27.
[20] 67 Fed. 698.
[21] U. S. v. Elliott, 62 Fed. 801, 803.
[22] U. S. v. Agler, 62 Fed. 824, 825.

and far-reaching in its express terms as to extend to like incidents and acts clearly within the expression and spirit of the law.[23]

On December 14, 1894, Eugene V. Debs and several other strike leaders were found guilty of contempt for violation of the injunction issued on July 2 in Chicago. Jail sentences varying from three to six months were imposed.[24] An appeal on a writ of habeas corpus was carried to the Supreme Court. Justice Brewer, speaking for the court, denied this petition on May 27, 1895. He justified the injunction on the ground that the federal government, which had constitutional authority over the mails and interstate commerce, was entitled to the aid of the courts in preventing interferences therewith. The court entered into no examination of the Sherman Act, upon which the Circuit Court mainly relied to sustain its jurisdiction. It declared that its failure to examine the matter must not be interpreted to mean that it dissented from the opinion of the lower court as to the scope of the act, but that it preferred to rest its judgment on the broader ground above stated.[25]

A perusal of the injunction order issued against the strikers, which is described in detail above,[26] indicates that persuasion and other activities that might be entirely peaceful were enjoined. The prohibition of peaceful activities by injunction has become common enough since 1894, but such a prohibition is especially important when considered in connection with the legality of labor activities under the Sherman Act. The courts in the Pullman cases held a railroad strike to be an unlawful conspiracy in violation of that statute. According to the accepted legal doctrine every act,

[23] U. S. v. Elliott, 64 Fed. 27, 30.
[24] U. S. v. Debs, 64 Fed. 724.
[25] In re Debs, 158 U. S. 564, 599-600.
[26] p. 66.

however peaceful and lawful in itself, if it is a part of a criminal conspiracy, becomes unlawful.[27] Hence peaceful persuasion in aid of the strike became unlawful and was enjoined. In later years, as the use of the act in labor cases expanded, the most innocent of activities carried on in connection with strikes or boycotts were enjoined, provided the courts concluded that the Anti-trust Law was being violated.

It is significant that not until the Pullman strike did the use of injunctions against labor unions become prominent enough to attract public attention. For the first time both trade unionists and lawyers devoted extensive consideration to the problems involved. Writers in both groups, especially the former, pointed out that such a use of injunctions, the justice of which they questioned in labor cases, was in this instance based upon an even more questionable application of a law passed to restrain trusts.[28]

Supreme Court Decisions in Cases Against Capital.— It was not until 1908, when it rendered its decision in the famous Danbury Hatters' case, that the Supreme Court expressed an opinion on the use of the Sherman Act against labor.[29] Prior to that date it had subjected the law to an extensive examination in an important series of cases involving business combinations. In view of the fact that these decisions were later frequently referred to by the courts in deciding the labor cases, and that in them the Supreme Court laid down a series of interpretative rules used in both

[27] Aikens v. Wisconsin, 195 U. S. 194 (1904).
[28] For important legal criticisms of the injunctions in the Pullman strike see Gregory, 11 *Harvard Law Review* 487; Dunbar, 13 *Law Quarterly Review* 374; Allen, 28 *American Law Review* 828.
[29] Loewe v. Lawlor, 208 U. S. 274.

labor and business cases, it is well to glance at the decisions in question.

The Supreme Court handed down its first opinion interpreting the Sherman Act in the case of United States v. E. C. Knight Company, decided on January 21, 1895.[30] The American Sugar Refining Company, already producing about 65 per cent of the sugar refined in the country, bought control of the Knight Company and three other concerns. This gave the trust control of 98 per cent of the production. The government brought suit to cancel the contract of purchase, alleging a violation of the Anti-trust Law. The Supreme Court permitted the contracts to stand, asserting that they related only to manufacture within a state and that there was neither a direct relation to interstate commerce, nor was there proof that there was any intention to restrain trade or commerce. Justice Harlan dissented vigorously, asserting that if such a ruling were adhered to the people would be at the mercy of selfish and greedy combinations.

On March 22, 1897, the Supreme Court rendered its decision in United States v. Trans-Missouri Freight Association.[31] The association was a combination of railroad companies the avowed purpose of which was to establish and maintain reasonable rates, rules, and regulations on freight traffic south and west of the Missouri River. The court declared, in answer to the position of the roads, that the Sherman Act applied to railroads; that it made illegal "every" contract, combination, or conspiracy in restraint of interstate trade or commerce, whether such a restraint was reasonable or not; and that the government was entitled to an injunction against the association. Four of the justices dissented, asserting their belief that only unreason-

[30] 156 U. S. 1.
[31] 166 U. S. 290.

able restraints were in violation of the statute. As will be clear later, the position of the minority became that of the majority by 1911, at least with regard to business combinations.

Three important decisions were handed down by the Supreme Court on October 24, 1898. In the first one, United States v. Joint Traffic Association,[32] the position in the Trans-Missouri case was affirmed. The Joint Traffic Association had fixed rates and regulations on traffic east of Chicago for thirty-one roads. The association questioned the constitutionality of the act on the ground that it deprived them of property guaranteed by the Fifth Amendment. The court held that the statute was a valid exercise of the power of Congress over interstate commerce, that the association was in restraint of interstate commerce, and that an injunction against the combination should issue. Three of the justices dissented, but wrote no opinion.

The second and third decisions involved business associations on the Live Stock Exchange in Kansas City. In Hopkins v. United States[33] the defendants were commission men who sold cattle for growers under rules which fixed commission charges, and provided that no business was to be done with non-members of the association. In Anderson v. United States[34] the defendants were members of an association of cattle buyers, rather than of commission merchants. The rules of the association forbade members to do business with merchants who dealt with non-members. In both opinions the Supreme Court, Justice Harlan dissenting, took the position that though the combinations had some effect upon interstate trade or commerce there was no suf-

[32] 171 U. S. 505.
[33] 171 U. S. 578.
[34] 171 U. S. 604.

ficiently "direct and immediate" restraint to bring them under the prohibition of the law. The court declared that the possible effect of the defendants' course of conduct upon interstate commerce was "quite remote, not intended and too small to be taken into account."[35] The following excerpt is especially pertinent, in view of the emphasis which courts later put upon the questions of intent and of the directness of the restraint:

Where the subject-matter of the agreement does not directly relate to and act upon and embrace interstate commerce, and where the undisputed facts clearly show that the purpose of the agreement was not to regulate, obstruct or restrain that commerce, but that it was entered into with the object of properly and fairly regulating the transaction of the business in which the parties to the agreement were engaged, such agreement will be upheld as not within the statute, where it can be seen that the character and terms of the agreement are well calculated to attain the purpose for which it was formed, and where the effect of its formation and enforcement upon interstate trade or commerce is in any event but indirect and incidental and not its purpose or object.[36]

The first case in which the Supreme Court ruled against an industrial combination of the sort which Congress had especially in mind in 1890, was that of Addyston Pipe and Steel Company v. United States, decided on December 4, 1899.[37] The six defendant corporations manufactured cast iron pipe, which they sold in thirty-six states. They had agreed not to compete with one another in making bids, and to share in the advantages of the high prices resulting. The court unanimously declared the combination to be

[35] Anderson v. U. S., 171 U. S. 604, 619.
[36] 171 U. S. 604, 615.
[37] 175 U. S. 211.

in violation of the Sherman Act. It pointed out that the arrangement eliminated all competition, that it increased prices unreasonably, and that its direct and immediate result was to control the sale of pipe in interstate commerce.

In Montague & Company v. Lowry,[38] the court had before it an organization of dealers in tiles, mantels, and grates, resident in California, and the manufacturers of these articles in other states. An agreement provided that the manufacturers would sell only to those dealers in California who were members of the association, and that the dealers would buy only from member manufacturers. The member dealers might sell to non-member dealers, but only at a price twice as high as they themselves were charged. Only those dealers were eligible to membership whose business was above a certain size. The plaintiff, Montague, finding himself ineligible and therefore compelled to pay the exorbitant prices, sued for damages under the Sherman Act. The Supreme Court, in a unanimous decision rendered February 23, 1904, ruled that the agreement violated the law, since it "directly affected and restrained interstate commerce."[39]

One of the most important business cases decided by the Supreme Court was that of Northern Securities Company v. United States,[40] in which an opinion was rendered on March 14, 1904. The corporation was a holding company which was organized to acquire control, by stock ownership, of the Northern Pacific and the Great Northern Railways, two competing lines in the Northwest. The government sought to have the company dissolved as a combination in restraint of interstate commerce. A majority of the court asserted that the combination suppressed competition

[38] 193 U. S. 38.
[39] 193 U. S. 38, 48.
[40] 193 U. S. 197.

and violated the Sherman Act. The government petition was granted. A dissenting minority of four justices supported the view that ownership of stock was not commerce.

On January 30, 1905, the Supreme Court rendered a decision in the case of Swift & Company v. United States.[41] The government sought an injunction against Swift and six other packing companies, which together controlled sixty per cent of the trade in fresh meats. It was charged that these companies had combined to lower prices for live stock and to monopolize interstate commerce in livestock and meats. The Supreme Court unanimously upheld the goverment, pointing out that the primary purpose of the combination was to restrain and monopolize interstate commerce, and that, despite the fact that the restraint alleged was imposed within a single state, its effect on such commerce was direct, and "not incidental, secondary, remote or merely probable."

The Position of the Supreme Court.—Those propositions laid down by the Supreme Court in the foregoing decisions which directly affected the later rulings of the courts in labor cases may be set forth briefly as follows:

(1) Manufacturing within a state is not commerce, and, accordingly, an agreement resulting in the control of manufacturing within a state cannot be considered a restraint of interstate commerce contrary to the law.[42]

(2) Every contract, combination, or conspiracy in restraint of interstate trade or commerce is illegal, regardless of whether, in the absence of the statute, it would be considered reasonable.[43]

(3) Where the subject matter of an agreement does not

[41] 196 U. S. 375.
[42] U. S. v. E. C. Knight Co., 156 U. S. 1.
[43] U. S. v. Trans-Missouri Freight Association, 166 U. S. 290; U. S. v. Joint Traffic Association, 171 U. S. 505.

directly relate to and act upon interstate commerce, where the purpose of the agreement is not to regulate or restrain commerce, and where the effect of the agreement upon it is indirect, incidental, and remote, the law is not being violated.[44]

(4) Where the subject matter of an agreement directly relates to interstate commerce, and where the effect is to restrain that commerce, the law is being violated.[45]

(5) Where the effect of a combination is to restrain interstate trade or commerce, the law is being violated even though the activities of the combination are carried on within a state, or these activities in themselves are not commerce.[46]

[44] Hopkins v. U. S., 171 U. S. 578; Anderson v. U. S., 171 U. S. 604.
[45] Addyston Pipe and Steel Co. v. U. S., 175 U. S. 211; U. S. v. Trans-Missouri Freight Association, 166 U. S. 290; U. S. v. Joint Traffic Association, 171 U. S. 505.
[46] Montague and Co. v. Lowry, 193 U. S. 38; Northern Securities Co. v. U. S., 193 U. S. 197; Swift and Co. v. U. S., 196 U. S. 375.

FROM THE DANBURY HATTERS' CASE TO THE RULE OF REASON

The Danbury Hatters' Case.—The momentous decision of the United States Supreme Court in the Danbury Hatters' case was the result of a nation-wide campaign of the Brotherhood of United Hatters of America to secure the closed shop. The campaign, which began in 1897, was so effective that, by 1903, 187 concerns were operating under closed shop conditions, with only twelve firms operating nonunion. To a considerable extent these results were obtained with the aid of highly organized boycotts against hats made under non-union conditions. The Danbury, Conn., firm of Loewe & Company was asked by the union officials to operate under closed shop conditions in 1902. The company refused to accede to the demand, and on July 25, 1902, 250 employees went out on strike at the call of the union.

The union soon initiated a secondary boycott against the firm's products. It found out to whom the company's goods were being sent and secured the aid of unions in the customers' towns to carry on the boycott. Union organizers traveled in different parts of the country and influenced unionists and dealers not to buy Loewe hats. The cooperation of the American Federation of Labor was secured. Advertisements announcing the boycott appeared in trade and labor journals and in the daily press, and circulars were broadcast. Retailers were told that none of their goods would be bought if they dealt with Loewe. Wholesalers were approached and threatened with loss of business. The hatters' agents and local union committees visited Loewe's customers for the purpose of influencing them not to buy the company's products. As a consequence of the boycott the company estimated its net losses by 1903 at over $88,000.[1]

On August 31, 1903, Loewe & Company filed a suit for damages under the Sherman Act in the Circuit Court at Hartford, Conn., against officers and members of the United Hatters. After various postponements Judge Platt, on December 7, 1906, rendered a decision dismissing the company's complaint.[2] In view of the later decision by the Supreme Court Judge Platt's reasoning is interesting. He pointed out that the defendants had tried to prevent production of the plaintiffs' hats at home, and, "with the assistance of their friends, to curtail, and, if possible, destroy, the distribution of such product after it had become settled into the stock of goods in the hands of plaintiffs' customers in other states." "There is no allegation," the court continued, "which suggests that the means of transporting plantiffs' product, or the product itself while being transported, were touched, handled, obstructed, or in any manner actually interfered with. There is no allegation that the defendants are in any way engaged in interstate commerce."

In response to the company's argument that by hindering production in one state and distribution by customers in other states the union had engaged in a combination to restrain interstate commerce, the court asserted (1) that the

---

[1] Loewe v. Lawlor, 208 U. S. 274; *Brief for Plaintiffs in Error,* Loewe et al. v. Lawlor et al., Supreme Court, October Term, 1907, pp. 6-9; Laidler, *Boycotts and the Labor Struggle,* New York, 1913, pp. 151-153.

[2] A brief summary of the various proceedings in this case will be found in Appendix C, Case 41.

manufacture of hats before they left the factory was not interstate commerce and the hats up to that time were not the subject of interstate commerce; (2) that the distribution of hats from customers in other states to ultimate consumers was not interstate commerce and the hats themselves during such distribution were not the subject of interstate commerce. "The real question," said the court, "is whether a combination which undertakes to interfere simultaneously with both actions is one which directly affects the transportation of the hats from the place of manufacture to the place of sale. It is not perceived that the Supreme Court has as yet so broadened the interpretation of the Sherman act . . . that it will fit such an order of facts as this complaint presents."[3]

The hat company appealed to the Supreme Court on a writ of certiorari, and on February 3, 1908, the most important opinion rendered up to that time in a labor case under the Sherman Act was handed down.[4] In a unanimous decision written by Chief Justice Fuller the court declared that in its opinion "the combination described in the declaration [was] a combination in 'restraint of trade or commerce among the several States,' in the sense in which those words are used in the act, and the action can be maintained accordingly." "[This] conclusion rests on many judgments of the court, to the effect that the act prohibits any combination whatever to secure action which essentially obstructs the free flow of commerce between the States, or restricts, in that regard, the liberty of a trader to engage in business."[5]

The court pointed out that the combination was in that class of restraints of trade illegal at common law which aimed at compelling third parties not to engage in trade

[3] Loewe v. Lawlor, 148 Fed. 924, 925.
[4] Loewe v. Lawlor, 208 U. S. 274.
[5] 208 U. S. 274, 292-293.

except under conditions imposed by the combination. The defendants had objected that even though their acts might be illegal at common law they did not come within the statute, since intrastate trade was affected, physical obstruction to transportation was not alleged, and they were not themselves engaged in interstate commerce. The court did not think this position tenable. It quoted from Justice Peckham's decision in the Addyston Pipe case[6] to the effect that "any agreement or combination which directly operates not alone upon the manufacture but upon the sale, transportation and delivery of an article of interstate commerce, by preventing and restricting its sale, etc., thereby regulates interstate commerce." Referring to the hatters' boycott the court declared that if "the purpose of the combination were, as alleged, to prevent any interstate transportation at all, the fact that the means operated at one end before physical transportation commenced, and at the other end after physical transportation ended was immaterial."[7]

The court, asserting that a case within the statute had been set up and that the defendants' demurrer to the complaint should have been overruled, reversed the judgment of the lower court, and directed that the case proceed accordingly.[8]

The most significant aspect of the decision is the fact that in it the Supreme Court for the first time definitely took the position that the prohibitions of the Anti-trust Law might be applied to the acts of trade unions. It is important, therefore, to present as fully as possible the Supreme Court's treatment of this point and the manner in which the question of the intent of Congress was presented to it.

[6] 175 U. S. 211, 242.
[7] 208 U. S. 274, 294-301.
[8] 208 U. S. 274, 309.

There is no evidence available to show that the counsel for the hatters directly raised the point that Congress did not intend that the act should reach labor unions. The only position of theirs which had even a slight bearing on the question was that which asserted that since the workers were not engaged in interstate commerce, had no aim to restrain it, and had used no means which directly did so, the Sherman Act did not affect them.[9]

James M. Beck and Daniel Davenport, counsel for the Loewe company, devoted the final section of their brief to a defense of the proposition that "members of a combination or conspiracy under the Anti-Trust Law are not exempt because they are not engaged in interstate transportation." In connection with this matter they presented the proposition that Congress had refused to exempt labor unions from the provisions of the Sherman Act.

"The legislative history of the Sherman Anti-Trust Law," they declared, "clearly shows that its applicability to combinations of labor as well as of capital was not an oversight." They pointed out that the early bills introduced by Senators Reagan and Sherman contained no exemption of labor unions; that Senator George on February 4, 1889, and Senators Teller and Hiscock on March 24, 1890, expressed the belief that the Sherman bills before the Senate on those dates would reach labor unions; and that on March 25, 1890, Senator Sherman, in order to meet these objections, introduced an exemption provision which was adopted. The brief then proceeded as follows:

Subsequently, on March 27, 1890, the bill, as amended, was recommitted to the Senate Committee on Judiciary, which on April 2, 1890, reported a substitute bill, *which wholly omitted*

[9] 208 U. S. 274, 280-283.

the amendment exempting organizations of farmers and laborers, and this bill, as reported, became a law on July 2, 1890. [Italics in the brief.] The exempting amendment was, however, not omitted until there had been a debate as to the propriety of discriminating in favor of labor organizations, in which Senators Stewart, Hiscock, Hoar, Teller and George, participated. It is significant that after the Sherman law was enacted bills were introduced in the Fifty-second Congress, H. R., 6640, Sec. 1; 55th Congress, Senate 1546, Sec. 8; H. R., 10539, Sec. 7; 56th Congress, H. R., 11667, Sec. 7; 57th Congress, S., 649, Sec. 7; H. R., 14947, Sec. 7, to amend the Sherman Anti-trust Law so that it would be inapplicable to labor organizations, and while one of these (H. R., 10539, Sec. 7) passed the House in the 56th Congress, none ever became a law.

Congress, therefore, has refused to exempt labor unions from the comprehensive provisions of the Sherman law against combinations in restraint of trade, and this refusal is the more significant, as it followed the recognition by the Courts that the Sherman Anti-Trust Law applied to labor organizations. [Italics in the brief.]

The brief then proceeded to quote from the decision in United States v. Amalgamated Council[10] to the effect that Congress had "made the interdiction include combinations of labor, as well as of capital; in fact, all combinations in restraint of commerce, without reference to the character of the persons who entered into them." The decisions rendered in the Pullman cases were also discussed in support of the plaintiffs' position.

Immediately preceding the presentation of the legislative history of the act the brief contained the following assertion: "Congress did not provide that one class in the community could combine to restrain interstate trade and another class could not. It had no respect for persons. It made

[10] 54 Fed. 994.

no distinction between classes. It provided that *'every'* contract, combination or conspiracy in restraint of trade was illegal."[11]

The Supreme Court thus had presented to it by the counsel for the company the proposition that the hatters' combination, as a labor union, might be reached by the Sherman Act. Its response to the argument was brief but extraordinarily significant. The court said:

Nor can the act in question be held inapplicable because defendants were not themselves engaged in interstate commerce. The act made no distinction between classes. It provided that "every" contract, combination or conspiracy in restraint of trade was illegal. The records of Congress show that several efforts were made to exempt, by legislation, organizations of farmers and laborers from the operation of the act and that all these efforts failed, so that the act remained as we have it before us.[12]

The court then referred to the case of United States v. Amalgamated Council, and quoted that portion of the decision which was given in the plantiffs' brief in support of the argument that the act reached labor combinations. It referred also to the decisions in the Pullman cases.

It seems fair to say that the statement of the Supreme Court concerning the congressional debates appears to have been based upon what the brief of the plaintiffs said, rather than upon a careful examination of the debates themselves. This was particularly unfortunate in view of the fact that in its history of the Sherman Act the counsel for the company made assertions which were misleading, as the following facts, already established, will show.

[11] For all the above references see *Brief for Plaintiffs in Error,* Loewe v. Lawlor, Supreme Court, October Term, 1907, pp. 30-34.
[12] 208 U. S. 274, 301.

(1) The provisos (there were two of them) exempting labor organizations which were added to the Sherman bill were attached to an anti-price raising measure. The Judiciary Committee bill, which became law, was not an anti-price raising measure, and probably did not seem to the Senate to require an exemption proviso on that account.

(2) The brief for the plaintiffs gives the impression that the labor exemption provisos were omitted as a result of a debate in which the "propriety of discriminating in favor of labor organizations" was discussed. The fact is that the labor provisos were not separately omitted, but were discarded with the rest of the Sherman bill by the Judiciary Committee. The Sherman bill was sent to the latter committee not because the provisos troubled the Senate, but because so many impertinent, obstructive, and probably unconstitutional amendments had been added to it as to necessitate a thorough overhauling of the measure.

(3) There was only one senator who objected to the adoption of a labor exemption proviso. Numerous senators took the opposite view, and the Senate on two occasions adopted such a proviso.

(4) Despite the frequent references in the Senate to the fact that the Sherman bill might reach labor and farmers' organizations, such a question was not mentioned in all the prolonged debates in the Senate and the House on the Judiciary Committee bill. The only reasonable explanation of this difference appears to be that the Sherman bill seemed to reach such organizations, whereas the bill actually passed did not, in the opinion of the members of Congress, do so.

(5) The brief for the plaintiffs asserted that it was significant that Congress, after the passage of the Sherman Act, had before it various proposals to exempt labor organizations, none of which it passed. It was declared further

that there was special significance in the fact that this refusal to exempt labor followed the application of the act to union activities. The brief neglects to point out, however, that five of these six proposals were bills to make illegal combinations to prevent competition and to raise prices. These five bills, in other words, were not mere proposals to exempt labor from the Act of 1890. They were, on the contrary, proposals to strengthen the anti-trust legislation. They each had a labor exemption proviso because their framers considered such a proviso necessary in an anti-price raising bill.

Counsel for the plaintiffs, as has been said, referred to five such measures.[13] They might have mentioned six more.[14] Every one of these eleven proposals were anti-price raising measures which exempted labor.[15] Only one of the proposals mentioned in the brief, S. 1546, introduced by Senator Allen in the 55th Congress on April 1, 1897, was restricted to the specific purpose of amending the Act of 1890 so as to exempt labor and farmers' organizations.[16] The fact that there is no record that this bill was reported out of committee may signify that the use of the act by the courts in labor cases appeared so desirable that the Senate wished no change. Or it may mean nothing more than the fact that the bill became

---

[13] H. R., 6640, in the 52nd Congress; H. R., 10539, in the 55th Congress; H. R., 11667, in the 56th Congress; S., 649 and H. R., 14947, in the 57th Congress.

[14] S., 1728, H. R., 89, H. R., 166, and H. R., 2636, in the 52nd Congress; H. R., 7938 in the 55th Congress; and H. R., 11988 in the 57th Congress.

[15] Copies of the bills here mentioned, in the order of their introduction, may be found in Bills and Debates Relating to Trusts, Senate Document, No. 147, 57th Congress, 2nd Session, 1902-1903, pp. 465 and 411, 469 and 449, 473 and 431, 477 and 417, 481, 581, 949, 953, 987, and 999.

[16] Bills and Debates, p. 557.

lost in the "legislative hopper" along with the usual multitude of bills. Even if one grants, however, that the Senate's refusal to pass the Allen measure shows that it was thought well to have the act apply to labor, the fact has little significance as to the intent of the Congress which in 1890 passed the Sherman Act. The evidence that that Congress had no desire to reach labor unions appears conclusive.

One cannot leave the discussion of the argument of counsel in the case without calling attention to the failure of the attorneys for the workers to present their case properly. They permitted counsel for the firm to present a misleading account purporting to show that Congress intended that the act should apply to labor; and they made no effective answer to that account. An adequate presentation of the hatters' case to the Supreme Court might have greatly changed the history of labor cases since 1908.

The decision in Loewe v. Lawlor[17] is of great importance because the Supreme Court took the position (1) that the Sherman Act applied to labor combinations, (2) that secondary boycotts affecting interstate commerce was illegal under it, and (3) that suits for damages might be brought against individual union members under its terms.

On the rendering of the decision the company's suit went back to the Circuit Court. After a trial lasting from October 13, 1909, to February 4, 1910, the jury, having been instructed by the court to return a verdict for the company, assessed the damages at $74,000. In accordance with the law this amount was trebled by the court. The addition of costs brought the total to over $232,000. The hatters appealed to the Circuit Court of Appeals, which, on April 10, 1911, reversed the judgment of the lower court. It ruled that there had been error in directing the jury to return a verdict for

[17] 208 U. S. 274.

the company.[18] After a new trial, which lasted from August 26 to October 11, 1912, another verdict against the hatters was returned. It resulted in the entering on November 15, 1912, of a judgment of over $252,000.

The hatters again appealed to the Circuit Court of Appeals, asserting that there was not sufficient evidence to prove that the Sherman Act had been violated, nor to justify holding the individual members of the union responsible for the acts of their officers in carrying out the boycott. On December 18, 1913, the court upheld the judgment of the court below.[19] The defendants thereupon appealed to the Supreme Court.

On January 5, 1915, the Supreme Court affirmed the results reached in the lower courts. The decision, which was rendered by Justice Holmes, reiterated the court's earlier declaration that the hatters' boycott violated the Sherman Act. It considered at length whether the individual members of the union should be held liable for the acts of their officers. It arrived at an affirmative conclusion, which was largely based on the fact that the members who knew of the boycott had continued to pay dues and support their officers while the boycott was being conducted.[20] Not until 1917 was the company able to collect the damages which had been awarded it.[21]

The Gompers Contempt Case.—The second pronouncement of the Supreme Court concerning the legality of union activities under the Sherman Act came on May 15, 1911, in the decision rendered in Gompers v. Bucks Stove and Range

[18] Lawlor v. Loewe, 187 Fed. 522.
[19] Lawlor v. Loewe, 209 Fed. 721.
[20] Lawlor v. Loewe, 235 U. S. 522, 534-536.
[21] Merritt, *History of the League for Industrial Rights,* New York, 1925, pp. 28-29.

Company.[22] As a result of a dispute of several years' duration between the members of the molders' union and the stove company, the American Federation of Labor, in May, 1907, placed the name of the firm in the "We Don't Patronize" list of its magazine, the *American Federationist*. Thereafter circulars were sent out and a nation-wide boycott took place.

In December, 1907, the company secured an injunction in the Supreme Court of the District of Columbia against the American Federation of Labor, its officers, and the molders. The defendants were enjoined from carrying on any activities in connection with the boycott. Advertising or publishing any information calling attention to the boycott was prohibited. The American Federation of Labor published the firm's name in the "We Don't Patronize" list in January, 1908. Other publicity was also given the boycott after the injunction was issued. As a result Samuel Gompers, Frank Morrison, and John Mitchell, officers in the Federation, were sentenced to jail for contempt of court in December, 1908. The sentences imposed upon them were one year, nine months, and six months respectively.

In March, 1909, the Court of Appeals modified the injunction, confining its terms to prohibiting the printing of the firm's name in the "We Don't Patronize" list in furtherance of the boycott. Toward the end of the same year the court upheld the sentences for contempt. Soon after this both contempt and injunction cases were merged and appealed to the United States Supreme Court. In 1910, after the death of its president, the Bucks Stove and Range Company came under new management. As a result the labor dispute was settled, and in January, 1911, the injunction proceedings were dismissed at the request of the firm. The contempt case, how-

[22] 221 U. S. 418.

ever, went on to the Supreme Court, which rendered a decision, delivered by Justice Lamar, on May 15, 1911. It dismissed the contempt cases against Gompers, Morrison, and Mitchell on technical grounds.[23]

Although the firm's petition for an injunction alleged that its interstate commerce was restrained, it had not asked for relief under the provisions of the Sherman Act. In their argument before the Supreme Court the defendants took the position that no court had the right to enjoin a boycott if "spoken words or printed matter were used as one of the instrumentalities by which it was made effective." This position appeared untenable to the Supreme Court. It pointed out that if the argument were sound no court could enjoin a boycott "even if interstate commerce was restrained by means of a blacklist, boycott, or printed device to accomplish its purpose"; and this notwithstanding the fact that the Sherman Act specifically directed the Attorney-General to seek injunctions against unlawful restraints of such commerce. The court called attention to the fact that among the acts of the unlawful Danbury Hatters' combination had been the circulation of advertisements. It went on to say:

the principle announced by the court was general. [The statute] covered any illegal means by which interstate commerce is restrained, whether by unlawful combinations of capital, or unlawful combinations of labor; and we think also whether the restraint be occasioned by unlawful contracts, trusts, pooling arrangements, blacklists, boycotts, coercion, threats, intimidation, and whether these be made effective, in whole or in part, by acts, words or printed matter.

The court's protective and restraining powers extend to every

[23] For an extensive description of this boycott and its results see Laidler, *Boycotts and the Labor Struggle,* New York, 1913, Chapter VIII.

device whereby property is irreparably damaged or commerce is illegally restrained. To hold that the restraint of trade under the Sherman anti-trust act, or on general principles of law, could be enjoined, but that the means through which the restraint was accomplished could not be enjoined would be to render the law impotent.[24]

It will be recalled that the injunctions issued in the Pullman strike operated to restrain various peaceful activities carried on in connection with the strike.[25] It was implied that if the strike itself violated the Sherman Act the methods used to carry it on were likewise enjoinable. This idea received explicit statement and emphasis in the Supreme Court's decision in the Bucks case. Though the statement was *obiter dictum*, it implied that any act, however peaceful, which was part of a conspiracy to restrain interstate trade unlawfully, itself partook of the illegal nature of the conspiracy.

Hitchman v. Mitchell.—The case of Hitchman Coal and Coke Company v. Mitchell, which was decided by the Supreme Court on December 10, 1917,[26] though always recognized to be of great importance, has not usually been thought to have had a close relationship to the Sherman Act. As a matter of fact the decision of the District Court in this case, had it been approved in its entirety by the Supreme Court, might have resulted in tremendously increasing the handicaps which the act imposes upon labor unions.

The coal company, which had for some time dealt with the United Mine Workers, found itself, in 1906, involved in a dispute with the union. After a strike, it resumed operations under agreements with each worker that he would not

[24] 221 U. S. 418, 438-439.
[25] See above, pp. 66, 69.
[26] 245 U. S. 229.

belong to the union so long as he remained in the employ of the company. In September, 1907, the union sent agents into the vicinity of the company's property for the purpose of organizing the workers. In October the company sued for an injunction in the Circuit Court (afterwards the District Court) for the Northern District of West Virginia. The court granted an injunction restraining all attempts to organize the company's employees without its consent.[27]

The order had been sought on the general equity ground of preventing damage to property rights, and, since diversity of citizenship existed, had been granted on that ground. On September 21, 1909, the court rendered a decision on a motion to modify. It pointed out that one of the charges against the union was that it was an attempt to monopolize labor in violation of the Sherman Act. In refusing to modify the injunction the court said that it was undesirable to pass on this charge until it had plenty of time for consideration.[28]

The court made the injunction permanent on December 23, 1912. In a lengthy opinion[29] it considered the legality of the United Mine Workers under the Sherman Act. The decision quoted extensively from the proceedings of one of the joint conferences of miners and operators in the Central Competitive Field. These excerpts stressed the need of organizing the non-union fields.[30] The court spoke as follows:

It is impossible to deny the conclusions to be drawn from all this. By reason of the natural advantages in the way of superior veins, roofs, and quality, West Virginia coals can be mined for something like 50 per cent less than those of Ohio, Western

[27] The injunction is briefly described in the Supreme Court decision. 245 U. S. 229, 261-262.

[28] Hitchman Coal and Coke Co. v. Mitchell, 172 Fed. 963.

[29] Hitchman Coal and Coke Co. v. Mitchell, 202 Fed. 512.

[30] 202 Fed. 512, 535-537.

Pennsylvania, Indiana, and Illinois, and then even her miners can make better wages. The officers and members of this union are almost wholly residents of Ohio, Western Pennsylvania, Indiana, and Illinois. In 1898 as an organization they entered into a direct contract with the operators of that field for and in consideration of an eight hour labor day and other concessions to organize the West Virginia miners, and, by reason of the control they would have under the union's laws over such miners when so organized, 'protect' these operators in Ohio, Western Pennsylvania, Indiana, and Illinois from the existing open competition even then threatening the markets of such operators especially in the West and the Lake regions.[31]

All the evidence in this record goes to show pretty conclusively that the 14 years' struggle of this labor organization since it entered into the compact with the operators of Ohio, Western Pennsylvania, Indiana, and Illinois in 1898 to unionize the operations in West Virginia has not been in the interest either of the betterment of mine labor in the state or of upholding that free commerce in coal between the states guaranteed by federal law, but to restrain and even destroy it in West Virginia for the benefit of these unionized competitive states. . . . Such a combination is clearly a common-law conspiracy, too far reaching to be reasonable, in restraint of trade, as well, in my judgment, a direct violation of the Sherman Anti-Trust Law.[32]

The court based its conclusion that the United Mine Workers was an unlawful organization (1) on its rules and principles, and (2) on its procedure and practices. Under the first head came such matters as the union's requirement that members surrender freedom of action, its assumption of the right to call strikes at its own pleasure, its limitation of the employer's right to hire and fire, etc. Under the second head the court concluded that the union was unlawful be-

[31] 202 Fed. 512, 541.
[32] 202 Fed. 512, 545-546.

cause "(1) it seeks to create a monopoly of mine labor such as to enable it, as an organization, to control the coal mining business of the country; and (2) has by express contract joined in a combination and conspiracy with a body of rival operators, resident in other states, to control, restrain, and, to an extent at least, destroy, the coal trade of the state of West Virginia."[33]

The court was of the opinion that the union's attempt to get Hitchman to deal with it and to organize his workers was carried out in pursuit of its unlawful purpose to monopolize mine labor and suppress the West Virginia coal industry. "By reason of its unlawful organization, purposes, and practices as hereinbefore set forth," said the court, "this organization, combination, or union, as now constituted, is unlawful, and under the law, therefore, has no right to seek plaintiff's employees to become members thereof or to become party to its unlawful purposes and practices." The injunction was made "perpetual."[34]

The defendants appealed from the decision to the Circuit Court of Appeals. On May 28, 1914, that court reversed the judgment of the District Court. It did not consider it necessary to discuss the Sherman Act at length. It pointed out, however, that only the government could sue for an injunction under the statute. It denied the position of the lower court that the United Mine Workers was an unlawful organization, and held that the only question should have been whether the union was guilty of unlawful acts. After considering this question it ruled against the issuing of the injunction. It held that the union had a right to induce the workers to join it, and that they might lawfully do so. The company, in recourse, had the right to discharge them. The

[33] 202 Fed. 512, 554.
[34] 202 Fed. 512, 556-557.

court thus thrust aside the question of the union's unlawful character under the Sherman Act.[35]

The Hitchman Company appealed from this decision to the Supreme Court, which, on December 10, 1917, reversed the Circuit Court of Appeals. Those portions of the injunction which restrained the union's attempt to organize the miners were upheld. The opinion of the court was of the first importance. It held that contracts whereby workers agreed with a company not to join a union while in its employ were valid and would be protected by the courts; and it asserted that the attempt of a union to induce such workers to become members was equivalent to inducing breach of contract and was enjoinable. In view of the decision of the District Court it is significant that no direct mention of the Sherman Act was made in Justice Pitney's opinion for the majority, although the court did refer to the union's unlawful purpose. It concerned itself with the unlawfulness of the union's activities, not of the union itself.

Justice Brandeis, with whom Justices Holmes and Clarke concurred, rendered a dissenting opinion. He took the position that the union, in attempting to get the Hitchman miners to promise to become members, was not guilty of an unlawful act and should not have been enjoined. He declared that the legality of the union under the Sherman Act should not have been passed upon by the District Court, and that no proof was shown that an unlawful conspiracy to injure the coal trade of West Virginia existed.[36]

Although the Supreme Court made no mention of the Sherman Act in its decision, the Hitchman case is worth noting. It was the first instance in which the United Mine Workers, which has been a defendant to more labor pro-

[35] Mitchell v. Hitchman Coal and Coke Co., 214 Fed. 685.
[36] Hitchman Coal and Coke Co. v. Mitchell, 245 U. S. 229.

ceedings under the Sherman Act than any other union, was
charged with violating that measure. It was the first case, as
far as the official reports show, in which an attempt to organize workers engaged in production within a state was
considered part of a conspiracy to violate the Sherman Act.
It was the first case, and as far as can be ascertained, the
only one, in which a union as such was said by the court to
be an unlawful organization under the Sherman Act.

It was this last point which possessed the most damaging
possibilities for labor unions. There had been, it is true, no
petition to dissolve the union as an unlawful organization.
The District Court, however, had declared that the union
was unlawful. If it had been sustained in this view, later
courts, had they been requested to do so, would have had a
legal basis upon which to issue injunctions ordering not
merely the cessation of the unlawful acts of unions, but the
dissolution of the unions themselves.

The Supreme Court had, when the District Court rendered
its decision in December, 1912, already approved numerous
injunctions which had ordered the dissolution of business
combinations.[37] The dissolution of labor unions as unlawful
combinations has frequently been effected in recent times,
especially in such countries as Turkey and China. The District Court in the Hitchman case laid the basis for such proceedings in the United States. The importance of the refusal
of the higher courts to consider the United Mine Workers
an unlawful organization is thus obvious enough.[38]

[37] See for example, Northern Securities Co. v. U. S., 193 U. S. 197
(1904); Standard Oil Co. v. U. S. 221 U. S. 1 (1911); American
Tobacco Co. v. U. S., 221 U. S. 106 (1911).

[38] It is quite probable that the Supreme Court, had it considered the
matter when the case came before it in 1917, would have found
that Section 6 of the Clayton Act, which declared that nothing

The Rule of Reason.—The history of this period would be incomplete without reference to the Supreme Court decisions in the Standard Oil and American Tobacco cases. These decisions were of great consequence, not only because of the importance of the businesses with which they dealt, but because of the "rule of reason" which the court enunciated. The decisions, which were rendered on May 15 and May 29, 1911, directed the dissolution of the oil and tobacco trusts as combinations unlawful under the Sherman Act. The opinion in the Standard Oil case entered into an exposition of the "rule of reason" to be applied in interpreting the Anti-trust Act. The principles laid down were reiterated in the American Tobacco case. The court took the position that only those agreements which were in undue or unreasonable restraint of interstate trade were prohibited by the statute. It held that the oil and tobacco combinations were unlawful according to this criterion. Excerpts from the Standard Oil decision will make the court's position clearer.

The statute . . . evidenced the intent not to restrain the right to make and enforce contracts, whether resulting from combinations or otherwise, which did not unduly restrain interstate or foreign commerce, but to protect that commerce from being restrained by methods, whether old or new, which would constitute an interference,—that is, an undue restraint.[39]

The merely generic enumeration which the statute makes of the acts to which it refers, and the absence of any definition of restraint of trade as used in the statute, leaves room for but one conclusion, which is, that it was expressly designed not to unduly limit the application of the act by precise definition, but while

---

in the anti-trust laws should be construed to forbid the existence of labor organizations, operated to prevent their dissolution.

[39] 221 U. S. 1, 60.

clearly fixing a standard, that is, by defining the ulterior boundaries which could not be transgressed with impunity, to leave it to be determined by the light of reason, guided by the principles of law and the duty to apply and enforce the public policy embodied in the statute, in every given case whether any particular act or contract was within the contemplation of the statute.[40]

In both the Standard Oil and American Tobacco cases Justice Harlan entered a vigorous dissent. He pointed out that the court, in the Freight Association and the Joint Traffic cases,[41] had declared that "every" combination in restraint of interstate trade was unlawful, that the Sherman Act itself used the word "every," and that the majority, in taking the position that only unreasonable restraints were illegal, was reversing itself and changing the policy adopted by Congress. In meeting this position the majority declared that though, in the cases cited, it had used words which, if taken out of their context, would lead to the view that it believed the act prohibited "every" restraint, the facts with respect to the combinations described in those cases showed them to be in unreasonable restraint of trade.

The court called attention to a statement it had made in the case of Hopkins v. United States,[42] uttered on the same day on which it had rendered a decision in the Joint Traffic case. It had said, "There must be some direct and immediate effect upon interstate commerce in order to come within the act." It continued as follows:

If the criterion by which it is to be determined in all cases whether every contract, combination, etc., is a restraint of trade within the intendment of the law, is the direct or indirect effect

[40] 221 U. S. 1, 64.
[41] 166 U. S. 290; 171 U. S. 505.
[42] 171 U. S. 578, 592; see above pp. 72-73.

of the acts involved, then of course the rule of reason becomes the guide . . .[43]

Thus the rule of reason merges with the rule that combinations having a direct, immediate, and (by implication) material effect upon interstate commerce are unlawful, while those whose effect is indirect, incidental, and (by implication) immaterial, are not unlawful.

Whether a direct restraint upon interstate commerce is necessarily equivalent to an unreasonable restraint, whether the criterion of directness has sufficient definiteness to be valuable, and whether the rule of reason has been satisfactorily applied or generally forgotten in the labor cases, are questions to which attention will be devoted in later chapters.

[43] 221 U. S. 1, 66.

CHAPTER VI

THE CLAYTON ACT AND THE DUPLEX CASE

The Labor Sections of the Clayton Act.—The Clayton Anti-trust Act[1] was passed after a prolonged agitation against what trade unionists considered the misuse of the injunction and the Sherman Act in labor cases. It became law on October 15, 1914, and was at once hailed by Samuel Gompers and other trade union leaders as labor's "Magna Charta."[2] The greater part of the new law was devoted to increasing the restrictions upon business combinations with a view to strengthening the Sherman Act.

There is no intention here of examining the Clayton Act with respect to its general effect upon the legal status of labor. Our primary task is to show the effect of its provisions upon the use of the Sherman Act in labor cases.

The pertinent sections of the Clayton Act are the following:

Section 6. That the labor of a human being is not a commodity or article of commerce. Nothing contained in the anti-trust laws shall be construed to forbid the existence and operation of labor, agricultural, or horticultural organizations, instituted for the purposes of mutual help, and not having capital stock or conducted for profit, or to forbid or restrain individual members of such organizations from lawfully carrying out the legitimate

[1] 38 Stat. 780.
[2] See for example an article by Gompers entitled, "The Charter of Industrial Freedom-Labor Provisions of the Clayton Anti-Trust Law," *American Federationist,* Vol. 21, p. 957.

objects thereof; nor shall such organizations, or the members thereof be held or construed to be illegal combinations or conspiracies in restraint of trade under the antitrust laws.

Section 20. That no restraining order or injunction shall be granted by any court of the United States, . . . in any case between an employer and employees, or between employers and employees, or between employees, or between persons employed and persons seeking employment, involving, or growing out of, a dispute concerning terms or conditions of employment, unless necessary to prevent irreparable injury to property, or to a property right, of the party making the application, for which injury there is no adequate remedy at law . . .

And no such restraining order or injunction shall prohibit any person or persons, whether singly or in concert, from terminating any relation of employment, or from ceasing to perform any work or labor, or from recommending, advising, or persuading others by peaceful means so to do; or from attending at any place where any such person or persons may lawfully be, for the purpose of peacefully obtaining or communicating information, or from peacefully persuading any person to work or to abstain from working; or from ceasing to patronize or to employ any party to such dispute, or from recommending, advising, or persuading others by peaceful and lawful means so to do; from paying or giving to, or withholding from, any person engaged in such dispute, any strike benefits or other moneys or things of value; or from peaceably assembling in a lawful manner, and for lawful purposes; or from doing any act or thing which might lawfully be done in the absence of such dispute by any party thereto; nor shall any of the acts specified in this paragraph be considered or held to be violations of any law of the United States.

Section 16. That any person, firm, corporation, or association shall be entitled to sue for and have injunctive relief, in any court of the United States having jurisdiction over the parties, against threatened loss or damage by a violation of the antitrust laws, . . . when and under the same conditions and principles as injunctive relief against threatened conduct that will cause loss or damage is granted by courts of equity, under the rules governing such proceedings, and upon the execution of proper bond against damages for an injunction improvidently granted, and a showing that the danger of irreparable loss or damage is immediate, a preliminary injunction may issue. . . .

Section 17 of the act provided that no preliminary injunction might be issued without notice to the opposite party. Sections 21 and 22 provided that in cases of contempt of court arising from the willful disobedience of an order of the court, the accused was entitled to ask for and receive a jury trial, on condition that the act committed by him was a criminal offense under the laws of the United States or of the state in which it was committed.[3]

A reading of Sections 6 and 20 of the Clayton Act might lead to the conclusions that the Anti-trust Act was no longer to be applied to labor organizations; that no injunctions were to be issued by the federal courts in labor disputes unless necessary to prevent irreparable injury to property or property rights, for which injury there was no adequate remedy at law; that no injunctions were to be issued preventing persons from quitting work singly or in concert, from engaging in peaceful picketing and persuasion, from carrying on primary or secondary boycotts, from paying strike benefits, from peaceably assembling, or from doing things which might lawfully be done in the absence of a labor dispute.

If such conclusions were correct labor would have found itself in as satisfactory a position as British labor was in after the passage of the Trade Disputes Act of 1906. Con-

[3] This latter provision was held constitutional by the Supreme Court in Michaelson v. U. S., 266 U. S. 42, decided October 20, 1924.

sidered only with relation to the Sherman Act, the provisions of Section 20 might have been thought (and were at first thought by unionists) to legalize a boycott such as that in the Danbury Hatters' case,[4] a railway strike such as that declared illegal in the Pullman strike cases, and acts of picketing and conducting a strike, such as were enjoined at that time.[5]

Despite the enthusiasm with which organized labor greeted the passage of the Clayton Act, events proved it to be devoid of the benefits anticipated. Not long after its passage Daniel Davenport, for years an outstanding attorney in cases against labor, and counsel for the Loewe company in the Danbury Hatters' case, declared in his testimony before the United States Commission on Industrial Relations that trade unions were given no advantages by the Clayton Act which they did not already possess.[6]

The failure of the Clayton Act to bring about any considerable improvement in the legal status of unions was not finally established until the Supreme Court rendered its decision, on January 3, 1921, in the case of Duplex Printing Press Company v. Deering,[7] soon to be described. So far as it specifically affected the Sherman Act in its application to trade unions, the Act of 1914 produced only one advantage for labor. It made it impossible to hold that a union as such was an unlawful organization under the anti-trust laws.[8]

The Increased Handicap to Labor.—It would be entirely incorrect, however, to assert that the Clayton Act had no

[4] Loewe v. Lawlor, 208 U. S. 274 (1908).

[5] U. S. v. Debs, 64 Fed. 724.

[6] *Report of the United States Commission on Industrial Relations,* 1916, p. 10713.

[7] 254 U. S. 443.

[8] See Hitchman v. Mitchell, 202 Fed. 512, 554 (1912); above, pp. 90-95.

important effect upon the application of the Act of 1890 to labor. The truth is that the law, so gratefully received as labor's "Magna Charta," greatly multiplied the burden of the Sherman Act. The latter law provided for three types of enforcement, criminal proceedings, injunction proceedings brought by the government, and damage suits brought by private parties. Section 16 of the Clayton Act added a fourth method, injunction suits brought by private parties. In the long run this particular provision of the act has probably had a greater effect upon labor than any other. Of a total of 64 proceedings of all kinds brought against labor under the Sherman Act after the passage of the Clayton Act, 34, or more than one half, were private injunction suits. The law may thus be said to have more than doubled the chances that labor activities would be hampered by the Sherman Act. This is indeed a curious, though probably the most important consequence of a law which labor greeted as its great charter of industrial freedom.[9]

The Duplex Case.[10]—The Duplex Printing Press Company was a manufacturer of newspaper presses with a plant in Battle Creek, Mich. There were only three other companies in the country manufacturing such presses. Between 1909 and 1913 the machinists' union induced these three to recognize and deal with it. They granted an eight-hour day and established a minimum wage scale. The Duplex Company refused to recognize the union and worked on an open shop basis. For the most part the firm operated ten hours

[9] For a further discussion of this matter see below, p. 218.
[10] Several labor cases involving the Sherman Act arose during the period between 1914 and the Supreme Court decision in the Duplex case in 1921. Following the general plan of this section of the study they will not be discussed here. They are all described in Appendix C.

per day. Two of the three other firms notified the union that they would be obliged to terminate their relations with it unless the Duplex Company signed a union agreement. In order to avert such a consequence the union, in 1913, called a strike at the Michigan plant and instructed its members and those of other unions to help it in boycotting the company's presses. Of the two hundred machinists working in the plant only eleven left the firm's employ.[11]

The machinists applied an elaborate program to enforce the boycott in and about New York City. In the words of Justice Pitney:

The acts embraced the following, with others: warning customers that it would be better for them not to purchase, or having purchased not to instal, presses made by the [firm], and threatening them with loss should they do so; threatening customers with sympathetic strikes in other trades; notifying a trucking company usually employed by customers to haul the presses not to do so, and threatening it with trouble if it should; inciting employees of the trucking company, and other men employed by customers of [the company], to strike against their respective employers in order to interfere with the hauling and installation of presses, and thus bring pressure to bear upon the customers; notifying repair shops not to do repair work on Duplex presses; coercing union men by threatening them with loss of union cards and with being blacklisted as "scabs" if they assisted in installing the presses; threatening an exposition company with a strike if it permitted [the Duplex Company's] presses to be exhibited; and resorting to a variety of other modes of preventing the sale of presses of [the firm's] manufacture in or about New York City, and delivery of them in interstate commerce, such as injuring and threatening to injure [the firm's]

[11] Duplex Printing Press Co. v. Deering et al., 254 U. S. 443, 460, 463, 479-480.

customers and prospective customers, and persons concerned in hauling, handling, or installing the presses.[12]

The Duplex Company petitioned for an injunction against the machinists in the District Court for the Southern District of New York. It charged the union with an illegal combination to monopolize the machinists' trade throughout the country and to compel the employers to operate union shops. On April 23, 1917, Judge Manton rendered a decision denying the petition. He pointed out that the conduct of the union had been peaceful. He believed it to be lawful and within the union's rights, and concluded that, under the terms of the Clayton Act, no injunction might be issued.[13]

The company thereupon appealed to the Circuit Court of Appeals, Second Circuit, which affirmed the decision of the lower court on May 25, 1918. Judges Hough and Hand constituted the majority, with Judge Rogers dissenting. Judge Hough asserted that the boycott was clearly a violation of the Sherman Act if that measure were strictly interpreted. He believed, however, that the Clayton Act had changed the situation by legalizing the secondary boycott. In response to the argument that the Clayton Act had forbidden injunctions only where the dispute involved an employer and his own employees, he declared that the act, since it contained the phrase "employers and employees," was meant to apply to these two classes. He also pointed out that there had been a dispute in Michigan between the company and its own employees. He concluded that no injunction was justified under the Clayton Act.[14]

Judge Rogers vigorously dissented from the opinion of

[12] 254 U. S. 443, 463-464.
[13] Duplex Printing Press Co. v. Deering et al., 247 Fed. 192.
[14] Duplex Printing Press Co. v. Deering et al., 252 Fed. 722, 747-748.

the majority. In his view the boycott was accompanied by threats and coercion, did damage to the company, and was unlawful. It was as clear a violation of the Sherman Act as the Danbury Hatters' boycott. In his opinion the Clayton Act did not make legal acts which were illegal before its passage. He believed, furthermore, that the Clayton Act forbade the use of an injunction only in a case involving an employer and his own employees. The dispute in the present case was not in this class. Referring to the plan of the machinists to make the presses unmarketable, the judge declared:

If this can be done under the laws of the United States, then it seems that no manufacturer of printing presses in this country can maintain an "open" shop, and no machinist engaged in the manufacture of such presses can earn his living at his trade, unless he consents to join a union, and be bound by all its rules and regulations, and the channels of interstate commerce are practically closed against the products of an "open" shop. If the truckmen are in the unions and cannot handle nonunion goods, of what use is it to ship goods from Michigan to New York? And if the unions have a right to say what goods their members shall handle, or shall not handle, what reason is there for saying that union men employed by railroads cannot refuse to handle any goods not made in an "open" shop?[15]

The Duplex Company appealed to the Supreme Court, which, on January 3, 1921, by a vote of six to three, reversed the judgment of the lower courts and directed that an injunction be granted to the company. The majority opinion declared that the machinists' boycott was a violation of the Sherman Act, and was unlawful despite the passage of the Clayton Law.

Counsel for the union contended that there had been no

[15] 252 Fed. 722, 745.

interference with interstate commerce. The members of the union had merely refused to transport and handle presses after they had reached the point of consignment. Though this caused some local embarrassment, interstate commerce had not been interfered with. If the opposite view were maintained "then teamsters and machinists' helpers employed by draymen could not legally combine or cease from working, as in every instance, no matter how local the situation, the contention would be raised that interstate commerce had been interfered with."[16]

Justice Pitney, speaking for the majority, pointed out that all the judges of the Circuit Court of Appeals had concurred in the view that the machinists' conduct "consisted essentially of efforts to render it impossible for complainant to carry on any commerce in printing presses between Michigan and New York; and that defendants had agreed to do and were endeavoring to accomplish the very thing pronounced unlawful by this court in Loewe v. Lawlor, . . ."[17]

The Justice asserted that Congress did not intend that secondary boycotts should be legalized by the Clayton Act, and declared that the first paragraph of Section 20, which prohibited the issuance of an injunction in "any case between an employer and employees, . . . involving, or growing out of, a dispute concerning terms or conditions of employment," confined this restriction upon the granting of injunctions only "to parties standing in proximate relation to a controversy such as is particularly described." Calling attention to the fact that the many thousands of machinists who had never worked at the factory of the company but who were involved in the boycott stood in no relation of employment to the firm, he declared that there was no dispute between

[16] Duplex Printing Press Co. v. Deering et al., 254 U. S. 443, 459.
[17] 254 U. S. 443, 464.

the employers of these machinists and the machinists themselves "respecting terms or conditions of employment." The Clayton Act was not intended to prevent the issuance of an injunction in such a case. "Congress had in mind particular industrial controversies, not a general class war."[18]

The Justice then proceeded to consider the phraseology of the second paragraph of Section 20 of the Clayton Act. After quoting from it, he declared:

The emphasis placed on the words "lawful" and "lawfully," "peaceful" and "peacefully," and the references to the dispute and the parties to it, strongly rebut a legislative intent to confer a general immunity for conduct violative of the Anti-trust Laws, or otherwise unlawful. The subject of the boycott is dealt with specifically in the "ceasing to patronize" provision, and by the clear force of the language employed the exemption is limited to pressure exerted upon a "party to such dispute" by means of "peaceful" and *lawful* influence upon neutrals. There is nothing here to justify defendants or the organizations they represent in using either threats or persuasion to bring about strikes or a cessation of work on the part of employees of complainant's customers or prospective customers, or of the trucking company employed by the customers, with the object of compelling such customers to withdraw or refrain from commercial relations with complainant, and of thereby constraining complainant to yield the matter in dispute. To instigate a sympathetic strike in aid of a secondary boycott cannot be deemed "peaceful and lawful" persuasion. In essence it is a threat to inflict damage upon the immediate employer, between whom and his employees no dispute exists, in order to bring him against his will into a concerted plan to inflict damage upon another employer who is in dispute with his employees.[19]

18 254 U. S. 443, 471-472.
19 254 U. S. 443, 473-474.

Referring to Section 6, Justice Pitney declared that its principal importance was

for what it does *not* authorize, and for the limit it sets to the immunity conferred. The section assumes the normal objects of a labor organization to be legitimate, and declares that nothing in the Anti-trust Laws shall be construed to forbid the existence and operation of such organizations or to forbid their members from *lawfully* carrying out their *legitimate* objects; and that such an organization shall not be held in itself—merely because of its existence and operation—to be an illegal combination or conspiracy in restraint of trade. But there is nothing in the section to exempt such an organization or its members from accountability where it or they depart from its normal and legitimate objects and engage in an actual combination or conspiracy in restraint of trade. And by no fair or permissible construction can it be taken as authorizing any activity otherwise unlawful, or enabling a normally lawful organization to become a cloak for an illegal combination or conspiracy in restraint of trade as defined by the Anti-trust Laws.[20]

The court directed that the union and its members should be enjoined from interfering or attempting to interfere with the sale, transportation, or delivery in interstate commerce of the company's presses, or their transportation, carting, installation, use, operation, exhibition, display, or repairing, or the performance of any contract made by the complainant respecting their sale, transportation, delivery, or installation, by causing or threatening to cause loss or inconvenience to anyone concerned with the presses; "and also and especially from using any force, threats, command, direction, or even persuasion with the object or having the effect of causing any person or persons to decline employment, cease employment, or not seek employment, or to refrain from work or cease

[20] 254 U. S. 443, 469.

working under any person, firm or corporation being a purchaser or prospective purchaser of any printing press or
presses from complainant, or engaged in hauling, carting,
delivering, installing, handling, using, operating, or repairing any such press or presses for any customer of complainant."[21]

Justices Brandeis, Holmes and Clarke dissented. Speaking
through Justice Brandeis, they held that the Clayton Act
was intended to improve the legal status of unions, and they
approved the decision of the lower courts. The dissenting
opinion supported the view that all those engaged in the
boycott had a common interest, and thus had a right to
refuse "to expend their labor upon articles whose very production constitutes an attack upon their standard of living
and the institution they are convinced supports it." They
concluded that that provision of the Clayton Act which restricted the issue of injunctions in disputes between employers and employees should operate to prevent an injunction
being issued in the Duplex case.[22]

The Supreme Court decision in this case was undoubtedly
the most important rendered in a labor case under the Sherman Act since the decision in the Danbury Hatters' case.
It definitely established the position that the legal status of
union activities under the Sherman Act had not been
changed by the passage of the Clayton Act. It reiterated the
declaration that a secondary boycott was illegal under the
Act of 1890. It made possible the greatly increased application of that measure to trade unions which has characterized
the period since the decision was rendered.

A German Conspiracy Case.—One may grant the possibility that one man, Senator Edmunds, in the Congress

[21] 254 U. S. 443, 478-479.
[22] 254 U. S. 443, 479, 481.

which passed the Sherman Law, expected that the act would apply to labor unions. It does not seem possible however, that anyone ever expected it to be used against a wartime conspiracy. That is nevertheless what happened in a criminal proceeding brought by the government, which resulted in the return of indictments on December 28, 1915, in the District Court of the Southern District of New York. A German agent, Rintelen, and seven others were charged with an illegal conspiracy to violate the Sherman Act by encouraging and fomenting strikes of munitions and shipping workers for the purpose of preventing the sending of munitions to the Allies.

The case was tried in April, 1917, and resulted in a verdict of guilty as to Rintelen and two other defendants, Lamar and Martin. They were each sentenced to prison terms of one year. Lamar and Martin appealed to the Circuit Court of Appeals, Second Circuit, which affirmed the judgment in a decision rendered on June 4, 1919.[23] The Supreme Court later refused to review the case on a writ of certiorari.[24]

The decision of the Circuit Court of Appeals is of particular interest for its discussion of what constitutes a violation of the Sherman Act. The conspirators had planned, by means of correspondence and publicity, and by distributing money among officers in control of various trade unions, to instigate strikes among workers manufacturing and transporting munitions. In order to accomplish this purpose Rintelen came to the United States with over half a million dollars to spend. He met the other defendants and they

[23] Lamar et al. v. U. S., 260 Fed. 561.
[24] 250 U. S. 673. Though the Lamar case involves a labor activity it is not included in Appendix C for the reason that there is no evidence to show that any of the defendants were themselves trade unionists.

agreed to carry out his desires. As a matter of fact the only result of the conspiracy was that Rintelen spent a great deal of money.

One of the arguments of Lamar and Martin in their plea before the Court of Appeals was that no strikes had resulted from their agreement. Circuit Judge Hough, speaking for the court, pointed out that the Supreme Court in the Nash case [25] had held that a conspiracy under the Sherman Act was established "by proving the forbidden meeting of minds." In the present case the existence of a crime had been proved when "the formulation of the plan, the formulation of purpose, the meeting of minds in an agreement to stop a trade always lawful, however repugnant temporarily to Germans," was shown.

Lamar and Martin contended that the Sherman Act was not meant to prevent agitation against the trade in munitions. In response the court said, "So far as the statute is concerned, the object or intent of the Sherman Act must, like that of every other written law, be gathered from its four corners as far as possible, and always if the words employed are clear and apt. Such is the case here, and no department of lawful commerce is left to be restrained or hindered by those who, for reasons that have not yet appealed to the Legislature, think it worthy of suppression."

The conspirators maintained that they had no intention of violating the Sherman Act; did not, indeed, have any suspicion that their acts did violate it. The court answered that "personal intent usually, and certainly here, means no more than an intention to do what was done; therefore, if . . . defendants intended to hinder and restrain export trade in war munitions, the fact that they had no suspicion of

[25] 229 U. S. 373.

thereby violating the Sherman Act is a matter of no importance, and is immaterial."

Finally, the defendants asserted that their agreement was
merely to bring about a peaceful quitting of work, and that
such an act was lawful under the Clayton Law. The court
replied that the Clayton Law had wrought no change in the
law of conspiracy as applicable to the case. It held that where
"the intent was solely to restrain foreign trade, and where
it is proved (as here) that the proposed instigation of strikes
bore no relation whatever to the welfare of the strikers, then
at most and best the strike becomes nothing more than an
instrument or means, legal in itself, but used only for an
illegal end." It is thus part of an illegal conspiracy to suppress
foreign trade, an object "as illegal as ever," which the Clayton Act assuredly "does not legalize."[26]

To summarize, the decision in the case of Lamar v. United
States indicates that so long as there exists an actual agreement or purpose to bring about a restraint of interstate or
foreign trade it is immaterial (1) that no actual restraint
resulted, (2) that Congress did not intend to prevent the
restraint of some particular kind of trade, (3) that the conspirators did not intend to violate the act, or (4) that the
restraint was to be accomplished by means otherwise lawful.
Though the conspiracy in this case was not one to carry
out a trade union purpose, the applicability of the court's
conclusions to labor activities may easily be made.

Two Business Cases.—Two important decisions rendered
by the Supreme Court in business cases during this period
are worth noting. Each of these decisions has a bearing
upon the application of the Sherman Act to labor.

The Eastern States Retail Lumber Dealers' Association
had adopted the practice of distributing among its members

[26] 260 Fed. 561.

a so-called "official report," which contained the names of wholesale dealers who sold lumber directly to consumers. The purpose of the report was to influence member retailers not to deal with such wholesalers. The government charged that the purpose was to restrain interstate commerce directly and unreasonably in violation of the Sherman Act. The association appealed to the Supreme Court, which upheld the view of the government in a decision rendered on June 22, 1914.[27] The court pointed out that while the Sherman Act did not reach "normal and usual contracts incident to lawful purposes and in furtherance of legitimate trade, it did broadly condemn all combinations and conspiracies which restrain the free and natural flow of trade in the channels of interstate commerce." Although there was no evidence of a boycotting agreement it was clear that the purpose of circulating the list was to influence members to boycott the listed wholesalers.

The resemblance of the purpose of the circulated reports to the purpose of an ordinary trade union boycott is apparent, as is also the similarity of the list to the "We Don't Patronize" list formerly published by the American Federation of Labor, which the Supreme Court implied was unlawful in its decision in Gompers v. Bucks Stove and Range Company.[28] This is one of the few cases which permit a close and direct comparison of the views of the Supreme Court in a labor case and a business case involving a similar practice. Here the position of the court corresponds to what one would expect from a reading of the labor boycott decisions.

In 1911 the government brought suit against the United

[27] Eastern States Retail Lumber Dealers' Association v. U. S., 234 U. S. 600.
[28] 221 U. S. 418, 438-439.

States Steel Corporation, seeking to have the corporation dissolved on the ground that it was engaged in an illegal restraint of trade and was a monopoly. In a decision rendered in the District Court for the District of New Jersey, in June, 1915, the government petition was denied. The government had called attention to the commanding position of the corporation in the market, and to various methods, such as the well-known "Gary dinners," whereby it had secured the stabilization of prices. The District Court[29] addressed itself to the question whether the size of a corporation and the percentage of its output to the total were criteria of its illegality under the Sherman Act. It pointed out that the Standard Oil and American Tobacco cases had established that combinations are unlawful when the public interest may be prejudiced by undue restraint of trade. It did not believe that the Steel Corporation did then or could in the future monopolize the steel trade. It concluded that mere size was not a criterion of illegality. The question was, had the corporation unduly restricted trade? This the court answered in the negative.

The government appealed the case to the Supreme Court, which rendered a decision on March 1, 1920.[30] Four of the justices affirmed the decision of the lower court, while a minority of three dissented. The majority asserted that the corporation was not a monopoly, that it had no power by itself to fix prices, and that it had committed no acts of aggression against its competitors. The fact that it was of impressive size was not sufficient to render it illegal under the Sherman Act. The court did not think public interest would be served by the dissolution of the corporation and its subsidiaries, that on the contrary, public interest might

[29] U. S. v. U. S. Steel Corporation, 223 Fed. 55.
[30] 251 U. S. 417.

suffer and foreign trade might be disturbed by such a procedure. It accordingly dismissed the government's petition.

The dissenting justices, speaking through Justice Day, differed from the majority on nearly every point. They called attention to the fact that as a result of the formation of the Steel Corporation prices had greatly increased, that for many years afterwards it had maintained and controlled prices, and that by combining with its competitors it could fix prices and restrain commerce "upon a scale heretofore unapproached in the history of corporate organization in this country." They agreed that size and power did not render a corporation unlawful, but when size and power were secured by conspiracies or combinations in restraint of trade the latter were unlawful. The decision of the majority, by placing the combination, organized in defiance of law, in an "impregnable position above the control of the law forbidding such combinations," necessarily resulted "in a practical nullification of the Act itself."

The decision in this case may be considered an application of the rule of reason laid down in the Standard Oil and American Tobacco cases.[31] Whatever may have been thought about the legality of the formation of the Steel Corporation, or of its price controlling methods, a majority of the court appeared to believe that the corporation had become what has been called "a good trust." It had no monopoly power, did not fix prices, and did not engage in unfair trade practices. In other words, it was not in unreasonable restraint of trade. The fact that it was the largest concern in the industry and the biggest in the whole country was not considered pertinent. The question was, was it an unreasonable combination in restraint of trade?

[31] See above, pp. 96-98.

Under the rule of reason the greatest of modern corporations was thus held to be unaffected by the act. It will be interesting to see how the rule of reason was applied, if at all, in the case of a railroad strike, or a coal strike, or the enforcement of an ordinary union rule.

CHAPTER VII

THE COAL STRIKE CASES

The period since the Supreme Court decision in Duplex v. Deering has witnessed the most extensive use of the Sherman Act in labor cases since its passage. There were only two important instances prior to the rendering of the Duplex decision in which the Supreme Court interpreted the act as applied to labor.[1] Since 1921 it has done so on six occasions.[2] In one of these cases the Supreme Court specifically applied the rule of reason to permit a labor agreement in restraint of trade.[3] Whereas the courts up to 1921 had for the most part applied the act to railway strikes and secondary boycotts, they now had before them numerous cases involving ordinary factory strikes, coal strikes, and trade agreements between employers and employees.[4] For the first time the act was used to prevent a strike of railway workers who were directly involved in a dispute with their em-

[1] Loewe v. Lawlor, 208 U. S. 274 (1908); 235 U. S. 522 (1915); and Gompers v. Bucks, 221 U. S. 418 (1911).

[2] United Mine Workers v. Coronado Coal Co., 259 U. S. 344 (1922); Coronado Coal Co. v. United Mine Workers, 268 U. S. 295 (1925); National Association of Window Glass Manufacturers v. U. S., 263 U. S. 403 (1923); United Leather Workers v. Herkert and Meisel, 265 U. S. 457 (1924); U. S. v. Brims, 272 U. S. 549 (1925); Bedford Stone Co. v. Journeyman Stone Cutters, 47 Sup. Ct. Rep. 522 (1927).

[3] National Association of Window Glass Manufacturers v. U. S.

[4] For example, the Herkert case; Borderland Coal Corporation v. United Mine Workers, 275 Fed. 871; and U. S. v. Brims, respectively.

ployers.[5] In this most recent period the application of the act to labor has gone so far as to be used against the most insignificant of labor activities.[6] Furthermore, the Supreme Court during this period had before it two business cases closely related to labor, and involving activities so much like those of labor that they give interesting opportunities for comparison.[7] Finally, the entire history of the Sherman Act is capped by the significant decision of the Supreme Court in the Bedford Stone case, rendered in April, 1927.[8]

Attention has been called to the fact that the United Mine Workers has been a defendant under the Sherman Act more often than any other labor organization. In the postwar period numerous decisions involving its activities have been rendered by the courts. Of these the decisions handed down by the Supreme Court in the Coronado case are of the first importance.

The Coronado Case.—The Bache-Denman Coal Company had a controlling interest in eight other corporations, operating mines in Arkansas. One of the companies in the group was the Coronado Coal Company. In March, 1914, Bache, the receiver for the controlling corporation, decided to cease dealing with the United Mine Workers and to put the properties on a non-union basis. He shut down some of the mines and prepared to open them on such a basis on April 6. Anticipating trouble, he employed guards and

[5] U. S. v. Railway Employees' Department, 283 Fed. 479; 286 Fed. 228 (1922). It will be recalled that the Pullman strike was a combination of a secondary boycott and a sympathetic strike.

[6] O'Brien v. U. S., 290 Fed. 185 (1923); U. S. v. Taliaferro, 290 Fed. 214 (1922).

[7] Industrial Association of San Francisco v. U. S., 268 U. S. 64 (1925); Anderson v. Shipowners' Association v. U. S., 47 Sup. Ct. Rep. 125 (1926).

[8] 47 Sup. Ct. Rep. 522.

bought rifles and ammunition. He posted notices ordering former employees to vacate the company houses. He gathered some thirty non-union miners at one of the plants ready to work.

The union officers called a public meeting, and a committee was appointed to visit the mine superintendent with a view to persuading the firm to change its plans. The committee, which went to visit the superintendent on April 6, was accompanied by a crowd which assaulted the guards, injured a number of employees, and forced the pulling of fires, with the result that all of the employees deserted the mine and it was completely filled with water.

During the month of June, the firm not having changed its plan to operate non-union, a movement developed among the union miners to make an attack upon the mine at which trouble had previously occurred. Early in the morning of July 17 this attack was begun. Many shots were fired into the premises. A coal wash-house was set on fire. By the afternoon all of the defending force had been driven away, the coal tipple set afire, and the whole plant destroyed by dynamite and fire. Several of the non-union employees were murdered.

In September, 1914, the companies brought a suit for damages against the United Mine Workers of America, District 21 of that organization and its officers, 27 local unions of the District and their officers, and 65 individuals. The suit, which was brought in the District Court of the Western District of Arkansas, charged the defendants with having entered into a conspiracy to restrain and monopolize interstate commerce in coal, and destroying the plaintiffs' property in consummation of this conspiracy. The complaint alleged that the value of the property destroyed amounted to

$740,000, and under the terms of the Sherman Act it asked for triple judgment, or $2,220,000.

The unions demurred to the suit, asserting that since they were unincorporated associations they could not be sued, and denying that they had violated the Sherman Act. The District Court sustained this demurrer.[9]

The plaintiffs thereupon appealed to the Circuit Court of Appeals, which reversed the judgment of the lower court in a decision rendered on July 21, 1916.[10] In response to the argument that the unions, being unincorporated associations, could not be sued, the court pointed out that they might be sued under the Sherman Act. The court further held that the destruction of property was part of the union policy to organize the whole industry and to handicap the non-union producers, and that there was no doubt that this constituted an illegal interference with interstate commerce. The case was remanded for further proceedings.

The trial of the suit in the District Court resulted in a verdict of $200,000, which was trebled by the court. To the judgment were added counsel fees of $25,000 and interest to the amount of $120,600. The defendants appealed from this result to the Court of Appeals, which upheld the judgment reached in the court below except as to the interest, which it did not allow. Its decision was rendered on April 28, 1919.[11]

The defendants then appealed on a writ of error to the Supreme Court, which rendered a unanimous decision, de-

[9] The foregoing facts appear in United Mine Workers v. Coronado Coal Co., 259 U. S. 344.

[10] Dowd v. United Mine Workers et al., 235 Fed. 1.

[11] United Mine Workers et al. v. Coronado Coal Co. et al., 258 Fed. 829.

livered by Chief Justice Taft, on June 5, 1922.[12] The court reversed the order of the lower courts awarding damages to the plaintiffs. One of the most important questions discussed was the suability of unincorporated associations such as trade unions. The Chief Justice described the structure and importance of the United Mine Workers, pointed out the legal recognition given unions, and referred to the Taff Vale judgment in which the House of Lords affirmed a decision holding unions suable. He concluded that they might be sued in the federal courts for their acts, "and that funds accumulated to be expended in conducting strikes are subject to execution in suits for torts committed by such unions in strikes." The court continued:

Our conclusion as to the suability of the defendants is confirmed in the case at bar by the words of sections seven and eight of the Anti-Trust Law. The persons who may be sued under Sec. 7 include "corporations and associations existing under or authorized by the laws of either the United States, the laws of any of the territories, the laws of any States, or the laws of any foreign country . . ." This language is very broad, and the words, given their natural signification, certainly include labor unions like these. They are, as has been abundantly shown, associations existing under the laws of the United States, of the territories thereof, and of the states of the Union. Congress was passing drastic legislation to remedy a threatening danger to the public welfare, and did not intend that any persons or combinations of persons should escape its application. Their thought was especially directed against business associations and combinations that were unincorporated to do the things forbidden by the act, but they used language broad enough to include all associations which might violate its provisions, recognized by the statutes of the United States or the states or the territories, of foreign

[12] United Mine Workers et al. v. Coronado Coal Co. et al., 259 U. S. 344.

countries as lawfully existing; and this, of course, includes labor unions, as the legislation referred to shows. [Thus it was that in the cases of United States v. Trans-Missouri Freight Association,[13] United States v. Joint Traffic Association,[14] Montague & Company v. Lowry,[15] and Eastern States Lumber Association v. United States,[16]] unincorporated associations were made parties to suits in the Federal courts under the Anti-trust Act without question by anyone as to the correctness of the procedure.[17]

Having thus concluded that the miners' union might properly be sued, the Chief Justice addressed himself to the question whether the defendants were really guilty of a violation of the Sherman Act. The first point to decide was whether the International Organization of the United Mine Workers was responsible for the acts of the miners. The court declared that there was no evidence to hold it responsible. It neither authorized the strike, prepared for it, nor paid its expenses. The strike was a purely local one for which the District Union paid the bills. After a further description of the evidence the court concluded that the District Union and the locals were responsible for the strike and the property damage involved.[18]

To hold that these unions were responsible, however, was not to maintain that they might be held for damages under the Sherman Act. That could be done only if it were proved that the unions had engaged in a conspiracy to restrain or monopolize interstate commerce in violation of the act. The plaintiffs had maintained that the events at the Arkansas mines were a result of the union policy to compel all

[13] 166 U. S. 290.
[14] 171 U. S. 505.
[15] 193 U. S. 38.
[16] 234 U. S. 600.
[17] 259 U. S. 344, 392.
[18] 259 U. S. 344, 393-403.

operators to deal with the union in order to prevent non-union coal from competing in the interstate market with union coal produced under higher costs. They cited records of the interstate conferences of miners and operators from 1898 to 1914 to show that there was a conspiracy between them to suppress competition from the non-union mines. The Supreme Court answered that, "Coal mining is not interstate commerce, and the power of Congress does not extend to its regulation as such." "Obstruction to coal mining is not a direct obstruction to interstate commerce in coal, although it, of course, may affect it by reducing the amount of coal to be carried in that commerce." The court continued as follows:

What really is shown by the evidence in the case at bar, drawn from discussions and resolutions of conventions and conference, is the stimulation of union leaders to press their unionization of non-union mines not only as a direct means of bettering the conditions and wages of their workers, but also as a means of lessening interstate competition for union operators which in turn would lessen the pressure of those operators for reduction of the union scale or their resistance to an increase. The latter is a secondary or ancillary motive whose actuating force in a given case necessarily is dependent on the particular circumstances to which it is sought to make it applicable. If unlawful means had here been used by the National body to unionize mines whose product was important, actually or potentially, in affecting prices in interstate commerce, the evidence in question would clearly tend to show that that body was guilty of an actionable conspiracy under the Anti-Trust Act. . . . But it is not a permissible interpretation of the evidence in question that it tends to show that the motive indicated thereby actuates every lawless strike of a local and sporadic character, not initiated by the National body but by one of its subordinate subdivisions.[19]

[19] 259 U. S. 344, 408-409.

After contrasting the case with Loewe v. Lawlor and Eastern States Lumber Dealers' Association v. United States, in which interstate commerce was the direct object of the conspiracies, the court declared that "coal mining is not interstate commerce and obstruction of coal mining, though it may prevent coal from going into interstate commerce, is not a restraint of that commerce unless the obstruction to mining is intended to restrain commerce in it or has necessarily such a direct, material and substantial effect to restrain it that intent reasonably must be inferred."[20]

The plaintiffs had contended that the fact that the miners had burned a railroad car laden with coal and billed to a town in Louisiana was significant as showing an intent to restrain interstate commerce. The court denied such significance, since Bache's men had used the car for defense during the battle and its burning was only a part of the general destruction.

It was further contended that the miners' obstruction to coal mining at the Bache-Denman mines resulted in keeping 75 per cent of their output out of interstate commerce, and that the miners must be charged with the intention to accomplish the natural result of their acts. The Supreme Court pointed out, in answer, that in a national production of from ten to fifteen million tons per week the 5,000 tons which the Bache-Denman mines produced in the most prosperous times "would have no appreciable effect upon the price of coal or non-union competition." If it be said that District 21 feared that, if Bache were successful, the defection among the union operators would spread and ultimately the whole district would become non-union, "and interstate commerce would then be substantially affected, it may be

[20] 259 U. S. 344, 410-411.

answered that this is remote" and there was no evidence in the record to show that the miners thought of it.

The court concluded that the evidence did not show that District 21 and the locals had been guilty of a conspiracy to restrain or monopolize interstate commerce, and that the jury should have been directed to return a verdict for the defendants. It remanded the case to the District Court for further proceedings.[21]

In October, 1923, a new trial took place in the District Court, which directed the jury to return a verdict in favor of the unions. The plaintiffs appealed from this decision to the Circuit Court of Appeals on a writ of error. They asserted that new evidence produced at the trial had changed the situation. The Circuit Court of Appeals, reviewing this evidence, concluded that there was nothing to justify a reversal of judgment in the light of the Supreme Court opinion, and it upheld the verdict for the defendants.[22]

The case then went to the Supreme Court again. On May 25, 1925, the court rendered another unanimous decision, which was delivered by Chief Justice Taft.[23] The plaintiffs asserted that new evidence indicated (1) that the International Organization of the United Mine Workers had been responsible for the original strike, (2) that the officers and members of the District Union had considered the strike necessary to prevent non-union competition in interstate commerce, and (3) that the productive capacity of the plaintiffs' mines was 5,000 tons daily, not 5,000 tons weekly, as the Supreme Court had thought, and that such an amount

[21] 259 U. S. 344, 411-413.
[22] Finley et al. v. United Mine Workers et al., 300 Fed. 972 (1924).
[23] Coronado Coal Co. et al. v. United Mine Workers et al., 268 U. S. 295.

was large enough to have a substantial effect upon interstate commerce.

The court concluded that the evidence was still not sufficient to justify holding the International responsible. As to the District Union the situation was different. The new evidence showed that the officers, speaking in convention, had considered it necessary to fight the operators to prevent nonunion coal from underselling union coal from neighboring states. Furthermore the evidence showing a production of nearly 5,000 tons a day was also significant. The court continued as follows:

The mere reduction in the supply of an article to be shipped in interstate commerce by the illegal or tortious prevention of its manufacture or production is ordinarily an indirect and remote obstruction to that commerce. But when the intent of those unlawfully preventing the manufacture or production is shown to be to restrain or control the supply entering and moving in interstate commerce, or the price of it in interstate markets, their action is a direct violation of the Anti-trust Act. . . . We think there was substantial evidence at the second trial in this case tending to show that the purpose of the destruction of the mines was to stop the production of nonunion coal and prevent its shipment to markets of other states than Arkansas, where it would in competition tend to reduce the price of the commodity and affect injuriously the maintenance of wages for union labor in competing mines.[24]

The court ordered the judgment in favor of the District Union and the defendants other than the International Organization reversed, and remanded the case for a new trial.

The third trial of the case was set for November 28, 1927. On October 17, 1927, however, the United Mine Workers

[24] 268 U. S. 295, 310.

and the plaintiffs settled the dispute out of court, the union agreeing to pay $27,500, the costs incurred for the trial planned for the following month. On the same day, as a result of the adjustment, the case was dismissed by order of the District Court. Thus ended litigation which had extended over a period of more than thirteen years.[25]

The Coronado dispute involved the most extensive litigation on record in a labor case under the Sherman Act. Its importance, however, does not arise on that account. The fact that the Supreme Court definitely established the principle that a trade union, an unincorporated association, might be sued for damages is of obvious significance. It is interesting that the terminology of the Sherman Act aided the court in reaching this conclusion. Since the court had long ago held that a trade union might be reached by the act it seemed logical to conclude that suits at law might be brought against it as a violator of the law under Section 7, which provided for such suits, and Section 8, which declared that "corporations and associations" were to be considered "persons" within the meaning of the law.

The possibility of damage suits against labor as a result of the first Coronado decision is not as dangerous as would at first appear. Only five such suits have been entered under the Sherman Act.[26] Of these five there have been only two in which the suits have been finally upheld.[27] Only one of these suits, the Danbury Hatters' case (it will be recalled that this suit was brought against individual unionists rather than

[25] *Monthly Labor Review,* Vol. 25, No. 6, December, 1927, p. 1291; *Report on Civil Liberties,* September-October, 1927, American Civil Liberties Union, p. 2; 9 *Law and Labor* 295.

[26] See Appendix C, Section III.

[27] Loewe v. Lawlor, 208 U. S. 274; and Coronado v. United Mine Workers, 268 U. S. 295.

against unions as such), resulted in the payment of substantial damages. It is of consequence that the Coronado suit, which, if damages asked for had been granted and trebled, would have cost the miners' unions over $2,000,000, was actually settled for $27,500. The fact that the hatters' case dragged out for twelve years and the Coronado case for thirteen years is evidence that an employer who sues labor for damages under the Sherman Act is embarking on a long and expensive enterprise which may in the end yield him little. That this has been generally understood appears when one recalls that the total number of damage suits under the act is a small fraction of the total number of private injunction suits.[28]

The Coronado decisions are probably more significant for their treatment of what constitutes a violation of the Sherman Act than for anything else. For the first time the Supreme Court had before it a labor case in which it had to decide whether an interruption of production within a state could be considered a violation of the Sherman Act. Its decisions were based upon two considerations. In the first place, was there an intent to restrain interstate commerce? Secondly, was the actual restraint upon interstate commerce so substantial that intent to restrain it must be inferred? In its 1922 decision it answered no to both questions. In its 1925 decision, on the basis of additional evidence, it answered yes to both questions. In other words, the court held that an interference with production within a state was a violation of the Sherman Act if the intent to restrain commerce existed.

The significance of such a position can hardly be overestimated. Any strike carried on with a view to secure

[28] See below, p. 212.

nation-wide recognition of a union is necessarily intended, in part, to prevent the competition of non-union goods with union goods in the interstate market. If union textile and shoe manufacturers in New England and union clothing manufacturers in Chicago and New York find their business threatened by the competition of non-union manufacturers in other districts, the obviously intelligent and necessary thing for the unions to do in order to protect the wages and conditions of their own members, is to attempt to organize the non-union producers. On the basis of the second Coronado decision, however, if such an attempt seriously obstructed production, it would be a violation of the Sherman Act.[29]

It is especially worth noting that the second Coronado decision held a coal strike to be a violation of the act, for, from 1898 on, the greatest single problem before the United Mine Workers has been to organize the non-union districts in order to protect its members. How the Sherman Act has been used to hinder such attempts to organize will appear from a consideration of the cases next to be described.[30]

The Borderland Case.—From 1920 on many operators of non-union mines in West Virginia brought suits for injunctions against the United Mine Workers under the Sherman

[29] See in this connection a decision restraining the Amalgamated Clothing Workers from attempting to organize the Philadelphia clothing workers, rendered on October 8, 1929. Alco-Zander Co. et al. v. Amalgamated Clothing Workers et al., 35 F (2) 203. Below, p. 250, Appendix C, Case 85.

[30] See Appendix C, Cases 16, 17, 18, and 24, for indictments under the Sherman Act against the miners' union which were not carried to trial. For another damage suit against the union see Pennsylvania Mining Co. v. United Mine Workers, 28 F (2) 851; Appendix C, Case 43.

Act. Their general complaint was that the miners were engaged in a conspiracy to restrain interstate commerce in coal mined under non-union conditions in West Virginia, and they sought injunctions to prevent the union's attempts to organize the state.

One of the most interesting of these suits was brought against the national and district unions, some of their officers, and several Indiana operators, in the District Court of Indiana, in September, 1921. The Borderland Coal Corporation, with mines in Mingo County, W. Va., complained on its own behalf and on behalf of 62 other companies in the same district, that a conspiracy in violation of the Sherman Act existed between the union and the union operators in the Central Competitive Field; and that this conspiracy was supported by means of the "check-off," whereby the operators deducted union dues from the wages of their employees and turned them over to the union. It was asserted that the union's attempt to organize West Virginia was accompanied by force and violence.

On October 31, 1921, Judge Anderson rendered a decision upholding the complaint as above set forth, but refusing to declare the United Mine Workers an unlawful combination in violation of the anti-trust acts. He issued a temporary injunction restraining the defendant operators from collecting and paying miners' dues to the union, and enjoining various union officers "and all other persons whomsoever" "from advising, assisting, encouraging, aiding, abetting, or in any way or manner, and by any and all means whatsoever by the use of any funds or money howsoever collected by the International Union, United Mine Workers of America, its officers, members, agents, or representatives, the unionization or the attempted unionization of the non-union mines in Mingo County, West Virginia, and Pike County, Kentucky. . . ."[31]

The officers of the United Mine Workers immediately appealed to the Circuit Court of Appeals, Seventh Circuit, which at once set aside the injunction pending its review of the case. On December 15, 1921, it rendered a decision reversing the order of the court below as to the check-off. The court declared that the company's property rights in interstate commerce had been injured by the destruction of mine property, by the use of force and intimidation, by secret attempts to get employees to violate their contracts with the firm, and by the sending in of money for these purposes. All of these acts should have been enjoined but were not. The company desired to keep the union from functioning, and to that end it sought and secured an injunction against the check-off and attempts to organize, both of which were lawful. The court concluded that the District Court had erred in not limiting the prohibitions to the acts directly interfering with the company's property rights in interstate commerce; in not limiting the prohibition of the sending in of money to its use for such interfering acts; and in enjoining the performance of existing check-off arrangements in the Central Competitive Field. The District Court was instructed to enter a decree in line with this opinion.[32]

The Red Jacket Cases.—On September 30, 1920, the Red Jacket Consolidated Coal and Coke Company filed a bill of complaint in the District Court of the Southern District of West Virginia against John L. Lewis, president of

---

[31] Borderland Coal Corporation v. United Mine Workers et al., 275 Fed. 871. The injunction is reproduced in 278 Fed. 56, and 3 *Law and Labor* 271-273, December, 1921.

[32] Gasaway et al. v. Borderland Coal Corporation, 278 Fed. 56; 3 *Law and Labor* 273.

the United Mine Workers, and other officers of the union, charging a conspiracy to restrain interstate commerce in non-union coal by interfering with the operation of the plaintiff's mines in West Virginia. A year later the Borderland Coal Corporation brought a similar suit. Shortly after the strike of bituminous miners began on April 1, 1922, other suits were brought against the union by operators with mines in Southern West Virginia. Four such suits were brought in April, one in May, three in June, and one in July, 1922. All of these suits were based on the Sherman Act, all were brought in the District Court of the Southern District of West Virginia, and all resulted in the granting of injunctions against the miners.[33]

Appeals from the injunction orders were taken to the Circuit Court of Appeals for the Fourth Circuit. In the case of Keeney v. Borderland,[34] the court, on June 8, 1922, decided that the questions at issue were so important that their settlement should await a trial on the merits. In the meantime it approved the granting of sufficient injunctive relief to protect property rights. It accordingly directed the court below to modify the injunctions in such a way as to restrain the defendants from interference with those seeking employment by menaces, threats, violence, injury, and molestation; from destroying property; from trespassing; and from persuading the employees to sever their contracts of employment. Similar modifications of the injunctions were directed in six other appeals, which were decided in July and December, 1922.[35]

---

[33] 7 *Law and Labor* 276.

[34] 282 Fed. 269.

[35] Dwyer et al. v. Alpha Pocahontas Coal Co. et al., and four other cases, 282 Fed. 270; United Mine Workers et al. v. Leevale Coal Co. et al., 285 Fed. 32.

On September 18, 1922, the Carbon Fuel Company brought suit against the union and numerous West Virginia coal companies which had signed agreements with the organization, charging a conspiracy to restrain interstate commerce, and asking for an injunction prohibiting the check-off. On the same day the District Court issued a restraining order prohibiting the union operators from paying and the union from receiving funds collected under the check-off system. After a further hearing the court, on March 20, 1923, rendered an opinion holding that the union and the union operators were engaged in an unlawful conspiracy in restraint of interstate commerce. The operators were again enjoined from paying over funds to the union to be used in carrying out the conspiracy. The union was enjoined from sending money into West Virginia to be used in organizing the non-union mines or to interfere with their operation, from attempting to secure trade agreements containing the check-off provision, and from calling strikes for the purpose of getting such agreements. All the defendants were further enjoined from "inciting, inducing, aiding, abetting, assisting, or encouraging any person, persons, organization, or association by letter, telegram, telephone, words of mouth or otherwise, to commit or do any of the acts or things hereinbefore inhibited, enjoined and restrained."

On March 24, 1923, immediately after the issuing of this injunction, Judge Waddill of the Circuit Court of Appeals ordered that an appeal be allowed and suspended the injunction until it should be heard.[36] On May 7, 1923, the higher court directed the District Court to issue an injunction similar to those it had ordered in the previous cases. It ordered, however, that in addition to the enjoining of illegal acts of interference with employees, trespass, and

[36] 5 *Law and Labor* 150-151.

inducing breach of contract, the union be restrained from aiding persons unlawfully occupying the houses of the companies.[37]

In the same month, May, 1923, the twelve suits just described, in all of which injunctions had been granted by the District Court of the Southern District of West Virginia, were consolidated for purpose of trial. Each of the suits except the first two, those of the Red Jacket and the Borderland Corporations, was brought by a number of companies. On consolidation a total of 316 companies were thus in the position of plaintiffs against the miners' unions. The trial of the cases produced voluminous evidence.

After long consideration the District Court, on October 16, 1925, rendered a decision. The miners were found to have conspired to restrain interstate commerce in coal. They were held to be causing employees to break their contracts and to quit work, and to have accomplished this by means of force and violence. All this was done so that the companies might be compelled to recognize the union. The court declared also that the companies were being hindered by the attempt of the union to keep its members in the houses belonging to the mine owners. Separate injunction decrees were granted by the court in each suit. The terms of these injunctions were like those approved by the Circuit Court of Appeals in the Carbon Fuel case above noted.[38]

The unions appealed from these decrees to the Circuit Court of Appeals, which rendered an opinion on April 18, 1927.[39] The complainants had asserted that the union was

---

[37] United Mine Workers et al. v. Carbon Fuel Co. et al., 288 Fed. 1020.

[38] 288 Fed. 1020.

[39] United Mine Workers et al. v. Red Jacket Consolidated Coal and Coke Co. and 11 other cases, 18 F (2) 839. Much of the fore-

itself illegal. The court, speaking through Judge Parker, answered that it did "not think that the International Organization, United Mine Workers of America, constitutes of itself an unlawful conspiracy in restraint of interstate trade or commerce because it embraces a large percentage of the mine workers of this country or because its purpose is to extend its membership so as to embrace all of the workers in the mines of the continent."[40] It continued as follows:

[When] the union turns aside from its normal and legitimate objects and purposes and engages in an actual combination or conspiracy in restraint of trade, it is accountable therefor in the same manner as any other organization, and we think that the evidence adduced in this case justifies the conclusion that the defendants have engaged in an actual combination and conspiracy in restraint of trade in a manner quite foreign to the normal and legitimate objects of the union. In this connection, it is not necessary that we consider whether complainants have established a conspiracy between the United Mine Workers and the operators of the central competitive field, or whether the acts of which complaint is made were done in furtherance of such conspiracy, for we think that the evidence sustains the finding of the District Judge that a combination or conspiracy existed among the defendants themselves, without regard to participation by the central operators to restrain and interfere with the interstate business of complainants. By this we do not mean, of course, that the union was unlawful of itself, but that defendants as officers of the union had combined and conspired to interfere with the production and shipment of coal by the nonunion operators of West Virginia, in order to force the unionization of the West Virginia mines and to make effective the strikes declared pursuant to the policy of the union. . . .

---

going information is contained in the first part of this decision. See also 7 *Law and Labor* 276.
[40] 18 F (2) 839, 843.

And there can be no question that the strikes called by the union in the nonunion fields of West Virginia in 1920 and 1922, and the campaign of violence and intimidation incident thereto, were merely the carrying out of the plan and policy upon which the defendants had been engaged for a number of years. . . .

The District Judge has found that the conspiracy existed, and that the acts complained of were done pursuant thereto. We think that these findings are sustained by the evidence. . . .

The defendants had asserted that the mining of coal was not interstate commerce and that a conspiracy to interfere with the operation of the coal mines was not one to restrain interstate commerce. They cited the Supreme Court decision in the first Coronado case[41] in support of this position. The Court of Appeals answered by referring to the second Coronado decision.[42] It pointed out that the total production of the plaintiffs' mines was more than 40,000,000 tons per year, more than 90 per cent of which was shipped in interstate commerce. It continued:

Interference with the production of these mines as contemplated by defendants would necessarily interfere with interstate commerce in coal to a substantial degree. Moreover, it is perfectly clear that the purpose of defendants in interfering with production was to stop the shipments in interstate commerce. It was only as the coal entered into interstate commerce that it became a factor in the price and affected the defendants in their wage negotiations with the union operators. And, in time of strike, it was only as it moved in interstate commerce that it relieved the coal scarcity and interfered with the strike. A conspiracy is in violation of the statute, where there exist an intent to restrain interstate trade and commerce and a scheme appropriate for that purpose, even though it does not act directly upon the instrumentalities of commerce . . . , and where the

[41] 259 U. S. 344 (1922).
[42] 268 U. S. 295 (1925).

necessary result of the things done pursuant to or contemplated by the conspiracy is to restrain trade between the states, the intent is presumed.[43]

Although the court did not approve every finding of fact made by the District Court, it declared that the evidence justified the decrees, which it affirmed. (It will be recalled that the decrees were practically identical with those which the Circuit Court of Appeals had itself directed in the earlier appeals.) The miners petitioned the United States Supreme Court for permission to appeal on a writ of certiorari, but that court denied the petition in a memorandum decision handed down on October 17, 1927.[44] The injunctions thus stood as modified by the Circuit Court of Appeals in 1923.[45]

The foregoing description of the application of the Sherman Act to the United Mine Workers warrants the assertion that no other labor organization has been so frequently brought into the courts under the act as has the miners' union. The extent to which it has been handicapped may be inferred from the foregoing discussion. All of these cases were based on the policy of the union to organize the non-union fields, a policy which must be carried out if the union is to protect its members in the union fields. By 1930 it has lost most of the ground it so laboriously won in previous years, and there can be no doubt that these great losses have been largely due to its failure to organize West Virginia. Neither can it be denied that this failure, at least in

---

[43] 18 F (2) 839, 844-846.

[44] United Mine Workers et al. v. Red Jacket Consolidated Coal and Coke Co. and 11 other cases, 72 L. ed. 112.

[45] United Mine Workers v. Carbon Fuel Co., 288 Fed. 1020. For a decision against the miners based on similar grounds see Pittsburgh Terminal Coal Corporation v. United Mine Workers, 22 F (2) 559 (1927). See Appendix C, Case 81.

part, was due to the obstacles which the federal courts put in its way with the aid of the Sherman Act. In such a highly competitive industry as mining the strength of unionism depends largely upon its ability to organize the whole industry. To the extent that the Sherman Act has hindered this it may be said to have hastened the destruction of collective bargaining in an industry greatly in need of it.

The district courts in the Indiana Borderland and the Carbon Fuel cases enjoined the check-off and the unionization of the non-union coal fields on the ground that these were part of the unlawful conspiracy. The circuit courts of appeals refused to permit these prohibitions, although they agreed that a conspiracy to violate the Sherman Act existed. The lower courts considered these activities to be unlawful under the act, while the courts of appeals seem to have decided that the act was merely a means of giving the desired jurisdiction, and directed the enjoining of acts illegal only under the common law. If the union attempt to organize the non-union fields was a conspiracy to violate the Sherman Act it seems reasonable to suppose that the organizing itself and the financial system which supported it were enjoinable. The result would obviously mean an exceedingly unreasonable restriction upon union activities, but it appears to follow from the original assertion that the union was engaged in an unlawful conspiracy. In this case it seems to have been unreasonable from an economic viewpoint to have held that the attempt to organize the non-union areas was a violation of the Sherman Act. The courts of appeals accepted the unreasonable original premise but not the unreasonable conclusion which logically followed from it. The matter indicates the extent to which confusion in matters both legal and economic has reigned when the courts have applied the Sherman Act to labor organizations.

CHAPTER VIII

FROM THE SHOPMEN'S STRIKE TO THE LEATHER WORKERS' CASE

The Shopmen's Strike.—It will be recalled that the Pullman cases involved a sympathetic strike of railway workers. The strikers had had no direct grievance against their employers. During the shopmen's strike of 1922, however, the Sherman Act was invoked in a railway strike involving an immediate grievance against the railways. On June 6, 1922, the Railroad Labor Board handed down a decision reducing the wages of railway shopmen throughout the country. The workers refused to accept the decision, and on July 1, when the new wage rates were to go into effect, and after the railway executives had refused to grant the demands of the men that the decision be ignored, they went on strike. The transportation system was severely handicapped, and for a time there was obstruction to the carrying of the mails. The roads partly recruited their forces with strikebreakers, but by the end of the summer the condition of the rolling stock, due to the failure to maintain repairs, was so bad as to slow up the service materially, and to endanger the safety of workers and passengers. Meanwhile President Harding had made several attempts to bring about an amicable settlement of the dispute, but without success.[1]

Failure to bring about a settlement resulted in a suit for an injunction against the strikers, which was brought by

[1] For an account of the strike see the author's *Labor Disputes and the President of the United States,* New York, 1924, pp. 226-247.

Attorney-General Daugherty in the District Court at Chicago, on September 1, 1922. Alleging various acts of violence and of interference with the mails and with interstate commerce, the government complaint declared that there was evidence of an illegal conspiracy to violate the Sherman Act and the Transportation Act of 1920. It was asserted that the strikers had conspired to quit the service and to disobey the decision of the Railroad Labor Board as a protest against that decision and as contempt for the board and the government.[2]

Judge Wilkerson at once issued a restraining order in accordance with the request of the Attorney-General. This order was probably the most sweeping one ever issued in a labor case. It ordered the officers of the union, their employees, and anyone acting with them, to refrain from doing the following acts:

interfering with the railways engaged in interstate commerce and the transportation of the mails, or with their employees or those seeking employment;

injuring, interfering with, or annoying any of the employees, "at any time or place, by display of force or numbers, the making of threats, intimidation, acts of violence, opprobrious epithets, jeers, suggestion of danger, taunts, entreaties, or other unlawful acts or conduct . . .";

loitering about exits from or entrances to railway property; "or aiding, abetting, directing, or encouraging any person or persons, organizations, or associations, by letters, telegrams, telephone, words of mouth, or otherwise to do any of the acts aforesaid"; or trespassing on the premises of the companies;

"inducing or attempting to induce by the use of threats, violent or abusive language, opprobrious epithets, physical violence or threats thereof, intimidation, display of numbers or force, jeers,

[2] *Government's Bill of Complaint* in U. S. v. Railway Employees' Department of the A. F. of L., September 1, 1922, Washington.

entreaties, argument, persuasion, rewards, or otherwise," any person to abandon railway employment or not to enter it;

engaging, directing, or encouraging others to picket;

congregating about railway property to picket;

doing injury to any employee, or going to his home to induce him not to work or seek work, by violence, threats, "or otherwise";

in any way hindering operation of the trains in interstate commerce or in carrying the mails, or encouraging anyone to do so;

"in any manner by letters, printed or other circulars, telegrams, word of mouth, oral persuasion, or suggestion, or through interviews to be published in newspapers, or otherwise in any manner whatsoever, encourage, direct, or command any person" to quit or not to enter railway employment.

In addition to these prohibitions, the officers of the shopmen's unions were forbidden to issue any instructions, requests, public statements or suggestions to the members as to what they should do after quitting employment, or calculated to get anyone to leave railway employment or not to enter it. They were also forbidden to use, or cause or consent to the use of, any of the union funds to promote or encourage the doing of any of the forbidden things.[3]

Put as briefly as possible the purpose of the restraining order was to prevent the continuance of the strike by prohibiting every possible means of carrying it on.

Shortly after the order was issued hearings were held on the granting of a preliminary injunction and on the shopmen's motion to dismiss the bill of complaint. On September 23, 1922, the District Court rendered a decision upholding

---

[3] *Restraining Order* in U. S. v. Railway Employees' Department of the A. F. of L., September 1, 1922, Washington.

the contentions of the government.[4] The shopmen had declared that they were not engaged in a conspiracy to violate the Sherman Act, that the court had enjoined peaceful acts in the exercise of which they had a constitutional right, and that the strike was one which they had a right to engage in under the terms of the Clayton Act.

The court's reply to these arguments stressed the many acts of violence committed during the strike. Judge Wilkerson asserted that the strike had restrained interstate commerce by "preventing the maintenance of rolling stock and equipment and thereby destroying the instruments by which passengers and property are carried over the rails." All of the acts enjoined were parts of an unlawful conspiracy to restrain interstate commerce. The peaceful acts were so mixed with the whole plan of intimidation that it would be an "idle ceremony" to go through the formality of enjoining the acts of violence and "leave the defendants free to pursue the open and ostensibly peaceful part of their program." Neither the Clayton Act nor the Constitution justified the performance of acts which were part of an illegal conspiracy. The court concluded:

It follows, therefore, that the motion to dismiss the bill must be denied. It follows, also, that the complainant is entitled to an injunction prohibiting the parties to this combination from committing the unlawful acts charged, the effect of which is to obstruct interstate transportation and the carriage of the mails or to restrain interstate commerce, as well as the acts charged which are lawful in themselves, when done in furtherance of a conspiracy to obstruct interstate transportation and the carriage of the mails or to restrain interstate commerce.[5]

[4] U. S. v. Railway Employees' Department of the A. F. of L., 283 Fed. 479.
[5] 283 Fed. 479, 495-496.

On January 5, 1923, the court denied a petition of the defendants that the government's bill be dismissed,[6] and on July 12, 1923, the injunction was made permanent.[7] In rendering the decision on the latter date Judge Wilkerson declared that the "manifest purpose" of the shopmen's strike, "as shown by the evidence, was to cripple and destroy interstate commerce, and to create by their assault a public opinion hostile to the decision of the Railroad Labor Board. The primary purpose of the combination, therefore, is unlawful, and it may not be carried out by means that otherwise would be legal."[8] (It should be noted in passing that the Transportation Act of 1920, which set up the Railroad Labor Board, did not require that its decisions be accepted. The refusal of the shopmen to accept the wage cut decision could therefore not have been a violation of the Transportation Act, despite the part which the subject played in the minds of both Judge Wilkerson and the Attorney-General.)

Long before July, 1923, the shopmen's strike had ended in failure. Though a number of roads, such as the Baltimore and Ohio and the New York Central, made agreements with the union ending the strike in September, 1922, the result on most of the country's roads was that collective bargaining with the shopmen's unions was at an end. Though men remained on strike for many months on some roads they won no concessions by their tenacity.

The restraining order in the shopmen's strike met with widespread criticism throughout the country. A move, which did not succeed, was set on foot in the House of Representatives to impeach the Attorney-General.[9] Labor's

[6] U. S. v. Railway Employees' Department, 286 Fed. 228.
[7] U. S. v. Railway Employees' Department, 290 Fed. 978.
[8] 290 Fed. 978, 982.
[9] New York Times, September 12 and 20 and October 22, 1922.

opposition to injunctions, always strenuous, became more intense. The injunction in the strike was probably a factor in the refusal of railway labor to tolerate the Railroad Labor Board.

In this case the doctrine of conspiracy under the Sherman Act was carried to the farthest possible extreme. Only thus could such activities as entreaties, interviews, telegrams, or telephone messages be enjoined. Once the court granted the government's assertion that the strike was a conspiracy to restrain interstate commerce, the road was open to it to declare unlawful every act, however peaceful, done in pursuance of the strike. So also did it feel free to enjoin violence, for if a letter might be a part of an unlawful conspiracy so might the use of physical force. The Sherman Act as applied to labor unions, by giving the courts a chance to consider certain activities conspiracies in restraint of trade, supplied them with an "omnium gatherum" in which to put every sort of act which was part of an alleged unlawful conspiracy to restrain interstate commerce.

It is worth noting again that this was the first instance in which the Sherman Act was used to forbid the carrying on of a railroad strike against a wage reduction. Many years before, in Waterhouse v. Comer,[10] a district court declared that the Sherman Act would prevent any railway strike, but this declaration was *obiter dictum*. During the Pullman strike the courts held that the act was being violated. In that instance, however, the railroad strikers were not attempting to protect their own wages, but to aid workers in another occupation. The Shopmen's Strike arose out of a refusal to accept a wage reduction. It could thus be considered neither a sympathetic strike nor a secondary boycott. The injunction issued against it appears to have completed the

[10] 55 Fed. 149 (1893).

array of direct precedents upon the basis of which the courts may invoke the Sherman Act to prevent any kind of railway strike which involves interstate transportation.[11]

Trifles.—It is an old legal maxim that the law does not concern itself with trifles. The courts have often declared, in interpreting the Sherman Act, that a restraint, intended or actual, upon interstate commerce, must be substantial to be prohibited by the act. It thus appears that the rule of *de minimis non curat lex* has been applied in the interpretation of the Sherman Act as in other matters. It is an indication of the readiness of the courts to use the Sherman Law in labor cases, however, that they have frequently prohibited unimportant labor activities by invoking its terms. Two labor cases are of especial interest merely because of the great insignificance of the acts in question.

In the summer of 1922 the members of the Brotherhood of Railway and Steamship Clerks employed by the Chesapeak and Ohio Railway went on strike, rather than accept a decision of the Railroad Labor Board. On August 5 the District Court of the Western District of Virginia issued an injunction against the members of the union and "all associated with them." They were enjoined from "abusing, intimidating, molesting, annoying, insulting, or interfering" with the railroad employees or with those seeking employment. The order was issued on the basis of the Sherman Act, presumably on the theory that the strike constituted a conspiracy in restraint of interstate commerce.

Taliaferro, a barber, had a shop near the freight house. The strikers brought him a large placard with the words, "No scabs wanted in here," prominently inscribed. He was

---

[11] There were numerous other proceedings under the Sherman Act against the shopmen. See Appendix C, Cases 29, 30, 31, 33, 35, 71, and 72.

asked to display the placard in his shop window, and being in sympathy with the strikers, he did so. Soon after a deputy marshal told him he was violating the injunction by keeping the sign in his window. Taliaferro, however, did not remove it. He was then charged with contempt of court for violating the injunction and was brought to trial.

On October 2, 1922, the District Court rendered a decision.[12] The court held that the word "scab" was insulting and annoying, and since the sign containing it was plainly visible to employees on the way to work, the injunction had been violated by Taliaferro. The defendant had contended that the court had authority to enjoin only acts which restrained interstate commerce. Admitting this, the court declared that it believed "that the act of molesting, annoying, and insulting numbers of those who were working for an interstate carrier during a widespread strike has an all sufficient tendency to restrict interstate transportation (and to retard the mails) to fully justify an injunction."[13] Taliaferro had demanded a jury trial under the terms of the Clayton Act, but it was denied, the court pointing out that since no crime had been committed the act was not applicable. The defendant was fined $200 for contempt of court. The case was carried to the Circuit Court of Appeals, Fourth Circuit, which, on May 21, 1923, rendered a decision affirming the judgment of the lower court.[14] The court made no reference to the Sherman Act in its opinion.

Early in 1922 a strike was in progress at a steel rolling mill in Newport, Ky., which is just across the Ohio River from Cincinnati. The management of the mill arranged to sell a steel billet to a Cincinnati manufacturer, the purchaser

[12] U. S. v. Taliaferro, 290 Fed. 214.
[13] 290 Fed. 214, 220.
[14] Taliaferro v. U. S., 290 Fed. 906.

to take delivery at the mill. An auto truck was accordingly sent from Cincinnati to get the billet. The driver received it from the mill, loaded it on his truck, and started back. Soon from six to ten men, acting as pickets, appeared on the road and asked the driver what he was carrying. On answering he was told that he couldn't go any further. He thereupon returned to the mill, unloaded the billet, and went back to Cincinnati without it.

In April, 1922, the government brought an indictment against five of the pickets in the District Court for the Eastern District of Kentucky, charging them with a conspiracy to restrain and obstruct interstate commerce in violation of the Sherman Act. They were tried by a jury and found guilty, four of them being sentenced to jail for terms of eight months each, and a fifth receiving a sentence of thirty days.

The defendants carried the case to the Court of Appeals for the Sixth Circuit, and charged error in the court below. On June 5, 1923, the Court of Appeals rendered a decision affirming the judgment. The defendants had argued that they had a right to picket under the Clayton Act. The court pointed out that the judge in the lower court had instructed the jury not to find the defendants guilty unless it believed that intimidation, rather than peaceful persuasion, had occurred, and the jury had found them guilty.

The defendants had asserted that they had not known that the shipment was destined for interstate commerce. The court answered that since their act was unlawful under the common law it is not important whether they knew that their act also violated federal law. Furthermore, the court believed that the picketers must have known that the billet was being carried across the state line.

Finally, the defendants had argued that the amount of

commerce involved was too insignificant to justify invoking the Sherman Act. The court answered by referring to its decision in Steers v. United States,[15] decided in 1911, in which it had held that the restraint of a single interstate shipment of tobacco by a cooperative society was a violation of the Sherman Act. It declared further "that the existence of the offense is found not in the amount of commerce restrained, but in the direct and absolute character of the restraint."[16]

Thus the Sherman Anti-trust Act, designed to prevent the exploitation of consumers by monopolies, was used to punish a barber who displayed a placard and some strikers whose picketing hindered the interstate shipment of a single billet of steel.[17]

The Window Glass Case.—The Window Glass case is the first case involving labor in which the Supreme Court clearly appears to have applied the rule of reason. In 1918 the United States government, desiring to reduce the production of articles not essential to the conduct of the war, brought about an agreement among the manufacturers and the workers in the handmade window glass industry under which half of the plants should operate during one part of the year and the remainder should operate during the other part. Finding that the system was beneficial the industry continued it. On September 16, 1922, an agreement was signed by representatives of the National Association of Window Glass Manufacturers and the National Association of Win-

---

[15] 192 Fed. 1.

[16] O'Brien et al. v. U. S., 290 Fed. 185. The Circuit Court of Appeals on July 18, 1923, denied a petition for a rehearing.

[17] Whether or not either of these acts should have been prevented by law is not at issue here. What does seem important is that they were punished under such a law as the Sherman Act.

dow Glass Workers. It was provided that half the factories should operate from September 15, 1922, to January 27, 1923, and the other half from January 29, 1923, to June 11, 1923. No operator was to produce during both periods unless he owned two separate plants, each of them running during only one period.

The government brought suit in the District Court (Northern District of Ohio, Eastern Division) against the two organizations, seeking an injunction dissolving what was alleged to be a combination in restraint of interstate commerce. The defendants asserted that the agreement related only to the production of hand-blown window glass, and not directly to interstate commerce; but that if interstate commerce was being restrained, such restraint was so indirect and incidental as not to violate the Sherman Act. They declared that the agreement, since it lawfully carried out the legitimate objects of a labor organization, was lawful under the Clayton Act, even though it might indirectly and incidentally curtail production or restrain interstate commerce. Finally, they maintained that even if interstate commerce were restrained and production curtailed, such restrictions were not so unreasonable under all circumstances as to be illegal.

Judge Westenhaver, of the District Court, on February 2, 1923, after considering the position of the defendants, rendered a decision granting the injunction.[18] He held that the inevitable result of the agreement was to halve the production of hand-blown window glass, to increase prices, and to cause a direct, not an incidental restraint of interstate commerce. "What the parties to this combination agreed to do, and have done," said the court, "has such a direct, material,

[18] U. S. v. National Association of Window Glass Manufacturers et al., 287 Fed. 228.

and substantial effect upon the production, distribution, and price of hand-blown window glass in interstate trade or commerce that an intent to restrain such trade or to curtail and restrain competition herein must be inferred." The court did not believe that the Clayton Act helped the defendants, since neither their object nor the means used to attain it was legitimate.[19]

The court devoted considerable attention to the assertion that the restraint in question was reasonable. The defendants had pointed out that there were less than half as many workers in the industry as were required to man all the factories throughout the year, that since the industry was a dying one, unable to compete successfully with the machine-made window glass industry, it was impossible to obtain new recruits willing to undergo the long period of training necessary. They claimed for these reasons that the arrangement was reasonable and that as a result of it production was increased and prices were not enhanced. The court answered these arguments by asserting that the system was bad for the manufacturers, that it prevented the most favorably situated factories from building up a permanent working force, that it placed the least efficient factory upon the same plane as the most efficient one, and that it tended to keep alive factories which had no economic justification for existence and supported them at the expense of the public. The contentions concerning production and price were not considered proved. The injunction sought by the government was accordingly granted.[20]

The manufacturers and the union appealed from this decision to the Supreme Court. On December 10, 1923, that

[19] 287 Fed. 228, 235.
[20] 287 Fed. 228, 238-239.

court handed down a unanimous opinion, delivered by Justice Holmes, reversing the decree of the District Court.[21] The court pointed out that the agreement did not concern sales or distribution, but that it was directed to the way labor should be employed in production. "If such an agreement can be within the Sherman Act, at least it is not necessarily so." The court continued as follows:

The dominant fact in this case is that, in the last quarter of a century, machines have been brought into use that dispense with the employment of the highly trained blower and the trained gatherers needed for the handmade glass, and in that and other ways have enabled the factories using machinery to produce window glass at half the cost of the handmade. The price for the two kinds is the same. It has followed, of course, that the companies using the machines fix the price, that they make much the greater part of the glass in the market, and probably, as was testified for the defendants, that the handmakers are able to keep on only by the sufferance of the others and by working longer hours. The defendants say, and it is altogether likely, that the conditions thus brought about and the nature of the work have driven many laborers away and make it impossible to get new ones. . . .

The defendants contend with a good deal of force that it is absurd to speak of their arrangements as possibly having any effect upon commerce among the States, when manufacturers of this kind obviously are not able to do more than struggle to survive a little longer before they disappear, as human effort always disappears when it is not needed to direct the force that can be got more cheaply from water or coal.[22]

The court declared that there were not men enough to enable the factories to run continuously, that serious losses

[21] National Association of Window Glass Manufacturers et al. v. U. S., 263 U. S. 403.

[22] 263 U. S. 403, 412.

in overhead costs would result if the plants were under-manned on full-time operation, and that the men would be in a poorer situation because of the uncertainties involved under the full-time system. "It is enough," it concluded, "that we see no combination in unreasonable restraint of trade in the arrangements made to meet the short supply of men." It ordered the injunction decree reversed and dis-missed the government's petition.[23]

The Supreme Court decision was of great significance be-cause it applied the rule of reason which had been described by it in 1911 to a case involving labor. The agreement be-tween the hand-blown window glass manufacturers and the trade union was national in scope. It had a direct relation to interstate commerce, for even though the agreement may not have decreased production or affected prices in general, it did operate to increase the production and therefore the in-terstate shipments of the less efficient plants and decrease those of the more efficient ones. It might have been con-sidered as much an agreement in restraint of interstate trade as a secondary boycott or an important coal strike. Yet the Supreme Court, giving careful consideration to the economic conditions of the industry and the economic and social ad-vantages of the agreement, concluded that it was not in un-reasonable restraint of trade. The rule of reason had encoun-tered a labor activity, though it had also encountered the activity of a manufacturers' association at the same time. The court, instead of confining itself, as has so often been done in the labor cases under the Sherman Act, to legal ver-balisms, made an economic study and arrived at an eco-nomically tenable conclusion. What significance such a ju-

---

[23] 263 U. S. 403, 413. Several federal indictments were returned on the basis of the same agreement in New York, but were not carried to trial. See Appendix C, Cases 28 and 32.

dicial technique would have if generally applied in these cases will be apparent later.[24]

The Leather Workers' Case.—The United Leather Workers International Union, after a fruitless attempt to reach an agreement with five companies manufacturing leather goods, called a strike, which began on April 10, 1920. The union, in the attempt to prevent the operation of the factories, established pickets consisting of from three to twenty strikers. The picketing was accompanied by the making of threats and various other alleged unlawful acts. In order to prevent this picketing and to secure workers needed to carry on production, the companies appeared before the District Court of the Eastern District of Missouri and asked for an injunction against the strikers. The only basis upon which such an injunction could be issued by the federal court was the alleged violation of the Sherman Act. The strike, declared the companies, had prevented the filling of orders under contracts equal in value to $327,000. Ninety per cent of the contracts called for delivery of goods through interstate commerce. It was alleged, therefore, that the union by calling the strike was engaged in a combination to restrain interstate commerce in violation of the Anti-trust Act.

[24] The position of the handmade window glass industry had become so desperate by 1928 that the national union, with only 879 remaining members, was officially disbanded by its executive board at the end of June, 1928. Even before the Supreme Court decision was rendered economic conditions in the industry had become so undesirable that the two shift system was discontinued with the consent of the union in order that the manufacturers might be free to operate as long as possible if it would help them in competing with the machine industry. "The Passing of the National Window Glass Workers," *Monthly Labor Review,* Vol. 29, No. 4, pp. 773, 783-784, 786, October, 1929.

On November 26, 1920, District Judge Faris rendered a decision ordering that a permanent injunction be granted. He declared "that the facts and circumstances disclosed a conspiracy within the meaning of the law, and that the direct and positive effect of that conspiracy was to hurt and injure the interstate commerce of plaintiffs, as that commerce has been defined in this circuit."[25]

The decision was largely based upon the opinions of the Circuit Court of Appeals in the Coronado case (the Supreme Court had not yet rendered a decision in that issue), to the effect that the coal strike was a conspiracy in violation of the Sherman Act.[26]

The union carried the case to the Circuit Court of Appeals for the Eighth Circuit. Judge Sanborn, with whom Judge Munger agreed, rendered a decision on October 19, 1922, affirming the judgment of the lower court.[27] A vigorous dissenting opinion was entered by Judge Stone. The defendants had argued that they had no purpose to restrain interstate commerce; their sole purpose had been to force the plaintiffs to employ only union men and to grant certain other demands. The majority of the court answered that "the natural and inevitable effect of the prevention by the defendants of the making by the plaintiffs of the articles they had made interstate contracts to sell, make, and deliver, was the prevention of their performance of their contracts and the prevention or partial prevention of their interstate commerce, and this result was so evident and unavoidable that the de-

---

[25] Herkert and Meisel Trunk Co. et al. v. United Leatherworkers International Union et al., 268 Fed. 662.

[26] Dowd v. United Mine Workers, 235 Fed. 1; United Mine Workers v. Coronado, 258 Fed. 829.

[27] United Leather Workers International Union et al. v. Herkert and Meisel Trunk Co. et al., 284 Fed. 446.

fendants could not have failed to know, to purpose, and to intend that this should be the result."[28]

The court cited the Supreme Court decision in the first Coronado case[29] to the effect that obstruction to mining was not restraint of interstate commerce unless this obstruction was intended to restrain such commerce, or had necessarily such a direct, material, and substantial effect to restrain it that the intent might reasonably be inferred. It continued as follows:

The case in hand falls directly under this rule. The obstruction and prevention of the manufacture of the articles which the plaintiffs had made interstate commerce contracts to make, sell, and deliver, and to pour into their existing currents of interstate commerce, could not have been without the knowledge of the defendants that their direct, material, necessary, substantial, and inevitable effect would be to restrain or to prevent the plaintiffs' interstate commerce in such articles and thus to deprive them of their income; nor could it have been made without their reasonably inferred intent and purpose to obtain that result.[30]

The necessary and inevitable effect of this prevention and restriction of the making of the articles the plantiffs had contracted to make, sell, and deliver, was to prevent for a time and drastically restrain their interstate commerce.[31]

The dissenting opinion of Judge Stone contained the following statement:

No attempt was made to prevent appellees from shipping any manufactured products or from receiving any raw material. There was no boycott of appellees' products or customers, no interference with interstate transportation, no purpose to inter-

[28] 284 Fed. 446, 451.
[29] 259 U. S. 344.
[30] 284 Fed. 446, 453.
[31] 284 Fed. 446, 457.

fere with such commerce. The conspiracy was confined to preventing manufacture. The purpose of the conspiracy was to accomplish unionization by preventing manufacture and in no way include as an object preventing appellees, by boycott or otherwise, from purchasing, selling, sending, or receiving products or materials. The jurisdictional question turns, therefore, on the point of whether a conspiracy for the sole purpose of unionizing a manufacturing plant is a restraint of interstate commerce because some of the articles which are prevented from being made are intended for interstate commerce and would normally enter therein.[32]

On the basis of a consideration of various decisions of the Supreme Court the judge concluded that there was no unlawful restraint of interstate commerce. Of much interest is the following declaration:

The consequences of a legal rule are often useful in testing its accuracy. There can be no shadow of doubt as to the consequences of the rule laid down in the majority opinion. The natural, logical and inevitable result will be that every strike in any industry or even in any single factory will be within the Sherman Act and subject to federal jurisdiction provided any appreciable amount of its product enters in interstate commerce. Moreover, if this be true as to the products produced in such industry or factory, it is entirely logical the same rule should apply to the raw materials used in such production if any of them are subjects of interstate commerce. In a practical sense, this would result in all strikes being subject to federal jurisdiction, because scarcely any factory is so small that some of its finished products do not enter interstate commerce.[33]

An appeal from the decision of the majority of the Circuit Court of Appeals was taken to the Supreme Court. On

[32] 284 Fed. 446, 458.
[33] 284 Fed. 446, 464-465.

June 9, 1924, that body handed down an opinion, delivered by Chief Justice Taft, reversing the judgment of the courts below.[34] Three of the justices, Messrs. McKenna, Van Devanter, and Butler, dissented, but wrote no opinion. The majority opinion affirmed in general the ideas of Judge Stone of the Court of Appeals. It was pointed out that there had been no interference with the shipment or the receipt of the companies' product in interstate commerce and that a strike intended to prevent manufacture was not a conspiracy in restraint of interstate commerce merely because the products normally went into interstate commerce and the strikers were aware of the fact.

The court made an extensive review of cases in which the concept of interstate commerce and of the restraint of such commerce had been considered, and then spoke as follows:

This review of the cases makes it clear that the mere reduction in the supply of an article to be shipped in interstate commerce, by the illegal or tortious prevention of its manufacture, is ordinarily an indirect and remote obstruction to that commerce. It is only when the intent or necessary effect upon such commerce in the article is to enable those preventing the manufacture to monopolize the supply, control its price or discriminate as between its would-be purchasers, that the unlawful interference with its manufacture can be said directly to burden interstate commerce.

The record is entirely without evidence or circumstances to show that the defendants in their conspiracy to deprive the complainants of their workers were thus directing their scheme against interstate commerce. . . .[35]

[34] United Leather Workers International Union, Local Union No. 66, et al. v. Herkert and Meisel Trunk Co. et al., 265 U. S. 457.
[35] 265 U. S. 457, 471.

The declaration of Circuit Judge Stone, that the effect of the logical application of the rule laid down in the Court of Appeals would be to bring within the Sherman Act every strike in a plant a substantial part of the products of which entered interstate commerce, was approved by the Supreme Court. "We can not think," it said, "that Congress intended any such result in the enactment of the Anti-trust Act, or that the decisions of the court warrant such construction."[36]

The Leather Workers' case shows clearly the uncertainty that exists with respect to the question of what type of a labor activity is likely to be considered a violation of the Sherman Act. The judge in the District Court held the strike to be a violation of the statute. Two judges of the Circuit Court of Appeals agreed while one held to the contrary. Six justices of the Supreme Court held it was not a violation, while three must have thought it was, though they failed to state their views except by dissent. Thus seven judges held the strike not to be a violation and six held to the contrary; and this emphatic disagreement came after many years of judicial interpretation.

It is obvious that the Supreme Court decision in the case, if it is carefully followed by other courts, will save labor from a much heavier burden than that normally imposed by the Sherman Act. To have held every strike a conspiracy in restraint of interstate commerce if it delayed the shipment of goods across state boundaries would have imposed an extraordinary handicap upon trade unions. The fact that the decision in the first Coronado case and the language of the statute permitted such an interpretation, according to the views of various judges, shows how much such a ruling as that of the Supreme Court in the present case was needed.

The case is illustrative of the manner in which the Sher-

[36] 265 U. S. 457, 472.

man Act has been used to extend the jurisdiction of the federal courts. The only way in which the companies could secure a federal injunction in this instance was to assert that some federal law was being violated. Since the picketing of the strikers would probably have been considered illegal by the state courts, a suit for an injunction in them would have resulted in the granting of a decree. Employers appear, however, to prefer an order issued by a federal court. The Sherman Act may be used by employers who, lacking the argument of diversity of citizenship, need some federal statute to justify bringing a suit in a court of the United States, and can convince the court that labor is violating the Anti-trust Law.

CHAPTER IX

THE BRIMS AND THE BEDFORD STONE CASES

United States v. Brims.—Manufacturers of millwork, building contractors, and the carpenters' union, all of Chicago, operated under an agreement which, in 1921, brought them into the District Court of the Northern District of Illinois (Eastern Division) on the charge of having violated the Sherman Act. This agreement provided that the manufacturers and contractors would employ only union carpenters, and that the carpenters would not install millwork produced under non-union conditions.

On September 2, 1921, an indictment was returned against substantially all of the millwork manufacturers, a number of contractors, and members of the carpenters' union. They were charged with violating the Sherman Law by making an agreement which enabled them to monopolize the trade in Chicago and to keep out of the city millwork made in other states. The trial of the defendants began on June 12, 1923. The case was dismissed as to a number of them, but a verdict of guilty as to the rest was returned by the jury on June 30, 1923. Fines aggregating $58,300 were imposed. Some of the defendants paid their fines, and the remainder appealed.[1]

---

[1] *The Federal Anti-trust Laws with Amendments,* Department of Justice, November 30, 1928, Washington, pp. 167-168. Hereafter referred to as B. B. (Blue Book). See Appendix C, Case 23. The case is identical with U. S. v. Andrews Lumber and Mill Co. et al.

The Court of Appeals for the Seventh Circuit rendered a decision reversing the conviction on June 4, 1925.[2] It called attention to the fact that the indictment charged a conspiracy to prevent plants located outside of Illinois from selling their products in Chicago, and that such a conspiracy was an obstruction to interstate commerce. The court did not believe that this charge had been proved.

Nonunion-made goods were made in Illinois, as well as outside of Illinois, union-made millwork was also produced outside of Illinois, as well as in the state. In other words, demand for millwork in Chicago could be supplied from all parts of the United States. . . . The agreement which the defendants entered into merely dealt with millwork which was the product of nonunion labor. It mattered not where the millwork was produced, whether in or outside of Illinois, if it bore the union label. The restriction was not against the shipment of millwork into Illinois. It was against nonunion-made millwork produced in or out of Illinois.[3]

Concluding that the evidence did not sustain the indictment, the court reversed the judgment.

The government appealed to the Supreme Court, which rendered a decision on November 23, 1926, reversing the Circuit Court of Appeals and sustaining the conviction of the defendants.[4] The opinion was delivered by Justice McReynolds. He pointed out that the manufacturers had found their business seriously impeded by non-union millwork made principally in Wisconsin and the South, though some was made in Illinois. This non-union millwork sold at a price lower than that at which the union manufacturers could sell. As a result their business was curtailed and they

[2] Brims et al. v. U. S., 6 F (2) 98.
[3] 6 F (2) 98, 100.
[4] U. S. v. Brims, 71 L. ed. 403.

had to employ fewer carpenters. The agreement was made in order to eliminate this competition.

The evidence, continued the justice, showed that as a result of the combination, "as intended by the parties, the so-called outside competition was cut down, and thereby interstate commerce directly and materially impeded." The local manufacturers, relieved from this interstate competition, found their output and profits increased; they gave special discounts to the local contractors; more union carpenters were employed; and their wages were increased. Outside non-union mills found the Chicago market greatly limited, the price of building was increased, and "as usual under such circumstances, the public paid excessive prices." In answer to the contention that the purpose of the agreement was to eliminate non-union millwork made in Illinois as well as out of it, the court declared that the "crime of restraining interstate commerce through combination is not condoned by the inclusion of intrastate commerce as well."

The case was ordered remanded to the Circuit Court of Appeals for further proceedings in line with the opinion. On October 22, 1927, that court affirmed the conviction of the defendants.[5]

The Brims case was the first one in which the Supreme Court passed judgment on an ordinary trade agreement between employers and employees under the Sherman Act. Its ruling is of considerable importance in view of the fact that there are many trade agreements with similar terms in operation in the building industry, as well as in other industries.

In the case of Boyle v. United States,[6] decided on April 4, 1919, the same Circuit Court of Appeals which had passed

[5] 21 F (2) 889.
[6] 259 Fed. 803.

on the millwork agreement, had upheld the conviction, under the Sherman Act, of electricians and manufacturers who had made an agreement that the shops be unionized and that the men install only union-made appliances. In that case the court had held the evidence to prove that the purpose of the agreement was to keep appliances made outside of Illinois from being shipped into Chicago. If the case had gone to the Supreme Court it would probably have been upheld.

In the Brims case the Supreme Court found both a purpose to keep outside millwork from coming into Chicago and a result actually in line with that purpose. A conspiracy to violate the Sherman Act thus appeared clearly to exist. Neither the Circuit Court of Appeals nor the Supreme Court considered whether or not such an agreement was economically justifiable as a means of protecting the wages of union workmen and was therefore permissible in the light of the rule of reason.

Two Employers' Association Cases.—Industrial relations in the building industry of San Francisco had for many years been affected by bitter struggles between employers and the unions. As a result of what they considered the undesirable practices of the unions the employers embarked on a vigorous anti-union campaign for the installation of the so-called "American Plan" or non-union shop. As a part of this campaign the employers organized the Industrial Association of San Francisco, and put into effect the "permit system," under which they made it practically impossible for building contractors dealing with the unions to secure materials necessary to carry on their business.

On May 26, 1923, the government filed suit for an injunction under the Sherman Act, alleging that the Industrial Association was engaged in a conspiracy to restrain interstate commerce in building materials.[7] On November 9, 1923, the District Court for the Northern District of California handed down a decision in favor of the government.[8] The court held that however little the defendants had intended to interfere with interstate commerce, the result of their action was such as to constitute a violation of the Sherman Act. They were enjoined from requiring any permit for the purchase of material or supplies produced outside the state, or for making, as a condition for the issuance of a permit, any regulation which would interfere with the free movement of such supplies into the state.

The employers appealed to the Supreme Court, which handed down a decision, written by Justice Sutherland, on April 13, 1925.[9] The court held that there had been no violation of the statute, and reversed the decree granting an injunction. Justice Sutherland asserted that the "thing aimed at and sought to be attained was not restraint of the interstate sale or shipment of commodities, but was purely a local matter, namely, regulation of building operations within a limited local area, so as to prevent their domination by the labor unions. Interstate commerce, indeed commerce of any description, was not the object of attack. . . ."[10]

Having concluded that there existed no illegal purpose, the justice went on to consider whether there had not actually occurred a direct and undue obstruction to interstate commerce. The lower court had stated several grounds for its belief that such an obstruction existed. It had been held, first, that permits were required for the purchase of materials produced in and brought from other states. In the

[7] B. B. p. 183.
[8] U. S. v. Industrial Association of San Francisco et al., 293 Fed. 925.
[9] Industrial Association of San Francisco et al. v. U. S., 268 U. S. 64.
[10] 268 U. S. 64, 77.

opinion of the Supreme Court there was no clear evidence to prove this except in the case of plaster. The evidence showed, however, that the permit requirement was confined to such plaster as had previously been brought into the state and "commingled with the common mass of local property, and in respect of which, therefore, the interstate movement and the interstate commercial status had ended."[11]

The District Court had asserted, secondly, that the permit requirement for materials produced in California interfered with the free movement of commodities from other states. This had reference principally to plumbing supplies, which were for the most part produced in other states. By refusing a permit to purchase other materials to an employer not operating under the "American Plan," the association made it useless for him to purchase plumbing supplies, with the result that the trade in them was diminished. The Supreme Court declared,[12] however, that the consequent "effect upon, and interference with interstate trade, if any, were clearly incidental, indirect and remote," precisely such an interference as it had held not to be in violation of the Sherman Act in the first Coronado decision,[13] and in the Leather Workers' case.[14]

Finally, the lower court had held that persons in other states had been directly prevented or discouraged from shipping into California. For example, lists of plumbing contractors who were not observing the "American plan" were sent to the plumbing supply houses, and some of them had refused to sell materials to such contractors. The Supreme Court pointed out that this practice had been abandoned be-

[11] 268 U. S. 64, 78.
[12] 268 U. S. 64, 80.
[13] 259 U. S. 344 (1922).
[14] 265 U. S. 457 (1924).

fore the suit was brought, and that the interferences which may have been unlawful, consisted of "some three or four sporadic and doubtful instances during a period of nearly two years," were not of sufficient weight to establish a conspiracy to restrain interstate commerce. The court accordingly reversed the decree and instructed the District Court to dismiss the suit.[15]

The Industrial Association case is another instance of the uncertainty involved in interpreting the Sherman Act. Evidence which was sufficient to convince the District Court did not convince the Supreme Court. A consideration of the evidence and of Justice Sutherland's treatment of it suggests that another justice might have made as good an argument against the association as he made for it. Perhaps the fact that the Supreme Court decision was unanimous indicated that the case was clear. Nevertheless one has the feeling that where the meaning of the statute is so indefinite and uncertain the decision of such a case is as likely to depend upon the court's social philosophy as upon any inescapable logic of legal interpretation.

Indeed, a study of the many cases brought under the Sherman Act impresses one with the ease of writing an apparently convincing opinion either for or against the same defendants. All that is needed is the shifting of emphasis to this or that scrap of evidence. Thus what to one judge appears as proof of an intent to conspire against interstate commerce, to another seems only the indication that such an intent was merely ancillary and unimportant. What to one judge indicates an actual restraint, to another indicates an effect so insignificant as to be negligible. In the Brims case the Circuit Court of Appeals believed that no purpose to restrain interstate commerce appeared, while the Supreme Court, on

[15] 268 U. S. 64, 82-84.

the same evidence, found clear proof of the contrary. In the Industrial Association case the lower court found that interstate commerce had been unlawfully restrained. Justice Sutherland on the contrary found the restraint to be so insignificant as to deserve no attention.

On November 22, 1926, the Supreme Court had another opportunity to pass upon the activities of employers' associations under the Sherman Act. Once again the decision was rendered by Justice Sutherland, but this time the result was a ruling in favor of labor.[16] Several shipowners' associations on the Pacific Coast operated a "Marine Service Bureau" through which they hired seamen. Anderson and the Seamen's Union complained that the association fixed wages, that the shipowners had surrendered all their rights to employ men to the Bureau, that no owner could hire any men except those sent from the Bureau, and that "when a seaman's turn [came], he [had to] take the employment then offered or none, whether it [was] suited to his qualifications or not, or whether he [wished] to engage on the particular vessel or for the particular voyage."

This arrangement was alleged to be a combination in restraint of interstate commerce and an injunction against it was sought in the District Court of the Northern District of California. The court dismissed the bill of complaint and the plaintiffs appealed to the Circuit Court of Appeals (Ninth Circuit). On January 18, 1926, that court affirmed the judgment of the court below, declaring that the conduct complained of did not constitute a violation of the Sherman Act.[17] The case was then carried to the Supreme Court,

[16] Anderson v. Shipowners' Association, 272 U. S. 359.
[17] Anderson v. Shipowners' Association, 10 F (2) 96.

which reversed the lower courts and remanded the case to the District Court for further proceedings.

The Supreme Court, having nothing before it but the allegations of the bill, pointed out that it appeared "that each shipowner and operator in this widespread combination [had] surrendered his freedom of action in the matter of employing seamen and agreed to abide by the will of the associations." "These shipowners," said the court, "having thus put themselves into a situation of restraint upon their freedom to carry on interstate and foreign commerce according to their own choice and discretion, it follows, as the case now stands, that the combination is in violation of the Anti-Trust Act." For ships and those who operate them are instrumentalities of commerce "and the immediate force of the combination both in purpose and execution, was directed toward affecting such commerce."[18]

Upon trial of the suit in accordance with the instructions of the Supreme Court the District Court, after considering the evidence, decided, on June 21, 1928, that the allegations in the bill of complaint had not been proven, and it refused to grant the decree.[19] The court pointed out that there was no proof that the associations fixed wages. Neither was it true that the shipowners had surrendered their rights of employment. Though they had hired men through the Bureau to a considerable extent they were under no agreement to do so exclusively, and many of them did not do so. Furthermore, though an occasional injustice may have occurred, it was not generally true that seamen had to take the jobs assigned to them or none, nor was it true that a seaman refusing a particular job lost his priority. In view of these facts, therefore, and on the basis of the Supreme

[18] 272 U. S. 359.
[19] Anderson v. Shipowners' Association, 27 F (2) 163.

Court's decision, the District Court concluded that no combination to violate the Sherman Act was proved. On March 18, 1929, this decision was affirmed by the Circuit Court of Appeals.[20]

The decision of the Supreme Court in the Anderson case, coming as it did on the heels of the Industrial Association and the Brims decisions, had the temporary effect of weakening the belief that the court was not likely to interpret the Sherman Act in a way favorable to labor. Certainly no one sympathetic to labor could complain of the decision. It is indeed conceivable that those on the opposite side of the controversy might have felt that the court had gone out of its way to rule against the employers' associations. The fact that in the end the seamen did not secure their injunction is another matter. On the basis of the evidence presented to it when the case was finally tried, the District Court appears to have been amply justified in concluding that no violation of the Sherman Act existed.

The Bedford Stone Case.—The decision of the Supreme Court in the Bedford case was one of the most important ever rendered in a labor proceeding under the Sherman Act. It gave rise to renewed public discussion as to the value of the law and as to its use against labor. As a result of the decision trade union criticism of the law and its interpretation by the courts was intensified.

Prior to 1921 the firms engaged in quarrying and cutting limestone in the Bedford-Bloomington district of Indiana operated under a trade agreement with the Journeyman Stone Cutters' Association of North America. In April, 1921, the employers and the union were unable to reach an agreement for a renewal of their contract, and a strike followed. About July 1 the firms set up organizations among their

[20] 31 F (2) 539.

employees and resumed operations despite the opposition of the Stone Cutters' Union.

One of the provisions in the constitution of the national union required that no member should handle stone "cut by men working in opposition" to it. The union, which had jurisdiction not only over the men working at the quarries, but also over those who installed the stone on buildings, began to enforce this clause in 1924. As a result members in other states refused to handle Bedford stone, and thus interrupted building operations.

The Bedford Cut Stone Company and twenty other concerns brought suit for an injunction in the District Court for the District of Indiana, asserting that the union was engaged in a conspiracy to restrain interstate commerce. Judge Anderson refused to grant the relief asked for, and the plaintiffs appealed to the Circuit Court of Appeals, Seventh Circuit. On October 28, 1925, that court rendered an opinion affirming the judgment of the court below.[21]

The court pointed out that there was no evidence that the quarrying or cutting of the stone, or setting it in buildings, or any other building operation, was interfered with; nor that any actual or threatened violence, picketing, or boycott had taken place. Though the acts of the defendants may have tended somewhat to restrain interstate commerce, they were within their rights in carrying them out. There was no evidence that the union had any purpose to restrain interstate commerce.

The companies appealed from this opinion to the Supreme Court, which, on April 11, 1927, handed down a decision declaring that the Stone Cutters' Union was guilty

[21] Bedford Cut Stone Co. et al. v. Journeyman Stone Cutters' Association of North America et al., 9 F (2) 40.

of violating the Sherman Act.[22] Justices Holmes and Brandeis dissented from the opinion of the majority, which was rendered by Justice Sutherland. The majority opinion pointed out that 75 per cent of the aggregate sales of the companies were made in interstate commerce. The evidence showed "many instances of interference with the use of petitioners' stone by interstate customers and expressions of apprehension on the part of such customers of labor troubles if they purchased the stone." Members of the union found working on the stone were ordered to stop and threatened with revocation of membership if they refused, and such orders seemed to have been enforced even against the desire of the local unionists to continue working.[23] It was apparent that the only purpose of these orders was to coerce or induce the local employers to refrain from purchasing the "unfair" stone.

The court declared that the fact that the means adopted to bring about the contemplated restraint of commerce operated after physical transportation had ended was immaterial. If interference with the product under such conditions had been for a purely local object with no intention, express or implied, to restrain interstate commerce, it would probably not have been a violation of the Sherman Law. But this interference had the restraint of interstate commerce as its primary aim. Prevention of the use of the petitioners' product was therefore only part of the conspiracy to destroy or narrow the petitioners' interstate trade. "In other words, strikes against the local use of the product were simply the means adopted to effect the unlawful restraint. And it is

[22] Bedford Cut Stone Co. et al. v. Journeyman Stone Cutters' Association et al., 47 Sup. Ct. Rep. 522.
[23] 47 Sup. Ct. Rep. 522, 523.

this result, not the means devised to secure it, which gives character to the conspiracy."

The defendants had contended that their sole and only purpose was to unionize the cutters and carvers of stone at the quarries. The court conceded that this was the ultimate end in view, but it was to be effected by an attack on the use of the product in other states for the purpose of bringing about the reduction of the companies' interstate business. "A restraint of interstate commerce [could not] be justified by the fact that the ultimate object of the participants was to secure an ulterior benefit which they might have been at liberty to pursue by means not involving such restraint."[24]

After considering various other cases brought under the Sherman Act and comparing them with the present one, the court declared that the principles established in the Duplex case[25] could be applied here. "The object there was precisely the same as it is here, and the interferences with interstate commerce, while they were numerous and more drastic, did not differ in essential character from the interferences here." Both cases involved a secondary boycott, which the court, in the Duplex case, defined as a "combination not merely to refrain from dealing with complainant, or to advise or by peaceful means persuade complainant's customers to refrain . . . but to exercise coercive pressure upon such customers, actual or prospective, in order to cause them to withhold or withdraw patronage from complainant through fear of loss or damage to themselves should they deal with it."[26]

The court, referring to the acts of the Stone Cutters' Union, concluded as follows:

[24] 47 Sup. Ct. Rep. 522, 524, 525.
[25] 254 U. S. 443.
[26] 47 Sup. Ct. Rep. 522, 526.

The strikes, ordered and carried out with the sole object of preventing the use and installation of petitioners' product in other states, necessarily threatened to destroy or narrow petitioners' interstate trade by taking from them their customers. That the organizations, in general purpose and in and of themselves, were lawful, and that the ultimate result aimed at may not have been illegal in itself, are beside the point. Where the means adopted are unlawful, the innocent general character of the organizations adopting them or the lawfulness of the ultimate end sought to be attained, cannot serve as a justification.[27]

The decree of the court below was reversed.

Justices Sanford and Stone made brief concurring statements. The former said, "I concur in this result upon the controlling authority of Duplex v. Deering, 254 U. S. 443, 478 . . . which, as applied to the ultimate question in this case, I am unable to distinguish."[28]

Justice Stone declared,

As an original proposition, I should have doubted whether the Sherman Act prohibited a labor union from peaceably refusing to work upon material produced by nonunion labor or by a rival union, even though interstate commerce were affected. In the light of the policy adopted by Congress in the Clayton Act, in respect to organized labor, and in the light of Standard Oil Co. v. United States, 221 U. S. 1, . . . and the United States v. American Tobacco Co., 221 U. S. 106, . . . I should not have thought that such action as is now complained of was to be regarded as an unreasonable and therefore prohibited restraint of trade. But in Duplex Printing Press Co. v. Deering, 254 U. S. 443, . . . these views were rejected by a majority of the court and a decree was authorized restraining in precise terms any agreement not to work or refusal to work such as is involved here. . . .

[27] 47 Sup. Ct. Rep. 522, 528.
[28] 47 Sup. Ct. Rep. 522, 528.

These views, which I should not have hesitated to apply here, have now been rejected again largely on the authority of the Duplex Case. For that reason alone, I concur with the majority.[29]

The dissenting opinion of Justice Brandeis, in which Justice Holmes concurred, devoted much attention to the application of the rule of reason to the case. Justice Brandeis said:

I have no occasion to consider whether the restraint which was applied wholly intrastate, became in its operation a direct restraint upon interstate commerce. For it has long been settled that only unreasonable restraints are prohibited by the Sherman Law. . . .[30] And the restraint imposed [here] was, in my opinion, a reasonable one. The Act does not establish the standard of reasonableness. What is reasonable must be determined by the application of principles of the common law, as administered in federal courts, unaffected by state legislation or decisions. . . . Tested by these principles, the propriety of the unions' conduct can hardly be doubted by one who believes in the organization of labor.

The justice pointed out that neither the individual stone cutters nor the unions had any contract with the stone companies or their customers. The stone cutters were thus free to work or not work on stone cut by non-members. The individual stone cutters were not free as regards their union, however, for they had agreed, on becoming members, not to work on non-union stone. It was the duty of the union to

[29] 47 Sup. Ct. Rep. 522, 528.
[30] The following decisions were cited in support of this view: Standard Oil Co. v. U. S., 221 U. S. 1; U. S. v. American Tobacco Co., 221 U. S. 106; Chicago Board of Trade v. U. S., 246 U. S. 231; U. S. v. Trenton Potteries Co., 47 Sup. Ct. Rep. 377.

urge its members to observe this obligation, for the companies were seeking to destroy it and the danger was great.

The plaintiff companies were "not weak employers opposed by a mighty union." They had large financial resources, and together shipped 70 per cent of all the cut stone in the country. They were not isolated concerns, but were combined in a local association affiliated with the national association of their industry. On the other hand, each of the 150 widely scattered stone cutters' locals with an average membership of only 33, was weak standing alone. Only through combining the 5,000 organized stone cutters in a national union and developing loyalty to it, could the individual stone cutter anywhere protect his job.

According to Justice Brandeis the way in which the stone cutters acted was clearly legal, unless it was illegal for them to agree not to work on non-union stone because it was an article of commerce; for there had been no trespass, breach of contract, violence, intimidation, or boycott. The union had also acted in a legal manner. The combination was wholly of persons in the same craft, united solely for self-protection. There was no attempt at boycott, nor was the aid of other crafts through a sympathetic strike sought. The contest was one between particular employers and employees, not a class struggle.

The facts complained of in the case were quite different from those in the Duplex case. According to the minority opinion:

The combination there condemned was not, as here, the co-operation for self-protection only of men in a single craft. It was an effort to win by invoking the aid of others, both organized and unorganized, not concerned in the trade dispute. The conduct there condemned was not, as here, a mere refusal to finish particular work begun "by men working in opposition to the union." It was the institution of a general boycott not only of the business of the employer, but of the businesses of all who should participate in the marketing, installation, or exhibition of its product. The conduct there condemned was not, as here, action taken for self-protection against an opposing union installed by employers to destroy the regular union with which they had long had contracts. The action in the Duplex case was taken in an effort to unionize an open shop. Moreover, there the combination of defendants was aggressive action directed against an isolated employer. Here it is a defensive action of workingmen directed against a combination of employers. The serious question on which the court divided in the Duplex Case was not whether the restraint imposed was unreasonable. It was whether the Clayton Act had forbidden federal courts to issue an injunction in that class of cases.[31]

After contrasting the present case with those in which the Supreme Court had ruled that the Sherman Act was being violated, Justice Brandeis concluded his opinion as follows:

Members of the Journeyman Stone Cutters' Association could not work anywhere on stone which has been cut at the quarries "by men working in opposition" to it without aiding and abetting the enemy. Observance by each member of the provision of their constitution which forbids such action was essential to his own self-protection. It was demanded of each by loyalty to the organization and to his fellows. If, on the undisputed facts of this case, refusal to work can be enjoined, Congress created by the Sherman Law and the Clayton Act an instrument for imposing restraints upon labor which reminds one of involuntary servitude. The Sherman Law was held in United States v. United States Steel Corporation, 251 U. S. 417, . . . to permit capitalists to combine in a single corporation 50 per cent. of the steel industry of the United States dominating the trade through its vast resources. The Sherman Law was held in United States

[31] 47 Sup. Ct. Rep. 522, 530.

v. United Shoe Machinery Co., 247 U. S., 32, . . . to permit capitalists to combine in another corporation practically the whole shoe machinery industry of the country, necessarily giving it a position of dominance over shoe manufacturing in America. It would, indeed, be strange if Congress had by the same act willed to deny to members of a small craft of working men the right to cooperate in simply refraining from work when that course was the only means of self-protection against a combination of militant and powerful employers. I cannot believe that Congress did so.[32]

In accordance with the decision of the Supreme Court an injunction was issued in the District Court for the District of Indiana on October 8, 1927. The unions, their agents, and all persons acting with or in aid of them, were enjoined from combining to hinder interstate commerce of the stone companies by any of the following means:

interfering with the use, sale, transportation, fabrication, or installation of the stone;

refusing to handle it, or refusing to work for anyone using it or upon any building where it was being used;

influencing anyone to quit work because the employer was using or was about to purchase such stone;

threatening loss or inconvenience to any firm using it;

informing each other or any firm that the complainants were unfair or should not be patronized;

imposing or threatening to impose a penalty whether fine, suspension, or expulsion, upon any worker because he handled such stone, or worked for an employer who bought it or upon a building where it was being installed;

doing any of the forbidden acts "either directly, or indirectly, or through by-laws, orders, directions, or suggestions to committees, associations, officers, agents or otherwise."[33]

[32] 47 Sup. Ct. Rep. 522, 531.
[33] 9 *Law and Labor* 297.

The Supreme Court decision in the Bedford case may be considered as the capstone of the long development in the application of the Sherman Act to labor. It doubtless ranks with the Danbury Hatters', the Duplex, and the second Coronado decisions as the most important interpretations of the statute against labor unions.

PART III

ANALYSIS AND CONCLUSIONS

CHAPTER X

LABOR ACTIVITIES AND LEGAL CRITERIA

A Classification of Restraints of Interstate Commerce.
—The activities of trade unions which have been affected by
the Sherman Act may be divided into three groups: (1)
those which interfere with some stage of interstate transportation or with the instrumentalities of interstate commerce; (2) those which interfere with the production of
goods destined for interstate commerce; and (3) those which
interfere with the marketing, installation, or use of goods
which have entered or normally would enter interstate commerce. Stated more briefly, though somewhat less accurately,
the labor activities in question may be considered as interferences with transportation, production, or marketing.[1]

This classification might also be applied to the activities
of business organizations which have encountered the prohibitions of the Sherman Act. Thus the Trans-Missouri
Freight Association, Joint Traffic Association, Northern Securities, and St. Louis Terminal Association cases were concerned with combinations said to be interferences with
interstate transportation.[2] The Standard Oil, American To-

---

[1] This classification is similar to that described in Terborgh, "The
Application of the Sherman Law to Trade-Union Activities,"
Journal of Political Economy, Vol. XXXVII, No. 2, p. 203,
April, 1929.

[2] U. S. v. Trans-Missouri Freight Association, 166 U. S. 290 (1897);
U. S. v. Joint Traffic Association, 171 U. S. 505 (1898); Northern
Securities Co. v. U. S., 193 U. S. 197 (1904); U. S. v. Terminal
Association of St. Louis, 224 U. S. 383 (1912).

bacco, Standard Sanitary, and International Harvester cases were concerned with combinations which, it was alleged, restricted the production of goods destined for interstate commerce, though in several of these cases sales were also said to be directly restrained.[3] Restraints upon marketing were said to exist in the Addyston, Swift, Montague, and Lumber Dealers' Association cases.[4] It is quite probable that not all the cases arising under the Sherman Act are comprehended under these three groups. In the labor cases the classification embraces every case with one exception.[5] It is thus sufficiently inclusive to serve the present purpose.[6]

[3] Standard Oil Co. v. U. S., 221 U. S. 1 (1911); U. S. v. American Tobacco Co., 221 U. S. 106 (1911); Standard Sanitary Manufacturing Co. v. U. S., 226 U. S. 20 (1912); U. S. v. International Harvester Co., 214 Fed. 987 (1914).

[4] Addyston Pipe and Steel Co. v. U. S., 175 U. S. 211 (1899); Montague and Co. v. Lowry, 193 U. S. 38 (1904); Swift and Co. v. U. S., 196 U. S. 375 (1905); Eastern States Retail Lumber Dealers' Association v. U. S., 234 U. S. 600 (1914).

[5] Barker Painting Co. v. Brotherhood of Painters, Decorators and Paperhangers, 23 F (2) 743 (1927). The defendants were accused of restraining interstate trade because of a rule whereby they insisted that any building contractor operating in different cities must pay in all cities wages equal to those paid in the city where they are highest. An injunction, granted at first, was later dismissed. The latter decision was sustained by the higher court. See Apendix C, Case 82. It will be observed that even this case might possibly be considered under a loose interpretation to cover an interference with production.

[6] Only those activities are described in this chapter which actually resulted in a use of the act against labor. In some instances no more than a temporary restraining order was issued. In others, however, the proceedings resulted in a permanent injunction, the levying of damages, or fine and imprisonment. Completely unsuccessful proceedings are not discussed in the text but may be cited in footnotes.

Interferences with Transportation.—The labor activities which may be classed as interferences with stages in interstate transportation or with the instrumentalities of interstate commerce may be placed in five groups.

1. *Strikes of transportation workers.* These include the strike of draymen which led to a sympathetic strike tying up commerce entering and leaving New Orleans in the winter of 1892-1893,[7] and the interference by striking taxicab drivers with the transfer of interstate passengers from one railway station to another in Toledo in 1925.[8] Except for these instances cases coming under this head involve strikes of railway workers. The Pullman strike of 1894, which gave rise to the first extensive use of the statute, was a sympathetic railway strike. It might also be regarded as a boycott of Pullman cars by railway workers.[9] In the railway shopmen's strike of 1922 the men quit employment because of a grievance over their own conditions.[10] This was probably also the case in the strike of members of the Brotherhood of Railway Clerks on the Chesapeake and Ohio Railroad in 1922.[11] The Sherman Act was invoked in a criminal prosecution against a railway train crew which deserted a passenger train in the desert at Needles, Calif., during the shopmen's strike of 1922. The men declared that they had quit the train because the equipment was in such disrepair

[7] U. S. v. Amalgamated Council, 54 Fed. 994 (1893).

[8] Toledo Transfer Co. v. Teamsters, 7 *Law and Labor* 33.

[9] U. S. v. Elliott, 62 Fed. 801, 64 Fed. 27; Thomas v. Cincinnati, 62 Fed. 803; U. S. v. Agler, 62 Fed. 824; In re Grand Jury, 62 Fed. 828, 62 Fed. 834, 62 Fed. 840; U. S. v. Debs, 64 Fed. 724; (all in 1894); and U. S. v. Cassidy, 67 Fed. 698 (1895).

[10] U. S. v. Railway Employees' Department, 283 Fed. 479, 286 Fed. 228 (1922), 290 Fed. 978 (1923).

[11] Referred to in U. S. v. Taliaferro, 290 Fed. 214 (1922).

on account of the strike that it was dangerous to operate.[12]

2. *Interference with transportation workers.* The case of O'Brien v. United States comes under this head. Here a small group of strikers on picket duty told a truck driver who was transporting a steel billet from Newport, Ky., to Cincinnati, Ohio, to turn back to the plant from which he had received the billet.[13] In United States v. Taliaferro the posting by a barber of a sign deriding railway strikebreakers was held to constitute an annoyance which tended to interfere with interstate commerce.[14] During the shopmen's strike an assault was made by some strikers on a roadmaster employed by the Kansas City Southern Railroad. They were tried for a conspiracy in restraint of interstate commerce and fined.[15]

3. *Interference with the instrumentalities of interstate commerce.* During the railway strike of 1922 some freight cars loaded with coal were set on fire. The act was punished as a conspiracy to restrain interstate commerce.[16] Shopmen on strike were also convicted under the Sherman Act for putting quicksilver in the boilers of locomotives undergoing repair.[17] Another instance of railway sabotage punished under the act was the dynamiting of the tracks of the International Railway Company, operating electric trains, in 1922.[18] In one case an electricians' union called a strike of

[12] Clements v. U. S. 297 Fed. 206 (1924).

[13] 290 Fed. 185 (1923).

[14] 290 Fed. 214 (1922); affirmed in 290 Fed. 906 (1923).

[15] U. S. v. A. L. Harvel, B. B., p. 179.

[16] U. S. v. Ed. Powell, B. B., p. 178.

[17] Williams v. U. S., 295 Fed. 302 (1923); contra: U. S. v. Hency, 286 Fed. 165 (1923).

[18] Vandell v. U. S., 6 F. (2) 188 (1925); Appendix C, Case 34. See also U. S. v. Dryllic et al., 6 *Law and Labor* 69.

building workers because the non-union employees of the Western Union Telegraph Company were installing call boxes, used for summoning messenger boys to take telegrams. The court considered the call boxes instrumentalities of interstate commerce and issued an injunction.[19]

4. *Interference with the starting of goods in interstate transportation.* The O'Brien case above mentioned, in which pickets were said to have prevented the transportation of a steel billet starting on its interstate journey, also belongs under the present head.[20] In the case of Buyer v. Guillan the refusal of union dock workers to handle goods ready to be shipped, because they were brought to the dock on trucks driven by non-union workers, was enjoined as a restraint of interstate commerce.[21]

5. *Interference with the final act of delivering goods in interstate transportation.* A strike which prevented the unloading of goods from railroad cars resulted in conviction under the Sherman Law. The strike was called as part of a plan of certain union leaders to extort money from a building material company.[22]

Interferences with Production.—Interferences with the production of goods destined to be shipped in interstate commerce may be divided into three groups.

1. *Strikes for the purpose of unionizing a wide area.* Numerous organizing campaigns conducted by the United Mine Workers in West Virginia and elsewhere have been held to be evidences of conspiracies in restraint of trade.[23]

[19] Western Union v. Electrical Workers, 2 F (2) 993 (1924).

[20] 290 Fed. 185.

[21] 271 Fed. 65 (1921).

[22] U. S. v. Norris, 255 Fed. 423 (1918); U. S. v. Michael Artery, B. B., p. 136.

[23] Borderland v. U. M. W., 275 Fed. 871 (1921); U. M. W. v. Red Jacket, 18 F (2) 839 (1927); Pittsburgh Terminal Coal Co.

2. *Local strikes.* Strikes confined to a single locality which have been held to constitute violations of the Sherman Act include three strikes of coal miners;[24] three strikes of machinists: one against a firm manufacturing munitions and electrical appliances,[25] another at the plant of an automobile manufacturer,[26] and a third against a manufacturer of tools and machinery;[27] a strike of leather workers;[28] and a strike of brick workers.[29]

3. *Agreements directly regulating production.* An agreement between the handmade window glass manufacturers and a trade union limiting the time during which the plants might operate was held to be in restraint of trade.[30]

---

v. U. M. W., 22 F (2) 559 (1927); consult Appendix C, Cases 57-68.

[24] Hitchman v. Mitchell, 202 Fed. 512 (1912); Dowd v. U. M. W., 235 Fed. 1 (1916); Coronado v. U. M. W., 268 U. S. 295 (1925); U. M. W. v. Pennsylvania Mining Co., 300 Fed. 965 (1924). In the last case the award of damages in the lower court was reversed.

[25] Wagner v. Machinists, 252 Fed. 597 (1918).

[26] Dail-Overland v. Willys-Overland, 263 Fed. 171 (1919).

[27] Gable v. Vonnegut, 274 Fed. 66 (1921); lower court granting an injunction reversed.

[28] Herkert and Meisel v. United Leather Workers, 268 Fed. 662 (1920); 284 Fed. 446 (1922); reversed by the Supreme Court, 265 U. S. 457 (1924).

[29] Danville Brick Workers v. Danville Brick Co., 283 Fed. 909 (1922). The Circuit Court of Appeals reversed the decision granting an injunction. In Silverstein v. Tailors' Union an injunction asked for in the District Court on the ground that a tailors' strike violated the Sherman Act was refused. 284 Fed. 833 (1922).

[30] U. S. v. Window Glass Manufacturers, 287 Fed. 228 (1923); reversed in 263 U. S. 403 (1923).

Interferences with Marketing.—Interferences by labor with the marketing, installation, or use of goods which have entered or would normally enter interstate commerce may be divided into three groups. All of the activities here considered are boycotts.

1. *Secondary boycotts of commodities.* The Danbury Hatters' boycott, in the course of which unions all over the country tried to persuade the public and dealers not to buy hats made under non-union conditions, was held to be in restraint of interstate trade.[31]

2. *Sympathetic strikes against non-union goods.* Sympathetic strikes of this nature may also be considered as backward boycotts of materials; *i.e.*, union workers, in order to aid unionists making goods which they handle, refuse to work with such goods if they are not union-made.[32] In the Duplex boycott truckmen and others refused to handle non-union presses.[33] The threat of calling a general building trades strike to prevent contractors from having non-union-made furnaces installed led to the issuance of an injunction under the Sherman Act.[34] This was also the result in a case involving the refusal of building trades workers in New York to work on buildings using stone not cut by the members of the local union which was a member of the building trades council.[35]

---

[31] Loewe v. Lawlor, 208 U. S. 274 (1908). See also Gompers v. Bucks, 221 U. S. 418 (1911) for a similar declaration, *obiter dicta*, as to the illegality of a secondary boycott.

[32] Wolman, *The Boycott in American Trade Unions*, Baltimore, 1916, p. 49.

[33] Duplex v. Deering, 254 U. S. 443 (1921).

[34] Columbus Co. v. Pittsburgh Building Trades Council, 17 F (2) 806 (1927).

[35] Decorative Stone Co. v. Building Trades Council, 18 F (2) 333 (1927); U. S. v. Journeyman Stone Cutters, 9 *Law and Labor*

3. *Refusal of members of a union to work on non-union materials which might be but are not made by members of their own trade organization.* This may be called a *lateral boycott of materials.*[36] Boycotts of this type which have been considered in restraint of interstate trade are of two types, those put into effect because of a rule or order of the union and those which are required by the terms of a trade agreement with employers. Of the first type are the refusal of union carpenters to work on trim made by non-union carpenters,[37] the refusal of sheet metal workers to install non-union-made furnaces,[38] and the refusal of stone workers on buildings to install Bedford stone quarried and cut by non-unionists.[39] Of the second type of lateral boycott are the following: a trade agreement between an electricians' union and the manufacturers of electrical appliances whereby the latter agreed to hire only union men and the former agreed not to install non-union appliances;[40] and a trade agreement between a carpenters' union, building contractors, and manufacturers of millwork, whereby the employers consented to

---

263 (1927). The courts refused to enjoin under the Sherman Act the refusal of building workers to work on buildings in which non-union-made organs were being installed. Aeolian v. Fischer, 27 F (2) 560 (1928); affirmed in 29 F (2) 679 (1928).

[36] Wolman, *op. cit.,* p. 58.

[37] Irving v. Neal, 209 Fed. 471 (1913); Paine v. Neal, 212 Fed. 259 (1913), 244 U. S. 459 (1917). The courts agreed that the Sherman Act was violated, but granted no injunction under it because the suits were by private parties and were brought before the passage of the Clayton Act, which permitted such suits.

[38] Columbus Co. v. Pittsburgh Building Trades Council, 17 F (2) 806 (1927).

[39] Bedford Stone v. Journeyman Stone Cutters, 47 Sup. Ct. Rep. 522 (1927).

[40] Boyle v. U. S., 259 Fed. 803 (1919); Appendix C, Cases 21 and 22.

employ union men and the carpenters agreed to work only on millwork made by unionists.[41]

A Summary of Labor Activities Considered Illegal.— The activities which have just been described, considered apart from their relation to production, transportation, or marketing, fall into one or several of the following groups.

1. *Strikes.* A. Local strikes due to the strikers' immediate grievances, such as those of miners, machinists, leather workers and brick workers. B. General strikes of members in one trade or industry, extending over a wide area, and carried on for the immediate benefit of the strikers, such as those of miners in West Virginia, and in the Central Competitive Field in 1927, and of the railway shopmen in 1922. C. Sympathetic strikes, such as the Pullman strike and those of truck drivers and building workers.

2. *Boycotts.* A. Secondary boycotts of commodities, such as those directed against non-union-made hats and stoves. B. Backward boycotts of materials, such as the refusal of truck drivers, building workers, and dock workers to handle goods made or hauled under non-union conditions. C. Lateral boycotts of materials, such as the refusal of carpenters, sheet metal workers, machinists, electricians, and stone workers to handle materials not made by members of their own unions.

3. *Picketing,* such as the act of picketers at a rolling mill who were said to have prevented the transportation of a billet, the posting of a placard deriding "scabs," and the assault of a strikebreaking roadmaster.

4. *Union rules or orders* against the handling of non-

[41] U. S. v. Brims, 272 U. S. 549 (1926); Appendix C, Case 23. See also U. S. v. Bricklayers' Union, 4 *Law and Labor* 95, Appendix C, Case 6.

union goods, such as those of carpenters, machinists, building workers, and railway workers (as in the Pullman strike).

5. *Trade agreements.* A. Those providing that only
unionists be employed and only materials made under union
conditions be used, such as the agreements made by the
electricians and carpenters. B. An agreement limiting the
period during which plants should operate, as in the handmade window glass industry.

6. *Sabotage*, such as the dynamiting of a roadbed, the firing of freight cars, and the placing of chemicals in
locomotive engines.

The Sherman Act has thus been used to prohibit, restrict,
or punish a large number of important trade union activities
and practices, many of which, such as local strikes, railway
strikes, organizing campaigns, certain union rules, and certain trade agreements, might not have been reached by other
statutes or by the common law.[42]

Judicial Disagreement.—It is apparent that though the
Sherman Act has operated to prevent certain interferences
with the transportation, production, and marketing of goods
in interstate commerce, there has been much disagreement
among the courts as to when such interferences constitute
restraints of trade and commerce in violation of the statute.
A few examples will demonstrate the extent of this disagreement.

In the following cases interferences with transportation

---

[42] There is record of one case in which union rules restricting
production were enjoined under the act along with trade agreements against non-union materials. Since no adequate report
of the court's opinion is available the basis for enjoining the
restrictive practices is conjectural. U. S. v. Bricklayers' Union,
4 *Law and Labor* 95; Appendix C, Case 6.

took place. In United States v. Railway Employees' Department it was held that the shopmen's strike of 1922 violated the Sherman Act.[43] This was denied, however, in Great Northern Railway Company v. the International Association of Machinists.[44] In Williams v. United States putting quicksilver in locomotive engines was held to restrain interstate commerce unlawfully.[45] A similar act was held not to violate the statute in United States v. Hency.[46]

As regards interferences with production, the District Court and the Circuit Court of Appeals which held a strike of leather workers illegal found themselves reversed by the Supreme Court.[47] A strike of machinists was held to be illegal in Wagner v. International Association of Machinists,[48] but another court held the opposite view in Gable v. Vonnegut.[49] A trade union agreement in the window glass industry which was considered illegal in the District Court was upheld in the Supreme Court.[50]

There are many instances of disagreement among the judges as to the legality of interferences with sale or use. For example, the lower court, which apparently did not believe that the hatters' boycott violated the Sherman Act,

[43] 283 Fed. 479 (1922).

[44] 283 Fed. 557 (1922).

[45] 295 Fed. 302 (1923).

[46] 286 Fed. 165 (1923).

[47] Herkert and Meisel v. United Leatherworkers, 268 Fed. 662 (1920); United Leather Workers v. Herkert and Meisel, 284 Fed. 446 (1922); 265 U. S. 457 (1924).

[48] 252 Fed. 597 (1918).

[49] 274 Fed. 66 (1921).

[50] U. S. v. Window Glass Manufacturers, 287 Fed. 228 (1923); National Association of Window Glass Manufacturers v. U. S., 263 U. S. 403 (1923).

was reversed by the Supreme Court.[51] The lower courts which held that the refusal of the journeyman stone cutters to work on Bedford stone was legal, found that the Supreme Court thought differently.[52]

What is Interstate Commerce?—Interstate commerce has often been defined by the courts. Although great disagreement exists as to the application of such definitions to specific activities in the cases under the Sherman Act, a consideration of them will nevertheless help to establish the criteria used in determining the question of legality.

It should be pointed out first that the courts have generally used the terms "interstate trade" and "interstate commerce" interchangeably, though, perhaps because "interstate commerce" is the term used in the constitutional provision which grants regulatory power to Congress,[53] they use that phrase most frequently. Thornton, in his treatise on "Combinations in Restraint of Trade,"[54] says, "No doubt the word 'trade' was . . . used [in the Sherman Act] in abundance of caution; for it is covered by the word 'commerce.'"

It should be noted further that though the present discussion is largely confined to the determination of legality in labor cases, the criteria established apply in all cases under the Sherman Act.

An oft-quoted definition of interstate commerce is that given by the Supreme Court in County of Mobile v. Kimball: "Commerce with foreign countries and among the states, strictly considered, consists in intercourse and traffic, including in these terms navigation and the transportation

---

[51] Loewe v. Lawlor, 148 Fed. 924 (1906); 208 U. S. 274 (1908).
[52] Bedford Stone v. Journeyman Stone Cutters, 9 F (2) 40 (1925); 47 Sup. Ct. Rep. 522 (1927).
[53] *Constitution of the United States*, Article I, Section 8, Paragraph 3.
[54] Cincinnati, 1928, p. 167.

and transit of persons and property, as well as the purchase, sale and exchange of commodities."[55]

Before the Sherman Act was passed the Supreme Court, in another frequently cited decision, that of Kid v. Pearsons, explained the distinction between commerce and manufacture. It said:

Manufacture is transformation—the fashioning of raw materials into a change of form for use. The functions of commerce are different. The buying and selling and the transportation incidental thereto constitute commerce; and the regulation of commerce in the constitutional sense embraces the regulation at least of such transportation. . . . If it be held that the term includes the regulation of all such manufactures as are intended to be the subject of commercial transactions in the future it is impossible to deny that it would also include all productive industries that contemplate the same thing. The result would be that Congress would be invested, to the exclusion of the States, with the power to regulate, not only manufactures, but also agriculture, horticulture, stock raising, domestic fisheries, mining —in short every branch of human industry. For is there one of them that does not contemplate, more or less clearly, an interstate or foreign market?[56]

On the basis of these widely approved statements it might be concluded (1) that interstate commerce includes transportation between states, and the sale or purchase of commodities between the citizens of different states; (2) that the production of goods is not commerce. Restraints of interstate transportation or interstate sales would thus be restraints of interstate commerce, but restraint of the produc-

[55] 102 U. S. 691, 702 (1881). See also U. S. v. Coal Dealers' Association, 85 Fed. 252 (1898).
[56] 128 U. S. 1, 20 (1888).

tion of goods at first glance appears not to be restraint of interstate commerce.

Would interference with the production of goods in one state and with their use or sale in others, accompanied by no direct interference with transportation, constitute a restraint of interstate commerce? In Loewe v. Lawlor the Supreme Court answered this question in the affirmative. It said, "If the purposes of the combination were, as alleged, to prevent any interstate transportation at all, the fact that the means operated at one end before physical transportation commenced, and at the other end after the physical transportation ended was immaterial."[57]

Might interstate commerce be considered restrained if the acts complained of occurred only within the boundaries of a single state? The answer is again in the affirmative, especially when the courts believe that the combination has interfered with the flow of interstate commerce.[58]

Would the fact that a combination restrained intrastate as well as interstate commerce, relieve it from the operation of the Sherman Act? The courts have answered this question in the negative. For example, in United States v. Brims, the Supreme Court declared that "[the] crime of restraining interstate commerce through combination is not condoned by the inclusion of intrastate commerce as well."[59]

Might the Sherman Act be violated by a combination of

[57] 208 U. S. 274, 301 (1908).

[58] U. S. v. Workingmen's Amalgamated Council, 54 Fed. 994, 995 (1893); Swift and Co. v. U. S., 196 U. S. 375, 399 (1905); Boyle v. U. S., 259 Fed. 803, 806 (1919); Bedford Stone v. Journeyman Stone Cutters, 47 Sup. Ct. Rep. 522, 524 (1927).

[59] U. S. v. Brims, 71 L. ed. 403, 405 (1926); also Montague v. Lowry, 193 U. S. 38, 45-46 (1904); Loewe v. Lawlor, 208 U. S. 274, 301 (1908).

persons not themselves engaged in interstate commerce? · This question was raised in the Danbury Hatters' case, when the hatters implied that they, being engaged in neither transportation nor marketing, were not reached by the act. The Supreme Court declared that this fact was of no consequence, since "[the] act made no distinction between classes."[60]

Despite the principles already laid down, we have not as yet reached the most definite criteria used by the courts in determining the existence of illegal restraint of interstate commerce. We know that interferences with marketing carried on within a state may be in violation of the Sherman Act, but not all such interferences are illegal. Production is not commerce, but we have seen that some interferences with production have been considered conspiracies in restraint of interstate commerce. And not every interference with transportation violates the Anti-trust Act.

When Is Interstate Commerce Illegally Restrained?— The courts have found the Sherman Act to be violated under one or another of the following sets of circumstances:

1. When there exists an intent to restrain interstate commerce and when the effect of such a restraint is direct, material, and substantial.

2. When the restraint upon interstate commerce is so direct, material, and substantial that the intent to restrain it must be inferred.

3. When there exists an intent to restrain interstate commerce, not accompanied by a substantial restraint.

The application of these criteria in particular cases may now be illustrated.

1. *Intent and substantial restraint.* In Anderson v. United

[60] Loewe v. Lawlor, 208 U. S. 274, 301 (1908).

States, decided in 1898, the Supreme Court declared that "where the undisputed facts clearly show that the purpose of the agreement was not to regulate, obstruct or restrain [interstate] commerce," and "where the effect of its formation and enforcement upon interstate trade or commerce is in any event but indirect and incidental, and not its purpose or object," the agreement would be upheld.[61]

In Ellis v. Inman, Poulsen & Company, a Circuit Court of Appeals, pointing out that the unlawful combination had the power to ruin the business of any contractor who imported lumber from the adjoining state, said, "Restraint of trade resulted therefrom, and the restraint was the direct and necessary result of a combination made to carry out that specific purpose."[62]

In the case of Gable v. Vonnegut, arising out of a suit for an injunction against strikers who, it was alleged, were violating the Sherman Act, the court pointed out that the record was "barren of evidence that the object of the strike was to interfere with interstate commerce," and that the interference with manufacture "merely incidentally and indirectly affected interstate commerce." It therefore reversed the judgment granting an injunction.[63]

The Supreme Court, in the first Coronado decision, ruled that no unlawful conspiracy to restrain interstate commerce existed, since the evidence available showed that there was no intention to restrain interstate commerce in coal and that the restraint which actually resulted was insignificant and incidental. When the case came before the court a second time, however, both the intent to restrain interstate com-

[61] 171 U. S. 604, 615-616.
[62] 131 Fed. 182, 188-189 (1904).
[63] 274 Fed. 66, 74 (1921).

merce and the substantial interference with it were found, and the Sherman Act was held to have been violated.[64]

In the Bedford case the Supreme Court declared that the prevention of the use of the companies' stone was the result of interferences by the stone cutters which "had for their primary aim restraint of the interstate sale and shipment of the commodity." It asserted that the strikes were "ordered and carried out with the sole object of preventing the use and installation of petitioners' product in other states." The combination was said to have "deliberately adopted a course of conduct which directly and substantially curtailed, or threatened thus to curtail, the natural flow in interstate commerce of a very large proportion of the building limestone production of the entire country, . . . and it must be held to be a combination in undue and unreasonable restraint of such commerce. . . ."[65]

It is clear that in each of these decisions it is both the elements of intent and substantial actual restraint which, in the opinion of the courts, render a combination illegal under the Sherman Law.

2. *Intent inferred from the existence of substantial restraint.* In the first Coronado decision the Supreme Court declared that an obstruction to coal mining is not a restraint of interstate commerce unless there is an intent to restrain it, or unless the obstruction "has necessarily such a direct, material and substantial effect to restrain it that the intent reasonably must be inferred."[66]

The District Court in the case of Silverstein v. Journey-

---

[64] U. M. W. v. Coronado, 259 U. S. 344 (1922); Coronado v. U. M. W., 268 U. S. 295 (1925).

[65] Bedford Stone v. Journeyman Stone Cutters, 47 Sup. Ct. Rep. 522, 524, 527, 528 (1927).

[66] U. M. W. v. Coronado, 259 U. S. 344, 411 (1922).

man Tailors' Union, in refusing to issue an injunction against strikers, pointed out that the evidence failed to show that the strike "necessarily had such a direct, material, and substantial effect to restrain [interstate commerce] that the appellees' intent so to do reasonably must be inferred."[67]

In the Window Glass case the District Court enjoined a trade agreement limiting production because it had "such a direct, material, and substantial effect upon the production, distribution and price of hand-blown window glass in interstate trade or commerce that an intent to restrain such trade or to curtail and restrict competition therein must be inferred."[68]

Referring to an interference with the installation of call boxes for use in connection with sending telegrams, Judge Wilkerson declared, "The intent to restrain interstate commerce therefore appears as an obvious consequence of the acts of the defendants."[69]

In the Pittsburgh Terminal case the court, in granting an injunction, asserted that the coal strike "necessarily had such a direct, material, and substantial effect upon interstate commerce that, even in the absence of averments of intent, such intent must be reasonably inferred."[70]

3. *Intent not accompanied by substantial restraint.* Perhaps the clearest expression of this rule occurs in the decision of the Circuit Court of Appeals in a case in which German conspirators were accused of violating the Sherman Act when they planned to bring about strikes of munitions workers. The court declared that "if the formulation of the

[67] 284 Fed. 833, 834 (1922).
[68] U. S. v. Window Glass Manufacturers, 287 Fed. 228, 235 (1923).
[69] 2 F (2) 993 (1924).
[70] 22 F (2) 559 (1927).

plan, the formulation of purpose, the meeting of minds in an agreement to stop a trade always lawful, however repugnant temporarily to Germans and to pacifists always, be a crime, the judgments complained of are right." "So far as the lack of success of the plaintiffs in error is relied on, it is enough to point out, what was specifically held in the Nash Case [229 U. S. 373], that conspiracy under the Sherman Act is proved by proving the forbidden meeting of minds."[71]

In the first Coronado decision the Supreme Court, in the same sentence in which it asserted that intent to restrain interstate commerce might reasonably be inferred from the existence of an actual substantial restraint, declared that "obstruction of coal mining, though it may prevent coal from going into interstate commerce, is not a restraint of that commerce unless the obstruction to mining is intended to restrain commerce. . . ."[72]

In the second Coronado decision the Supreme Court said, "The mere reduction in the supply of an article to be shipped in interstate commerce by the illegal or tortious prevention of its manufacture or production is ordinarily an indirect and remote obstruction to that commerce. But when the intent of those unlawfully preventing the manufacture or production is shown to be to restrain or control the supply entering and moving in interstate commerce, or the price of

[71] Lamar v. U. S., 260 Fed. 561, 562, 563 (1919).

[72] U. M. W. v. Coronado, 259 U. S. 344, 411 (1922). See also Silverstein v. Journeyman Tailors, 284 Fed. 833, 834 (1922), for another clear statement emphasizing the principle that illegality would arise either from intent, or from an effect so substantial as to lead to an inferred intent. The sentence from the first Coronado decision here quoted is referred to in most of the important cases on the act arising since 1922.

it in interstate markets, their action is a direct violation of the Anti-trust Act."[73]

Summary.—It may thus be concluded that restraint of production, restraint of transportation, and restraint of marketing may each constitute a violation of the Sherman Act; but they will do so only if the courts find (1) the existence of an intent to interfere with interstate commerce accompanied by substantial restraint, (2) the presence of a restraint so material that intent must be inferred, or (3) the existence of an intent alone.[74] Though the theory of determining illegality appears to emphasize intent in preference to effect, the doctrine of inferred intent, since it is based on the existence of actual effect, shows the latter to be as important as intent itself.[75] That these criteria are too general and indefinite to produce certainty is clear when one considers the divergence of opinion among the various courts respecting the legality of the same combination.[76]

[73] Coronado v. U. M. W., 268 U. S. 295, 310 (1925).

[74] For a discussion of the relation of these criteria to the development of the rule of reason see Chapter XII below.

[75] The use of these principles of unlawful intent and unlawful restraint in interpreting the Sherman Act indicates that the courts, in reaching their conclusions, are making a special application of the general doctrine of conspiracy.

[76] It is difficult, if not impossible, to prophesy what position a particular court will take. It is this factor which probably accounts for the large number of cases under the act which are appealed to the higher courts. Of the 58 proceedings against labor under the statute in the lowest courts which are recorded in the Federal Reports, appeals were taken to the higher courts in 40 cases. Ten of these reached the Supreme Court, several of them on two different occasions.

CHAPTER XI

LEGAL PROBLEMS

Does Legality under Common Law Affect Legality under the Sherman Act?—In Chapter III attention was given to the assertion that Congress, in passing the Sherman Act, intended among other things to enact the common law with respect to labor activities affecting interstate transactions.[1] It was there shown that there was no justification for that position. But regardless of the actual intent of Congress it is conceivable that the courts may have assumed that the Anti-trust Law really did enact the common law. A study of the decisions, however, produces little evidence that they have generally acted upon such an assumption. Ordinary strikes, organization campaigns, and trade agreements, for example, which have occasionally been declared unlawful under the Sherman Act, were not, for many years prior to 1890, considered illegal under the common law.

It would nevertheless be incorrect to assert that legality under the common law has been without effect upon the interpretation of the statute. Under common law the courts have frequently held that secondary boycotts, coercion, violence and intimidation have been illegal.[2] Has this fact influenced the courts to decide that the Sherman Act was being

[1] See above, pp. 47-50.
[2] For a brief discussion of this question and for a list of supporting cases see Commons and Andrews, *Principles of Labor Legislation*, 3rd Edition, New York, 1927, pp. 112-122.

violated in cases where the evidence showed such unlawful activities?

A statement by the late Chief Justice, William Howard Taft, in a volume entitled, *The Anti-Trust Act and the Supreme Court,* published in 1914, bears on this point. He declared,

> It is quite clear that the mere striking to secure better wages or other terms of employment, and thus embarrassing the operation of a railroad engaged in interstate commerce, would not be within the statute, because such a combined action was not unlawful at common law, and it has come in modern days to be recognized as a legitimate means by which working-men through united action may put themselves on a level of resource and power with their employer. But when they go further and seek by striking and united withholding of patronage to coerce others who have no normal relation to the fight to assist them in it and injure their employer, they step over the line of lawfulness, and if by such means they obstruct the interstate trade of their employer they violate the act.[3]

A writer in the *Harvard Law Review* declares that legitimate methods of organizing the non-union mines should not be held to violate the Sherman Act, but when such methods as violence are used the balance shifts and an injunction should be issued under the law.[4]

In the Bedford Stone case the Circuit Court of Appeals, refusing to direct the issuance of an injunction against the stone cutters, pointed out that "no actual or threatened violence [appeared], no picketing, no boycott, and nothing of that character." "The tendency in greater or less degree . . . to restrain interstate commerce may be conceded," it

[3] Taft, *The Anti-Trust Act and the Supreme Court,* New York, 1914, p. 97.
[4] 35 *Harvard Law Review* 459.

declared, "but, so long as it does not appear that appellees resorted or threatened to resort to unlawful acts or means to accomplish their lawful purpose, there was no impropriety in Judge Anderson's refusal to grant a temporary injunction, and his order denying same is accordingly affirmed."[5]

This position was not accepted by a majority of the Supreme Court, but it was heartily endorsed by Justice Brandeis in his dissenting opinion. He asserted that the stone cutters' methods were legal. "They were innocent alike of trespass and of breach of contract. They did not picket. They refrained from violence, intimidation, fraud and threats. They refrained from obstructing otherwise either the plaintiffs or their customers in attempts to secure other help. They did not plan a boycott against any of the plaintiffs or against builders who used the plaintiffs' product." "There was no attempt to seek the aid of members of any other craft, by sympathetic strike or otherwise."[6]

Underlying the foregoing statements there appears to be the idea that common law legality is a factor of importance in determining legality under the Sherman Act. It is not usual, however, to find such clearly stated expressions of the principle in the decisions. Despite this fact it is likely that where the determination of legality is so uncertain as it is under the Anti-trust Law, the courts are readily influenced by evidence of violence and "coercion" to conclude that the defendants have intended to restrain interstate commerce or have brought about a substantial restraint of it, and have thus violated the statute.

There is indirect support for this conclusion in the fact that in many of the labor decisions the courts have devoted

[5] Bedford Stone v. Journeyman Stone Cutters, 9 F (2) 40 (1925).
[6] Bedford Stone v. Journeyman Stone Cutters, 47 Sup. Ct. Rep. 522, 528, 529 (1927).

much space to a description of the acts of violence or "coercion" such as might normally be considered unlawful under the common law. This is especially true in such decisions as those on the railway strikes and the Duplex boycott.[7] If the existence of violence and "coercion" is of no significance in determining the legality of an act it is difficult to explain why the courts should bother to describe such evidence at length, as they often do. It seems valid, therefore, to conclude that the courts are often influenced by such evidence, whether consciously or not, in arriving at their decisions.

As we shall see, the common law has affected the application of the Anti-trust Act to labor activities in other ways than that just discussed.

The Doctrine of Conspiracy in the Labor Cases.—The Sherman Act declared unlawful "every contract, combination in the form of trust or otherwise, or conspiracy, in restraint of trade or commerce among the several States." It is as unlawful conspiracies that labor combinations are usually reached. The emphasis of the courts on the element of intent indicates the extent to which the doctrine of conspiracy has been applied in these cases. It is an old rule under that doctrine that where an unlawful conspiracy exists, every act which is a part of or carried out in connection with the conspiracy is itself illegal.[8] Applying this rule in the labor cases under the statute the courts have frequently enjoined many acts which, though innocent and peaceful in

---

[7] See the following decisions for examples: U. S. v. Debs, 64 Fed. 724 (1894); U. S. v. Cassidy, 67 Fed. 698 (1895); Loewe v. Lawlor, 208 U. S. 274 (1908); Dail-Overland v. Willys-Overland, 263 Fed. 171 (1919); Duplex v. Deering, 254 U. S. 443 (1921); U. S. v. Railway Employees' Department, 283 Fed. 479 (1922); O'Brien v. U. S., 290 Fed. 185 (1923).

[8] Aikens v. Wisconsin, 195 U. S. 194 (1904).

themselves, are considered part of an unlawful conspiracy in restraint of interstate commerce.

Thus, in the Pullman strike, the courts enjoined the strikers from persuading railway workers to quit work.[9] In the Bucks Stove case the Supreme Court declared that "spoken words or printed matter" might be enjoined if they were part of a combination to restrain interstate commerce.[10] In the case of the Borderland Coal Corporation v. United Mine Workers the check-off and an organization campaign were enjoined by the District Court as part of an unlawful conspiracy in violation of the Sherman Act.[11] The injunction in the shopmen's strike of 1922, on the same grounds, enjoined such acts as entreaties, persuasion, argument, use of letters, telegrams, and interviews.[12] Whatever one may think of the reasonableness of forbidding acts like these it is clear that a judge who believes that a conspiracy exists has the firm support of legal principle in enjoining them.

Nevertheless the courts have frequently hesitated to press the doctrine of conspiracy under the Sherman Act to its logical conclusions. In the case of the Borderland Coal Corporation v. United Mine Workers Judge Anderson, as we have seen, enjoined the check-off system and the union attempt to organize West Virginia.[13] When the case was carried to the Circuit Court of Appeals the injunction against these activities was reversed, the court asserting that they were entirely lawful. It declared that what should have been

[9] U. S. v. Debs, 64 Fed. 724 (1894).
[10] Gompers v. Bucks, 221 U. S. 418, 439 (1911).
[11] 275 Fed. 871 (1921).
[12] Restraining Order in U. S. v. Railway Employees' Department, Washington (1922); U. S. v. Railway Employees' Department, 283 Fed. 479 (1922).
[13] 275 Fed. 871 (1921).

enjoined were such illegal acts as the destruction of mine property, the use of force and intimidation, the secret attempt to get men to violate their contracts, and the spending of money to do these things. It accordingly directed that an injunction restraining these acts be issued.[14]

This position of the Circuit Court, however reasonable it may seem, does not appear to be logical. The court assumed throughout that an illegal conspiracy to restrain interstate commerce existed, and that it was the existence of the conspiracy which justified the issuance of an injunction. But if the arrangement between the union operators and the miners' union was an illegal restraint of interstate commerce, every act whereby it was carried out was illegal. The check-off and the organization campaign were assuredly parts of the conspiracy, as were acts like violence and intimidation. If authority to enjoin the latter acts existed under the Sherman Act so did authority to enjoin the former. To have been strictly logical the court should have affirmed the injunction issued in the lower court. But it considered that injunction unreasonable. The element of unreasonableness really enters farther back. It seems unreasonable to have considered the arrangement between the miners and the operators and the attempt to organize West Virginia an illegal conspiracy at all. Once a court decided that an illegal conspiracy in violation of the statute existed, any act by means of which the conspiracy was carried out might properly be enjoined. The Circuit Court of Appeals, which considered the check-off a lawful act, should logically have concluded that no illegal conspiracy existed, and that therefore no injunction might be issued under the Sherman Act, or that an illegal conspiracy did exist and that therefore all activities which were in aid of it might be enjoined.

[14] Gassaway v. Borderland, 278 Fed. 56, 65 (1921).

There are numerous other instances of a similar failure on the part of the courts to carry the doctrine of conspiracy under the Anti-trust Law to its logical conclusions. In the case of the Carbon Fuel Company v. United Mine Workers, the District Court, in 1922, enjoined the operation of the check-off and attempts to organize West Virginia, on the ground that they were parts of an illegal conspiracy in violation of the act. Two days later the injunction was suspended by a judge of the Circuit Court of Appeals, and in 1923 that court directed that only such acts as threats, violence, trespassing and inducing breach of contract be enjoined.[15] This case was later consolidated with eleven others, all arising under the statute, and in 1927 the Circuit Court of Appeals, declaring that the miners were engaged in an unlawful conspiracy, affirmed the injunction last described.[16] The court found an illegal conspiracy, but it refused to permit acts which were ordinarily lawful to be enjoined.

Similarly, in the Pittsburgh Terminal Coal case, the court, despite the existence of what it considered an illegal conspiracy in restraint of interstate commerce, enjoined only the attempt of the union to keep strikers in the houses owned by the operators.[17] In the case of the Dail-Overland Company v. Willys-Overland Company, though the court found the striking machinists engaged in an unlawful conspiracy, it did no more than enjoin illegal acts of picketing.[18]

In every one of these cases, and in numerous others which

[15] 5 *Law and Labor* 150-151; U. M. W. v. Carbon Fuel Co., 288 Fed. 1020 (1923).

[16] U. M. W. v. Red Jacket, 18 F (2) 839 (1927); Appendix C, Cases 57-68.

[17] Pittsburgh Terminal Coal Corp. v. U. M. W., 22 F (2) 559, 565 (1927).

[18] 263 Fed. 171, 189 (1919).

might be mentioned, the courts, once convinced that the Sherman Act was being violated, would have been legally justified in enjoining every act carried on in aid of the alleged conspiracy. Actually they hesitated to do this, probably because they considered it undesirable to restrain activities apparently reasonable and justifiable. In the end, they restrained only those acts which were unlawful under the common law. Thus it is clear that common law legality enters to determine, in numerous cases, what will be enjoined under the Anti-trust Act. It is also clear that in such cases the courts have used the act only as a means of conferring jurisdiction in labor disputes and have then acted as though they were protecting rights under the common law.

Obtaining Jurisdiction by Means of the Sherman Act. —Federal courts obtain jurisdiction only in cases where there exists diversity of citizenship between the parties in dispute, or where a federal statute is violated. As a rule employers contemplating legal action against labor would prefer to bring a case in a federal rather than in a state court. Legal procedure in federal courts is usually handled with more dispatch. An order issued by a United States court is likely to command greater respect than that of a state court, perhaps because the ordinary citizen stands in greater awe of the federal than of the local government. Since the order of a federal court will be enforced by federal officers, it is likely to be more effective. Such an order also has effect over a wider area than one issued by a state court. A single injunction issued by a federal court reaches such activities as a nation-wide railway strike or boycott, and often stands a fair chance of being enforced, whereas a state court, though it might attempt to prevent such activities, would meet with many obstacles in reaching contemners of its order outside state boundaries. If an employer can invoke the jurisdiction of a federal court and secure an order enjoining a wide-spread boycott, he may accomplish results which could probably not be obtained except by bringing a multiplicity of suits, at great expense, in numerous state courts. For these reasons a suit in a federal court is of greater advantage to the employer than one in a state court.

Often, however, a labor case lacks diversity of citizenship. In order to bring it into a federal court employers will allege the violation of a federal statute. The Sherman Act has in later years become more and more useful to employers in such circumstances. This is probably the reason why, since the passage of the Clayton Act, which permitted private suits for injunctions, so many ordinary strike cases have been brought into the courts by employers under the Sherman Act.

In many instances, as has been seen, the courts have issued injunctions similar to those which would have been issued under the common law if the federal courts had possessed jurisdiction because of diversity of citizenship. This appears from a consideration of the injunctions in the cases described in the latter part of the previous section. Other instances may be mentioned. In the Herkert case the lower court appears to have issued an injunction against unlawful picketing.[19] In the Duplex decision the Supreme Court directed the issuance of an injunction against what it considered a secondary boycott.[20] In the case of the Columbus Heating and Ventilating Company v. Pittsburgh Building Trades Council an injunction prohibiting a threatened sympathetic strike and boycott was approved.[21] It is fair to conclude,

[19] Herkert and Meisel v. United Leather Workers, 268 Fed. 662 (1920).
[20] Duplex v. Deering, 254 U. S. 443, 478 (1921).
[21] 17 F (2) 806 (1927).

therefore, that the Anti-trust Law has given employers an opportunity to get injunctions from federal courts when they would otherwise have had to go to the state courts.

Violation of the Sherman Act is punishable by fine and imprisonment. Since certain acts of violence affecting interstate commerce have been held to violate the statute the federal courts have taken jurisdiction over cases of criminal acts which were unlawful under local statutes. Thus they have punished an assault upon a roadmaster,[22] the burning of cars filled with coal,[23] the dynamiting of railroad tracks,[24] and the putting of quicksilver in locomotive engines.[25] The Sherman Act has thus operated to bring into the federal courts criminal cases which would normally be tried in state courts.

Finally, of course, the law, interpreted to prohibit various labor activities previously legal under common law and under state and federal statutes, has brought into the federal courts a considerable body of labor disputes which would otherwise not have come into the courts at all.

Methods of Enforcement: Extent and Effectiveness.— Upon the basis of the cases described in Appendix C a count has been made to show the relative success of the various methods of enforcing the Sherman Law. The cases include all of which record could be found in the official reports to December 10, 1928, those described in the bulletin on the anti-trust laws published by the Attorney-General in November, 1928, and a few additional cases mentioned in the

[22] U. S. v. Harvel (1922), B. B. p. 179, Appendix C, Case 33.
[23] U. S. v. Powell (1922), B. B. p. 178, Appendix C, Case 31.
[24] U. S. v. Reilly (1924), B. B. p. 180; Vandell v. U. S., 6 F (2) 188 (1925).
[25] U. S. v. Williams (1923), B. B. p. 177; Appendix C, Case 30; Williams v. U. S., 295 Fed. 302 (1923).

monthly journal, *Law and Labor*. Only cases first reaching
the courts prior to December, 1928, are covered. Though
there may be other cases in which labor has been in the position of defendant under the Sherman Act which have
escaped notice, they are probably not numerous.

Of the original proceedings against labor brought in the
federal courts of first instance there have been 10 government suits for injunctions, 30 cases of criminal indictments,
4 damage suits,[26] and 39 suits for injunctions brought by
private parties. Excluding those instances in which no decision had been made in the lowest courts by 1928, there
have been 9 government injunction suits, 27 criminal cases,
4 damage suits, and 39 private injunction suits.

Using the term "ultimately successful" to describe proceedings in which, whether or not they went to the higher
courts, the law was finally invoked against the defendants,
there were eight ultimately successful government injunction suits, or 89 per cent of all such suits, excluding the
pending case. Of the criminal prosecutions, 14 out of 27, or
52 per cent, were ultimately successful, the remaining cases
being noll prossed or dismissed, or ending in verdicts of
not guilty for all defendants. Of the four suits for damages
only one, that in Loewe v. Lawlor,[27] can be considered to
have been ultimately successful. The lower federal courts
issued injunctions in 32 out of 39 private suits. These were
finally reversed by the higher courts in six cases; but in two
instances in which the district courts refused injunctions the
higher courts directed that they be issued. There were thus

---

[26] In one case, Decorative Stone v. Building Trades Council, 18 F
    (2) 333, a suit for injunction was accompanied by a request
    for damages, which was denied. This case is not counted here
    among the damage suits. See Appendix C, Case 80.
[27] Appendix C, Case 41.

28 out of 39 ultimately successful private injunction suits, or 71 per cent. On the basis of the foregoing data, one may therefore conclude that there is most chance of ultimate success in injunction suits against labor, and least in damage suits.

Considering the available data from another aspect, one finds that 51 out of a total of 79 of the decided proceedings, or over 64 per cent, were ultimately successful. Of these 51 approximately 16 per cent were government suits, 27 per cent were criminal prosecutions, two per cent were damage suits, and 55 per cent were private injunction suits. Thus private injunction suits constituted more than half of the successful proceedings.

The nature of all the proceedings is also interesting. Of the total of 83, 12 per cent were government injunction suits, 36 per cent were criminal prosecutions, 5 per cent were damage suits, and 47 per cent were private injunction suits. It is thus clear that labor has most to fear from private injunction suits, not only because the chances of ultimate success from the employer's viewpoint are greater, but because nearly half of all proceedings against labor under the statute have been of that nature.

As between government suits for injunctions and criminal prosecutions the former have in the past been more successful from the government's point of view. It is probable that this difference is due to the fact that federal judges are more likely to grant an injunction to a United States attorney than a jury is to return a verdict of guilty. At any rate the government has experienced no difficulty in getting a lower court to grant an injunction on request. On the other hand, it has experienced numerous acquittals of defendants who have been tried by juries. The realization of government attorneys that they need a good case to secure convictions from a jury is probably responsible for the considerable proportion of indictments which have been noll prossed or dismissed without being carried to trial.[28]

The severity of the punishments imposed upon labor defendants as a result of criminal prosecutions under the Sherman Act is worth noting, especially since such prosecutions are the second most important method of enforcing the Sherman Act against labor. Of the fourteen successful prosecutions the sentences are known in twelve cases. In eight of these major punishments were imposed, those in the other four being relatively unimportant. The minor penalties include a total fine of $110 divided among 72 defendants, a fine of $25, imprisonment for ten days in one case and four hours in another. The most common major punishment consists in the imposition of large fines aggregating several thousands of dollars. In other cases the records show prison sentences of one year, ten months, and eight months. The act obviously has teeth in it in the case of successful criminal prosecutions.[29]

Damage Suits Against Labor.—Section 7 of the Sherman Act provides that any person whose property or business is injured by an activity which violates the law may sue and recover triple damages as well as the costs of the suit and a reasonable attorney's fee.

In 1908, when the Supreme Court, in Loewe v. Lawlor,[30] declared that the members of a trade union were liable in damages for injuries sustained by an employer due to a violation of the Anti-trust Act, fear that the precedent would impose a severe handicap on trade union activities was widely expressed. Again, when the Supreme Court, render-

[28] Consult Appendix C, Cases 11-40.
[29] Appendix C, Cases 11-40.
[30] 208 U. S. 274.

ing the first Coronado decision, held in 1922 that a trade union, though it was an unincorporated association, might be sued for damages,[31] the same fear was given expression.[32]

The data given in the preceding section demonstrates, however, that labor has been only slightly affected by damage suits under the Sherman Act. In all there have been no more than five such suits (including the Decorative Stone case), only one of which resulted in ultimate success.[33]

The hatters, who finally had to pay damages of over $250,000, will receive little satisfaction from the realization that such suits are generally unsuccessful. Even in their case, however, the employer, who entered suit in 1903, was not able to collect damages until 1917. The Coronado Company's suit against the United Mine Workers came into the District Court in 1914. It went through several trials in the lower court and five appeals to the Circuit Court of Appeals and the Supreme Court, and though it involved the possibility of an award of more than half a million dollars, the plaintiffs, rather than undergo the costs of a new trial and possible new appeals, were willing to settle the case for $27,500 in 1927, thirteen years after it first entered the District Court. In the third damage suit the Pennsylvania Mining Company, which brought suit because of losses suffered in 1915, found a verdict in its favor reversed by the

[31] U. M. W. v. Coronado, 259 U. S. 344.

[32] In this connection see Wolman, *The Boycott in American Trade Unions*, Baltimore, 1916, pp. 134-135; and Commons and Andrews, *Principles of Labor Legislation*, 3rd Edition, New York, 1927, pp. 130-133. Commons and Andrews call especial attention to the fact that since unions are unincorporated, they have no limited liability and every member may therefore be mulcted until the total sum awarded is collected, if possible. This, they believe, aggravates the menace to labor.

[33] See Appendix C, Cases 41-44.

Circuit Court in 1924, experienced a new trial as a result of which no damages were awarded, and finally, in 1928, thirteen years after the original trouble, learned that the higher court had once more definitely decided against it. In the fourth instance, the case of Christian v. International Association of Machinists, the suit was finally dismissed on motion of the plaintiff at his own cost, without ever coming to trial.[34] In a fifth case, that of the Decorative Stone Company v. Building Trades Council, a suit for an injunction was accompanied by a request for damages. The injunction was granted by the District Court, but the request for damages was denied. The plaintiff carried its request for damages to the Circuit Court of Appeals, which upheld the lower court on the ground that the anti-trust acts made no provision for damages in an action for an injunction.[35]

Surely such a record as that of these five cases should not cause labor and its sympathizers much worry about the menace of damage suits.

The bringing of such suits is attended by numerous disadvantages to the plaintiffs which do not accompany suits for injunctions. In the first place, an injunction order can be obtained more quickly. The delay due to the necessity of impaneling jurymen and selecting a jury does not appear in injunction proceedings. It is likely, furthermore, that an employer's attorney will find it harder to convince a jury than a single judge, which is all that would be required in a suit for an injunction. In case an injunction order is appealed, the higher court, if it disapproves, can direct a modification of the order which the lower court can put into effect speedily. If a higher court finds error in a judgment

[34] Letter from the Clerk of the United States District Court at Covington, Kentucky, May 17, 1929.

[35] 18 F (2) 333 (1927); 10 *Law and Labor* 54; Appendix C, Case 80.

of damages, however, it is not possible to direct a modification which can be effected with dispatch. It is necessary instead to go through all the delay and expense of a new trial by jury. In the Coronado suit, for example, the fact that the Supreme Court twice ruled that there had been error in rendering judgment against some of the united defendants necessitated retrials of all of them. The great delay involved in damage suits increases the attorney's fees and court costs, which must be paid by the plaintiff in the likely event that he loses his suit. Added to all these disadvantages is the high degree of uncertainty which attends the interpretation of the Sherman Act by the courts. It is difficult to prophesy when a court will find error in a judgment under the act. Damage suits under it, therefore, stand more than the usual chance of meeting with reversals of judgment and the attendant delays, retrial, and expenses.

In view of these circumstances, and of the history of damage suits against labor under the statute, it is easy to understand that not even the tempting possibility of triple damages is likely to induce employers to sue labor at law. It is the private suit for an injunction, not the damage suit, which constitutes the gravest menace to labor under the Sherman Act. And for that menace the Clayton Act is responsible.

The Effect of the Clayton Act.—Section 16 of the Clayton Act permits private parties to sue for injunctions under the anti-trust acts. Prior to that time injunction suits could be brought only by the government.[36] This is one of the most important reasons for the increased use of the Sherman Law against labor in recent years. Further data based on the cases arising since 1914 which are recorded in Appendix

[36] Appendix A, The Sherman Act, Section 4.

C will demonstrate the importance of the Clayton Act in this connection.

Of a total of 39 private injunction suits against labor under the Sherman Act all but five were brought after the passage of the Clayton Act. Injunctions were refused in four of these five cases because the courts held that they had no authority to grant them. That granted in the fifth case, to the extent that it was based on the statute, was reversed in the next higher court.[37]

In the 83 cases which have been brought against labor since 1890, 64, or over 77 per cent, have been brought in the fourteen years since the passage of the Clayton Act. Thirty-four of these 64 cases, or 53 per cent, were private injunction suits.

Since 1914 there have been 49 proceedings in the district courts which were immediately successful.[38] Twenty-eight of these, or about 57 per cent, were private injunction suits. Of a total of 43 ultimately successful proceedings since 1914, 28, or 65 per cent, were private injunction suits.

Of the 34 private injunction suits brought since the passage of the Clayton Act, 32, or 94 per cent, were immediately successful, and 28, or 82 per cent, were ultimately successful.

These figures show that about seven-eighths of all the private injunction suits and all of the ultimately successful ones have been brought since the Clayton Act was passed; that more than half of all the Sherman Act cases against labor since 1914 have been private suits for injunctions; that such suits have constituted more than three-fifths of all the

[37] Appendix C, Cases 45-49.
[38] By an "immediately successful" proceeding is meant one which results either in conviction, an injunction, or a judgment of damages before the case is carried to a higher court. In numerous suits, of course, no appeals were made.

successful proceedings against labor; and that more than four-fifths of such private injunction suits have been successful. The Clayton Act, instead of relieving labor of the burden of the Sherman Law, has thus greatly increased it.

Legality of Unions *Per Se.*—Reference was made in Chapter VI to the one positive gain for labor in the Clayton Act, so far as it was related to the Act of 1890. It will be remembered that the District Court in the Hitchman case declared that the United Mine Workers was an unlawful organization *per se* under the Sherman Law.[39] If this declaration had been affirmed by the higher courts, proceedings for the dissolution of labor unions might have resulted, and such organizations would have been faced with a significant menace to their existence. The Circuit Court of Appeals, however, reversed the lower court on this point.[40] When the Clayton Act was passed it contained, in Section 6, a provision stating that "nothing contained in the antitrust laws shall be construed to forbid the existence and operation of labor, agricultural, or horticultural organizations. . . ."[41] In view of this statement the Clayton Act has at least made it unlikely that trade unions will be dissolved under the Sherman Law.

"An Adequate Remedy at Law."—The first paragraph of Section 20 of the Clayton Act declared that no federal court should issue an injunction "in any case between an employer and employees or between employers and employees, or between employees, or between persons employed and persons seeking employment, involving, or growing out of, a dispute concerning terms or conditions of employment unless necessary to prevent irreparable injury to property, or

[39] Hitchman v. Mitchell, 202 Fed. 512 (1912).
[40] Mitchell v. Hitchman, 214 Fed. 685 (1914).
[41] 38 Stat. 730.

to a property right, of the party making the application, for which injury there is no adequate remedy at law. . . ." The phrase "no adequate remedy at law" should be especially noted.

It has already been shown that in the Danbury Hatters' and the Coronado decisions the Supreme Court held respectively that the members of a union and a union itself might be sued at law for damages incurred through violations of the Sherman Act. May not the right of employers to bring such suits be considered an "adequate remedy at law"? If it is so considered does not the Clayton Act operate to prohibit the issuance of an injunction by a federal court in a labor dispute under the Sherman Act?[42]

It may be said in answer to this question that the courts might not consider damage suits an adequate remedy because of the delay with which they are accompanied. The difficulty of collecting damages from a multitude of propertyless workmen might also be stressed. But where the union concerned has large funds there is property available adequate to permit the payment of substantial damages. It would not be necessary to bring a multiplicity of small suits in such cases, a factor which has often led a court to issue an injunction. A single suit against a responsible union, as in the Coronado case, or against a large number of individual union members, as in the Hatters' case, would be sufficient. If a large union should be held responsible the plaintiff would undoubtedly be able to collect. In the case of a suit against individual members the fact that money was forth-

---

[42] The possibility that the Coronado decision, by opening the way for damage suits, might bring about a decrease in the use of the injunction in labor cases, is clearly stated in Mason, *Organized Labor and the Law*, Durham, 1925, pp. 231-232; and in a comment on the decision in 32 *Yale Law Journal* 59, 64.

coming with the help of other unions to make it possible for the hatters to pay over $250,000 is a strong argument in favor of the position that a damage suit is an adequate remedy at law. Equity courts have frequently refused to exercise jurisdiction in cases where the bringing of a damage suit, which they considered an adequate remedy, was open to a plaintiff.[43]

In the Duplex decision[44] the Supreme Court took the position that the first paragraph of Section 20 of the Clayton Act, which has been referred to above, cannot be applied to every kind of labor dispute. It has reference only to disputes between an employer and his own employees. "Congress," said the court, "had in mind particular industrial controversies, not a general class war."[45] Assuming that this interpretation of Section 20 will be followed in the future as it has in the past, it is clear that the argument of the foregoing paragraph would not be applicable to all activities which have been enjoined under the Sherman Act.

The courts would not consider secondary boycotts or sympathetic strikes, such as those in the Duplex v. Deering or the Western Union case,[46] disputes between an employer and his own employees. In such cases the prohibition of injunctions where there is an adequate remedy at law would not apply. On the other hand, in cases like Wagner v. International Association of Machinists,[47] Dail-Overland v. Willy-Overland,[48] Herkert and Meisel v. United Leather

---

[43] For a discussion of what the courts might consider an adequate remedy at law see Corpus Juris, Vol. 21, pp. 41, 42, 45, 50-60.

[44] Duplex v. Deering, 254 U. S. 443 (1921).

[45] 254 U. S. 443, 472.

[46] Western Union v. Electrical Workers, 2 F (2) 993.

[47] 252 Fed. 597 (1918).

[48] 263 Fed. 171 (1919).

Workers,[49] and those involving mine strikes, which were concerned with direct disputes between employers and their own employees, the first paragraph of Section 20 of the Clayton Act would apply. Thus, if the courts were to accept the position that a damage suit constituted an adequate remedy at law, they would not issue injunctions in immediate disputes between employers and employees.

It is to be noted that if the foregoing argument applies to labor injunctions under the Sherman Act it also applies to the use of injunctions issued by the courts under the principles of the common law. The first Coronado decision, in laying down the rule that unions might sue and be sued, used a line of reasoning which may in large part be applied to damage suits in general, not alone to damage suits under the Anti-trust Law. The prohibition in the Clayton Act against the issuing of injunctions is not confined to injunctions under the Sherman Act. That act is in fact not mentioned in Section 20. If damage suits are to be considered adequate remedies at law, Section 20 has general application in all direct labor disputes.

Should unions in the future raise the foregoing argument in order to avert the issuance of injunctions? Against such a policy it may be asserted that in so doing they would be calling the attention of their opponents to the possibility of a damage suit. On the other hand, it is a fair assumption that attorneys for employers are already fully aware of the latters' right to bring such an action. If the courts should accept the argument that a damage suit against labor is an adequate remedy at law it is probable that the number of these suits would increase. In view, however, of the delay and expenses involved they would certainly not be brought as frequently as injunction suits now are. Furthermore the

[49] 268 Fed. 662 (1920).

effect which an injunction has of immediately handicapping the trade union would not be present in a damage suit. Such a suit would probably not come to trial until after the union had had the opportunity of carrying out its activities.

The Sherman Act, besides providing for damage suits, also permits criminal prosecutions by the government, as well as government suits for injunctions. Does not a criminal suit furnish a sufficiently adequate remedy at law to make unnecessary the issuance of an injunction to the government under the terms of Section 20 of the Clayton Act?

Whatever the reception which the courts might give to the line of argument here set forth labor unions would lose nothing by pressing it. It offers at least the possibility that the Clayton Act may in the end produce some net gain of consequence for labor.

The Uncertainties of the Sherman Act.—The advantages of certainty in the application of a law do not need an elaborate presentation. It is sufficient to point out that a violation of a law is less likely to occur if there is knowledge of what constitutes such a violation and an assurance that the courts will be quick to punish it; that where a high degree of certainty exists cases are less likely to be appealed, with an attendant economy of time and money of the parties and of the energies of the courts; that greater respect for the laws and the courts exists where judges are likely to agree in the interpretation and enforcement of a statute; and finally that to the extent that certainty of interpretation exists, it becomes less likely that the economic or social bias of the court will enter into the determination of cases.

The Sherman Act has been so encumbered with uncertainty as to be notorious. This has been especially true in the labor cases. It was shown in the previous chapter that there has been wide disagreement among the courts as to the illegality of similar and often identical labor activities. Another test of the uncertainty attendant upon the cases under the act is the extent to which the district courts, the circuit courts of appeals, and the Supreme Court have disagreed with each other in interpreting the law. In six cases the circuit courts of appeals reversed the judgments of district courts.[50] Eight times the Supreme Court reversed the decisions of the courts below. This last is especially significant in view of the fact that there have only been ten decisions rendered by the Supreme Court in labor cases under the statute.[51]

Another indication of the uncertainty of the courts with respect to the effect of the statute is the number of cases in which the higher courts have divided. The record of the circuit courts of appeals is a good one on this point, for in

[50] Mitchell v. Hitchman, 214 Fed. 685 (1914); Dowd v. U. M. W. 235 Fed. 1 (1916); Gable v. Vonnegut, 274 Fed. 66 (1921); Danville Brick Workers v. Danville Brick Co., 283 Fed. 909 (1922); U. M. W. v. Pennsylvania Mining Co., 300 Fed. 965 (1924); and Brims v. U. S., 6 F (2) 98 (1925).

[51] Those decisions of the Supreme Court in which the lower court was reversed are Loewe v. Lawlor, 208 U. S. 274 (1908); Duplex v. Deering, 254 U. S. 443 (1921); U. M. W. v. Coronado, 259 U. S. 344 (1922); National Association of Window Glass Manufacturers v. U. S., 263 U. S. 403 (1923); United Leather Workers v. Herkert and Meisel, 265 U. S. 457 (1924); Coronado v. U. M. W., 268 U. S. 295 (1925); U. S. v. Brims, 71 L. ed. 403 (1926); Bedford Stone v. Journeyman Stone Cutters, 47 Sup. Ct. Rep. 522 (1927). The remaining two decisions, in which the lower court's opinion was affirmed, were Lawlor v. Loewe, 235 U. S. 522 (1915); and Paine v. Neal, 244 U. S. 459 (1917). In the latter case the court upheld the refusal to grant an injunction to a private party in a suit begun before the passage of the Clayton Act. See Appendix C, Case 49.

only three out of 27 recorded decisions was there a division. In the Supreme Court, however, unanimous decisions were rendered in six cases and divided ones in four. The fact that three of these four were the very important Duplex, Herkert and Meisel, and Bedford Stone cases is especially significant.[52]

The basic cause of this uncertainty and difference of opinion is the terminology of the Sherman Act, especially that of Section 1, which prohibits "Every contract, combination in the form of trust or otherwise, or conspiracy, in restraint of trade or commerce among the several states." A multitude of disputes over the meaning of the terms "trade," "commerce," "restraint of trade or commerce," "interstate trade or commerce," and over the significance of the adjective "every," has accompanied the history of the statute since the beginning. The use of the term "conspiracy" further increased the field for disagreement because it introduced the notion of intent and gave the courts the opportunity to decide whether or not an illegal intent existed. The plain truth is that the Senate Judiciary Committee which framed the Act of 1890, despite the fact that on it sat such eminent lawyers as Senators Edmunds, Hoar, George, and Vest, produced a measure which events have proved was extremely ill-drawn. The only defense to be made for them, and it is not an altogether inadequate one, is that they were in entirely uncharted legal territory, trying to produce federal anti-trust legislation which should be at once effective and constitutional.

The immediate elements of uncertainty in the application of the Anti-trust Law have centered on the following questions: Does an illegal intent to restrain interstate commerce

[52] The fourth was Paine v. Neal, 244 U. S. 459.

exist? Is the actual restraint upon interstate commerce direct, substantial, and significant? Assuming violation of the act what activities should be enjoined? The first two questions are of course the most important, and at least one of them must be answered in every case.

It is in answering these questions that the need for the rule of reason arises. When a statute is so vague that arguments apparently sound can be found both for and against the view that a particular activity violates it, the court must exercise a degree of discretion which is unnecessary where a statute is definite and well understood. It is compelled, if it seeks to prevent an unjust and indiscriminate application of a vague statute, to look beyond the mere words of the law to the economic and social facts of each case and to apply the standard of reasonableness.

CHAPTER XII

THE RULE OF REASON

The Development of the Rule of Reason.—The Sherman Act, containing as it does a prohibition of "every" contract, combination, and conspiracy in restraint of interstate commerce, would, if literally enforced, have resulted in rendering an enormous number of innocent transactions and activities unlawful. It is impossible to conceive of a business transaction between the citizens of different states which does not affect interstate commerce. If such a transaction should result in influencing prices, or reducing the number of competitors, it might logically be considered a contract in restraint of interstate commerce. If a manufacturer in New York should buy a competing plant in Ohio he would be guilty of restraining interstate commerce. So would a local chamber of commerce which should decide to urge merchants to patronize home industries.

It is clear, when one considers the result of a literal interpretation of the Sherman Act, that its enforcement on such a basis would have been both undesirable and impossible. What was needed was a reasonable application of the law. A beginning in this direction came when the Supreme Court rendered its decisions in the Hopkins and Anderson cases in 1898.[1]

In the Hopkins case the court declared that only those contracts were illegal "whose direct and immediate effect is a restraint upon . . . [interstate] trade or commerce. . . .

[1] Hopkins v. U. S., 171 U. S. 578; Anderson v. U. S., 171 U. S. 604.

The effect upon the commerce spoken of must be direct and proximate."[2] In the Anderson case the court, referring to agreements which affected interstate commerce but were not intended to do so, said, "If an agreement of that nature . . . should possibly, though only indirectly and unintentionally, affect interstate trade or commerce, in that event we think the agreement would be good. Otherwise, there is scarcely any agreement among men which has interstate or foreign commerce for its subject that may not remotely be said to, in some obscure way, affect that commerce and to be therefore void."[3]

In these decisions the court recognized that not every contract affecting interstate commerce should be considered unlawful. Only those whose effect was direct and "not too small to be taken into account"[4] should be so regarded. But the Sherman Act mentioned neither the size of a restraint nor the directness of its effect on interstate commerce. It declared against "every" such restraint. The Supreme Court in refusing to condemn every restraint laid down the policy that each restraint must be judged by itself. Was it direct? Was it important? Was it intentional? As soon as questions like this were to be asked the court found itself compelled to condemn some restraints and approve others. In order to decide a case it had to set up some standard of judgment apart from the mere existence of the restraint itself.

It was not, however, until 1911 that such a standard was clearly enunciated by the Supreme Court. In the Standard Oil case the court, referring to its decision in Hopkins v. United States, declared that "if the criterion by which it is to be determined in all cases whether every contract, com-

[2] 171 U. S. 578, 592-594.
[3] 171 U. S. 604, 616.
[4] 171 U. S. 604, 619.

bination, etc., is a restraint of trade within the intendment of the law, is the direct or indirect effect of the acts involved, then of course the rule of reason becomes the guide. . . ."[5] Considering the nature of the defendants' activities, it concluded that there existed a combination in unreasonable restraint of trade. In the American Tobacco case the court, in the light of the rule of reason, concluded that acts of the combination were so harmful to "individual liberty and the public well-being" that there was no doubt as to its being unreasonable and in unlawful restraint of trade.[6]

With these decisions the rule of reason became the accepted standard for determining whether a business combination violated the Anti-trust Law. If the restraint upon interstate commerce was "unreasonable" or "undue" it was illegal. In the Standard Oil and American Tobacco cases it was the undesirable, harmful character of the restraints, as well as their directness and importance, which appeared to render the combinations unlawful. In applying the rule of reason, however, the courts have not always considered whether a restraint was socially harmful. Their attention has usually been centered upon the question of whether it was direct and substantial.

The best standard of reasonableness would be one which included both elements. The technique of applying such a standard would be as follows: It should first be determined whether the restraint was direct, material and substantial. If it were found to be indirect and insignificant, purely incidental to the accomplishment of some local object, the matter should be dismissed as not affected by the statute. If, however, the restraint were found to be direct and consequential, it would be necessary, before determining that it

[5] Standard Oil Co. v. U. S., 221 U. S. 1, 66.
[6] U. S. v. American Tobacco Co., 221 U. S. 106.

was illegal, to decide whether or not it was also socially harmful. Only in cases where both directness and substantiality on the one hand and harmfulness on the other are found to exist, should a restraint of interstate commerce be considered unlawful.

A rule of reason, to be truly useful in reaching intelligent and socially tenable conclusions, should involve the application of the foregoing criteria. For to hold all sorts of unimportant restraints unlawful is to burden the courts with a multitude of unimportant cases; and to hold substantial restraints unlawful unless they are actually harmful to society is to hamper activities which may be of social benefit.

It cannot be said that the courts have clearly enunciated and commonly applied a standard of reasonableness of the kind just advocated. As shown in Chapter X, the only generally accepted criteria used have been those respecting intent to restrain and the direct and substantial character of the restraint. Nevertheless, there have been signs, apart from the decisions rendered in 1911, that it was such a standard of reasonableness that the courts often had in mind in reaching decisions.

One of the best illustrations of this is the majority opinion in the case of the Maple Flooring Manufacturers' Association v. United States, rendered on June 1, 1925.[7] The government had complained that the association, which disseminated information among its members as to prices, production, and costs, was acting in violation of the Sherman Act. The Supreme Court held that the association was lawful. The following excerpt from its opinion shows the nature of the considerations which a satisfactory rule of reason requires:

[7] 268 U. S. 563.

It is the consensus of opinion among economists and of many of the most important agencies of government that the public interest is served by the gathering and dissemination, in the widest possible manner, of information with respect to the production and distribution, cost and prices in actual sales, of market commodities, because the making available of such information tends to stabilize trade and industry, to produce fairer price levels, and to avoid the waste which inevitably attends the unintelligent conduct of economic enterprise. Free competition means a free and open market among both buyers and sellers for the sale and distribution of commodities. Competition does not become less free merely because the conduct of commercial operations becomes more intelligent through the free distribution of knowledge of all the essential factors entering into the commercial transaction. General knowledge that there is an accumulation of surplus of any market would undoubtedly tend to diminish production, but the dissemination of that information cannot, in itself, be said to be restraint upon commerce in any legal sense. The manufacturer is free to produce, but prudence and business foresight based on that knowledge influence a free choice in favor of more limited production. Restraint upon free competition begins when improper use is made of that information through any concerted action which operates to restrain the freedom of action of those who buy and sell.[8]

The court, believing that the effects of the association's activities were socially desirable, therefore took the position that there had not been an unlawful restraint of interstate commerce.[9]

[8] 268 U. S. 563, 582-583.
[9] For other instances of an attempt to apply the rule of reason see especially the unanimous opinion, written by Justice Brandeis in Board of Trade v. U. S., 242 U. S. 231 (1918), the dissenting opinion in American Column and Lumber Co. v. U. S., 257 U. S. 377 (1921), and the majority opinion in the Cement

The Rule in Labor Cases.—Though one finds the developed rule of reason frequently used in cases involving business it is rare to encounter it in labor cases. The courts have asked, in such cases, whether there was present an intent to restrain interstate commerce, or whether the actual restraint was direct and substantial. In accordance with the answers to these questions they have found some labor activities lawful and others unlawful. In only one important labor decision does one find the rule of reason applied in such a way as to take account of the question whether a substantial restraint is necessarily harmful, and therefore unreasonable. It is not insignificant that that decision involved an agreement between manufacturers and a union. It was not, in other words, exclusively a labor case.

In 1923 the Supreme Court rendered a decision in the case of the National Association of Window Glass Manufacturers v. United States.[10] As we saw in Chapter VIII the court had before it an agreement between the trade union and the manufacturers' association in the handmade window glass industry under which the plants in the industry were divided into groups, each of them permitted to operate only during the part of the year assigned to it. The District Court declared that such an agreement brought about an unlawful and unreasonable restraint of interstate commerce, a restraint which was direct, material, and substantial.[11] The Supreme Court, devoting its attention principally to the underlying economic conditions, found that the industry was a declining one, that there were not available a number of workers sufficient to man all the plants if they operated

Manufacturers' Protective Association v. U. S., 268 U. S. 86 (1925). See also U. S. v. Steel Corporation, 251 U. S. 417 (1920).
[10] 263 U. S. 403.
[11] U. S. v. Window Glass Manufacturers, 287 Fed. 228 (1923).

full time, and that such operation meant overhead losses to the firms and undesirable uncertainties to the men. "It is enough," said the court, "that we see no combination in unreasonable restraint of trade in the arrangement made to meet the short supply of men."[12]

It is obvious that the question of the directness of the restraint and its importance did not seem pertinent to the Supreme Court. "If such an agreement," it said, "can be within the Sherman Act, at least it is not necessarily so. . . . To determine its legality requires a consideration of the particular facts."[13] The facts considered were those which bore directly on the conditions of the industry and the benefits to be derived from the agreement. The conclusion that the restraint was not unreasonable was clearly based upon the belief that the agreement was justifiable and not socially harmful.[14]

It may be asserted that the Supreme Court, in rendering its decisions in the Window Glass and Maple Flooring cases, was concerned with considerations of economic and social consequence only to the extent that such considerations bore on the questions of substantiality and directness of restraint. This may possibly be true. It is a fact, however, that in each of these decisions the court paid considerable attention to the social and economic advantages of the arrangements before it. No such attention was required to determine whether the restraints were direct or substantial. These decisions,

[12] 263 U. S. 403, 413.

[13] 263 U. S. 403, 411.

[14] The minority opinion of Justice Brandeis in the Bedford Stone case, 47 Sup. Ct. Rep. 522, 528 (1927), is in many respects an excellent application of the rule of reason to a labor activity. See above, Chapter IX, pp. 175-178. It should be compared with his decision for the court in Board of Trade v. U. S., 242 U. S. 231 (1918).

therefore, appear to bear out the conclusion that the court, in rendering them, was applying the rule of reason in an advanced form.

If the rule of reason in this form is worth applying at all it is worth applying in every case under the act, whether a trade union or a business combination is involved. What its complete application to proceedings against labor would involve remains to be considered.

The Rule and the Doctrine of Intent.—The importance which the courts assign to the element of intent in cases of restraint of trade has been demonstrated. The application of the rule of reason in its highest form demands that this entire notion of intent be abandoned in deciding cases under the Sherman Act. In saying this there is no wish to question the desirability of considering intent in many fields of the law. Undoubtedly the law, in its progress from its early stages, has increasingly emphasized it as essential to the existence of various crimes and torts. But regardless of its usefulness, or indeed of its necessary presence in certain fields of law, sound policy, as we shall endeavor to show, demands its abandonment in cases under the Sherman Act.

It is not inconsistent to favor the abandonment of intent in some kinds of cases and not in others. There is, for example, an essential difference between the offense of conspiring to restrain interstate commerce and an offense like conspiring to murder. In the case of the latter there can be no quarrel between men of judgment as to the evil and anti-social nature of the act. Proof of murder, once demonstrated, would lead, without argument among judges, to the condemnation of the offenders. The presence of an intent to murder, even though unaccompanied by the commission of the act, is evil in itself because of the enormity of the crime contemplated. If no actual murder has taken place, but the intent to bring it about exists, the courts seem fully justified in imposing some punishment, for they might reasonably conclude that only chance or the lack of suitable circumstances has prevented the commission of the crime.

In all cases under the Sherman Act, and in cases involving the activities of trade unions not arising under the act, the situation is entirely different. The acts which are to be judged are not such as are universally held to be evil and anti-social. It would be impossible to find even an approach to unanimity of opinion as to whether strikes, boycotts and unionizing campaigns, or price agreements, traffic associations and the combination of business competitors, are under all circumstances to be considered evils deserving of punishment as crimes. Under certain conditions many courts might hold these activities to be unlawful, but they would hardly consider them despicable crimes. The notion of intent, however, has frequently been the sole factor leading a court to consider such activities unlawful under the Sherman Act. Strikes or boycotts affecting interstate commerce have been held quite legal under the Sherman Law because the court has believed that there was no intent to restrain interstate commerce; and, as we have seen, where one court will find intent another will not.

Decisions under the Anti-trust Act have, as in crimes under the common law, frequently distinguished between "intent" or "purpose" on the one hand, and "motive" on the other. "Intent" has been used in the sense of "immediate aim," "motive" in the sense of "ultimate aim." A few examples will illustrate the distinction.

In Boyle v. United States,[15] the court said, "The reasons which actuated the parties to thus conspire and combine

[15] 259 Fed. 803, 807 (1919).

may have been and doubtless are quite different. . . . But it was not the motive, but the common and concerted action of the parties for the unlawful purpose of restraining interstate commerce for which plaintiffs in error were indicted and convicted."

In the first Coronado decision[16] the Supreme Court pointed out that the organization of non-union mines was attempted not only as a direct means of bettering wages and conditions, but also as a means of lessening interstate competition from non-union operators, in order thus to lessen the pressure from the union employers for a reduction of wages or their resistance to a wage increase. No intent to restrain interstate commerce in coal was discovered. In the second Coronado decision[17] the Supreme Court found that the union leaders had considered it necessary to fight the company in order to prevent non-union coal from underselling union coal mined in neighboring states. The evidence previously presented had indicated that the strike was local in origin and motive. The new evidence proved the existence of an intent to restrain interstate commerce.

In the Bedford Stone decision[18] the Supreme Court declared that the primary aim of the union was to restrain interstate sale and shipment of stone, although it was willing to concede that the "ultimate end in view" was "to unionize the cutters and carvers of stone at the quarries."

The District Court, in the case of United States v. Journeyman Stone Cutters' Association,[19] declared, "The Supreme Court cases say the motive is immaterial, and all that is required . . . to be shown is intent to restrain inter-

[16] 259 U. S. 344, 408-411 (1922).
[17] 268 U. S. 295, 305-308 (1925).
[18] 47 Sup. Ct. Rep. 522, 524-525 (1927).
[19] 9 *Law and Labor* 263, October, 1927.

state commerce. . . ." "It may be said, and it is likely true, that economically and morally those motives . . . were all right." But "the unlawful conspiracy or unlawful restraint depends only upon an intent to interfere with the flow of interstate commerce. . . . So, the motive, good or bad, does not make it any the less the duty of the court to sustain the government's case."

Though the distinction between intent and motive is not often clearly enunciated by the courts in cases under the Sherman Act, it is commonly assumed to exist. The courts do not deny that the ultimate aim of the labor defendants may be to benefit their own conditions, but they are not interested in this matter. What they are concerned with is the question whether or not an intent to restrain interstate commerce exists.

This distinction between ultimate motive and immediate intent and the emphasis upon the latter are believed to be neither sound nor productive of reasonable decisions. By attempting to find an intent to restrain interstate commerce the court is usually assigning to the defendants an aim of which they are not conscious. This is especially true when the court, failing to find direct evidence of such an intent, infers that it exists from the fact that interstate commerce is directly and materially restrained. Practically every labor activity, be it strike, boycott, or trade agreement, has for its fundamental aim the improvement of wages or conditions. Whatever methods are used have this as their end. These methods, even when they involve a restraint of interstate commerce, are not aims or ends in themselves. They are means to ends. It is not psychologically sound to assume that every time a person uses a particular means for the purpose of accomplishing an ultimate aim he consciously intends to bring about results other than those which are the object of all his acts.

Even if one grants, for example, that a secondary boycott, such as that in the Danbury Hatters' case, restrains interstate commerce unreasonably, nothing is to be gained by considering intent. The boycott was begun in order to benefit the union workers. It was not begun in order to restrain interstate commerce. Interstate commerce might be held to have been unjustifiably restrained. But such a restraint was not the object of the combination. At worst it was a means of accomplishing the object. To speak of it as being intended is to assign to the boycotters an aim which they did not possess. If the actual restraint was unreasonable and unjustifiable the boycott might properly be considered unlawful, but surely no mere intent to restrain trade could have made it so, since no such intent in the real sense of the word existed.

Every time a court looks for intent to restrain interstate commerce it takes unto itself a function which it is not trained to perform well. It attempts to conduct a research into the minds of men. Many years of inquiry by skilled psychologists and scientists, well-trained individuals whose lives have been spent in their single field of study, have so far failed to produce an accurate technique capable of determining men's thoughts and purposes. Not even the psychoanalysts would assert that they have discovered a method so complete and unfailing as to be adequate for that purpose. The courts, however, have not hesitated to assign intent from secondary evidence, or to infer its existence only from the appearance of results. They have classified aims and purposes, distinguished between intent and motive, sought to discover the former, and on the basis of such a procedure they have declared acts lawful or unlawful.

If they had arrived at results which could be commonly accepted and were uniform one might hesitate to criticize them, for it is entirely conceivable that judges, trained to deal with human beings, might contribute something valuable to the controversial and unsettled principles of psychology. But the judicial technique of discovering intent under the Sherman Law has been very clearly marked by inadequacy and inaccuracy. If the technique is both adequate and accurate how can we explain the failure of one court to discover the very intent which another court, on the basis of the same evidence, has vigorously declared to exist? If such disagreements were rare they might not be regarded as throwing any discredit upon the technique itself. But, as has been amply shown, they are common and to be expected. The only reasonable conclusion is that the courts do not have the means of locating and analyzing intent accurately.

It is only as a thought or an aim is translated into action of some kind that society is affected. Intent is a purely subjective thing, hidden, often impossible to find and describe. Effects are objective and measurable. The search for intent carries the courts into a field of obscure, generally unascertainable data. Guessing at the facts, and easily controverted assertions are the outcome. Judgments based upon such a search have no necessarily close relationship to the social consequences of the acts of which the defendants are accused. On the other hand, the analysis and weighing of effects would carry the courts into a field where, though some uncertainty doubtless exists, knowledge can be obtained and the results of acts measured. Judgments based upon such a technique would bear a direct relationship to the social consequences of what had been done by the defendants. Uncertainties would be reduced and legal procedure would have a closer relation to economic and social realities.

The first requirement, therefore, if the rule of reason is to be satisfactorily applied in cases under the Sherman Act, is the abandonment of judicial considerations of intent. This applies equally to all the cases, whoever may be the defendants, whether labor unions or business combinations.[20]

The Rule of Reason, Social Bias, and Uncertainty.— Assuming that reasonable procedure means the abandonment of the search for intent, what remains to be done by the courts in applying the rule of reason in its highest form? The answer to this question has already been outlined. Where the restraint upon interstate commerce exists it should be ignored if it is insignificant and of no importance. If the restraint is direct, material, and substantial, the courts should then consider whether the consequences of the restraint are socially harmful. They should ask the following questions: If the activity complained of is permitted to continue would it produce consequences harmful to society? If it were prohibited or punished would society be deprived of any beneficial consequences? Which are more to be desired: the benefits resulting from permitting the activity, or the benefits resulting from prohibiting it?

Such questions cannot be satisfactorily answered unless the courts are fully acquainted with general social and economic conditions, and with the special circumstances leading to the activity in question. They cannot be answered *in vacuo*. They require a study of effects and an understanding of causes.

[20] For an excellent brief criticism of intent as used in the labor cases under the act see Terborgh, "The Application of the Sherman Law to Trade-Union Activities," *Journal of Political Economy*, Vol. XXXVII, No. 2, April, 1929, pp. 203, 222-224.

It may be asserted that uncertainty would still exist, that considerations of social desirability would lead to decisions based on the social philosophy of the courts, and that what a liberal judge would consider lawful a conservative judge would consider unlawful. All this would be true, but it is not enough to counterbalance the advantages of the procedure suggested. Under the system of interpreting the Antitrust Law used in the past the social philosophy of the courts has also frequently been a determining factor. A liberal judge might see no intent to restrain trade while a conservative one might assert its existence. The former might consider the effect upon commerce of no consequence, while the latter might regard it as direct and material. It is not suggested that social philosophy has entered into every case. It is probably not clearly evident in most of them; but it exists nevertheless, and several important Supreme Court decisions under the statute (for example those in the Duplex and Bedford Stone cases) appear to have been strongly influenced by it.

The proposed technique would have the great advantage of bringing the factor of social philosophy out into the open. It would not be hidden behind profitless discussion as to intent and the directness of the restraint.

The facts as to the social effects of an act are capable of being studied and discovered. They are of an objective character. Political science, sociology, and economics can contribute the technique necessary to discover them. Thus, if decisions based upon the consideration of social consequences are susceptible to bias, the evidence is available whereby every man can reach conclusions upon the basis of data open to all. If labor or capital thinks the courts unfair the remedy lies in the education of judges, lawyers, and public along the lines of a just policy.

The rule of reason as advocated cannot eliminate uncertainty, but it would place the problem upon a more acceptable basis. Under the old technique disagreement occurs over one matter, intent, concerning which no adequately objective knowledge is possible, and over another, directness and substantiality of restraint, concerning which some objective knowledge can be obtained. By adding the element of social consequence and omitting that of intent, a factor concerning which knowledge can be acquired is substituted for one of which this is not true. Disagreements would be concerned with a sum of facts much more susceptible of objective determination. Uncertainty due to the possibility of such disagreement would be preferable to the old uncertainty.

The Rule of Reason and Judicial Legislation.—The objection may be raised to the rule of reason here advocated that the courts, if they were to determine which restraints were socially harmful and which beneficial, would be guilty of a pernicious form of judicial legislation. Would they not, in applying such a technique, be performing a function which properly belongs to the legislature? As an expression of general principle such an objection might appear to be valid. The principle, however, cannot be and has not been applied in the case of the Sherman Act. As soon as the Supreme Court, in rendering the Hopkins and Anderson decisions in 1898, decided that not "every" combination in restraint of trade could be considered illegal, despite the declaration of the act, it was placed in the position of having to decide which restraints were legal and which illegal. It was thereupon compelled to enter upon a career of what might be called judicial legislation. As long as the Anti-trust Act was on the statute books there was no other course open to it, unless, indeed, it was to decide against all conceivable restraints of interstate commerce.

The court had before it, when it chose to disregard the word "every" in the first section of the act, a statute which was extremely ambiguous. Wrestling with this ambiguity the court, in order to give the statute a more precise meaning, developed the criteria of directness and substantiality of restraint. Still not content with the situation it expanded these criteria into another, the rule of reason, under which the socially and economically harmful aspect of the restraint was taken into consideration to some extent. In the Window Glass and the Maple Flooring cases the court placed great emphasis upon the social and economic consequences of the restraints before it, and comparatively little emphasis upon the question of directness and substantiality.

In view of this development the application by the courts of an advanced rule of reason, under which only those restraints which were both socially harmful and substantial would be considered unlawful, would not be likely to result in what should properly be called "pernicious judicial legislation." Judicial legislation in regard to the Sherman Act, as has been seen, commenced many years ago. It has continued to date. An advanced rule of reason, consciously applied to all labor and capital cases, would result in diminishing rather than in increasing whatever perniciousness may at present be thought to exist in the determination of cases under the Sherman Act.

The Supreme Court, had it given the act a literal interpretation and held illegal "every" combination in restraint of interstate commerce, would, by such a policy, have demonstrated at the beginning the unsatisfactory character of the measure as Congress passed it. Congress might then have been compelled to amend the law in order to make clear its real intention and to make the act definite enough to render judicial legislation unnecessary. Had such a policy been followed there is reason to believe that the resulting situation would have been more satisfactory to all parties. The court, however, appears to have decided that Congress could not have meant what it said, and it entered its long career of judicial legislation in connection with the act. It is hardly likely that it will at this late date turn its back upon the policy of many years and begin to interpret it literally. Until Congress, therefore, decides to enact a basic remedy for the situation there is much to be gained if the courts will proceed according to a developed rule of reason.

CHAPTER XIII

THE RULE OF REASON APPLIED TO LABOR
ACTIVITIES

Collective Bargaining.—In most of the labor cases under the Sherman Act the activities complained of have had for their purpose the securing of collective bargaining, the prevention of its destruction, or the fulfillment of the aims for which it was established. It is obvious, therefore, that the fundamental social facts which the courts must be aware of if they are to apply the advanced rule of reason in labor cases have to do with the causes for the establishment of trade unions and with the economic and social need for collective bargaining. If a judge is not aware of these facts he is likely to believe trade unions public nuisances and collective bargaining unnecessary. If he has such beliefs his decisions can have no relation to the realities of modern life.

It is worth while to summarize briefly the reasons why trade unionism, which is generally considered essential for successful and effective collective bargaining, is supported by economists.

In the first place, it is recognized that the individual worker applying for a job is not able to secure for himself the advantageous terms which a union can secure for him. The employer is his superior in bargaining skill and knowledge of competitive conditions, and he is able to wait until a worker willing to accept his terms appears. The worker, on the other hand, has not the means to support himself if he waits too long. Trade unionism operates to equalize the bargaining power of employer and workers. Union leaders bargaining for the workers possess skill and knowledge. The realization by the employer that an insistence on unreasonable terms may bring on a strike induces him to yield to reasonable demands. In short, trade unionism generally makes possible wages and working conditions more favorable than those which the individual workers can secure for themselves. Since the wages and conditions in American industry are by no means always satisfactory, any reasonable method whereby they can be improved deserves support. On that ground alone trade unionism is to be considered socially desirable.[1]

This general argument for trade unions has been stated as follows by the late Chief Justice Taft, in American Steel Foundries v. Tri-City Central Trades Council:[2]

Labor unions are recognized by the Clayton Act as legal when instituted for mutual help and lawfully carrying out their legitimate objects. They have long been thus recognized by the courts.

[1] In recent years some employers have established shop committee plans, which have often been thought to provide a form of collective bargaining that makes trade unionism unnecessary. Many students of these plans, although they consider them generally superior to individual bargaining, nevertheless believe that their dependence upon employers, the narrow and often unimportant range of subjects over which they have control, and the fact that they have no economic support coming from beyond the individual establishment, render them inferior to the trade unions from the workers' viewpoint. See for example, Selekman, *Employee Representation in Steel Works*, New York, 1924; Lauck, *Political and Industrial Democracy*, New York, 1926; Myers, *Representative Government in Industry*, New York, 1924, Chapters 4 and 12; Fitch, *Causes of Industrial Unrest*, New York, 1924, pp. 146-151; Blum, *Labor Economics*, New York, 1925, pp. 329-337.

[2] 257 U. S. 184, 209 (1921).

They were organized out of the necessities of the situation. A single employee was helpless in dealing with an employer. He was dependent ordinarily on his daily wage for the maintenance of himself and family. If the employer refused to pay him the wages that he thought fair, he was nevertheless unable to leave the employ and to resist arbitrary and unfair treatment. Union was essential to give laborers opportunity to deal on an equality with their employer. They united to exert influence upon him and to leave in a body in order by this inconvenience to induce him to make better terms with them.

If the application of the rule of reason in labor cases appears to demand approval of trade unionism and collective bargaining, what does it mean when applied to the important trade union activities which have often been considered unlawful under the Sherman Act?

Ordinary Strikes.—Various local strikes for better wages and conditions or for the recognition of the union have been held by the lower courts to violate the Anti-trust Act. In the Herkert case the Supreme Court held one such strike legal.[3] In the second Coronado decision, however, it held that a local mine strike was illegal because it had for one of its purposes the prevention of the competition of non-union coal with union coal in interstate commerce.[4]

Ordinary strikes should not be considered illegal under the Sherman Act. Most cases involving them should be dismissed at once on the ground that their effect upon interstate commerce is not important. Even when they result in a substantial restraint of commerce because they prevent the shipment of large quantities of goods, they should not be regarded as unlawful. The strike is the most important and

[3] United Leatherworkers v. Herkert and Meisel, 265 U. S. 457 (1924).

[4] Coronado v. U. M. W., 268 U. S. 295 (1925).

most effective weapon of a trade union. Without the possibility of its use as a weapon in reserve, effective collective bargaining is not possible. If collective bargaining is socially desirable the ordinary strike, the most important means of securing its existence, must be permitted. Its effect upon interstate commerce is no more harmful than the shutting down of an industrial plant by an employer. No court has ever considered such an act a restraint of interstate commerce.

Organization Campaigns.—The United Mine Workers have frequently been brought into the federal courts charged with a conspiracy in restraint of interstate commerce because of their attempt to organize the non-union coal producing areas, especially that of West Virginia. The courts have held that such attempts violated the Sherman Act and have issued injunctions on the assumption that such a violation gave them jurisdiction.[5]

Organizing campaigns over wide areas would usually have a sufficient effect upon interstate commerce to make it necessary for the courts to decide whether or not they were socially harmful. If collective bargaining is desirable it is difficult to see how an attempt to extend it throughout an industry can be considered undesirable. In an industry in which the competitive area is local, as in building, the extension of collective bargaining to all areas, though of advantage to the workers in any particular locality, is not an urgent necessity to the workers already organized. When, however, an industry is of such a nature that the competitive area is national, when, in other words, Illinois coal competes with that of Kentucky, or shoes made in Massachusetts with those produced in St. Louis, it is of great importance to the

[5] U. M. W. v. Red Jacket, 18 F (2) 839 (1927); a writ of certiorari was refused by the Supreme Court, 72 L. ed. 112 (1927).

organized workers that the unorganized areas be unionized. Otherwise they are continually faced with the danger that their employers, unable to compete with firms paying the low non-union rates, may be compelled to end trade agreements and may refuse to continue collective bargaining.

The members of the Amalgamated Clothing Workers of America, the national union in the men's clothing industry, produce a commodity the market for which is nation-wide. Their union has accordingly felt the constant need of organizing the non-union areas, not only in order that the clothing workers in those areas might be benefited, but in order to protect the standards of the workers in the organized sections. After a long and careful preparation the union initiated a series of strikes in the non-union clothing shops of Philadelphia in the summer of 1929. On September 4, 1929, a number of concerns brought suit in the federal District Court in Philadelphia for restraining orders against the national unions and its officers. On September 9 Judge Kirkpatrick granted the decrees asked for, one of which was based on an alleged violation of the Sherman Act. The union was enjoined from all attempts to bring about or to carry on strikes in the plants of the complainants. On October 8 Judge Kirkpatrick rendered a decision stating his reasons for issuing the decrees. He called attention to the official statements of the union, which declared that it was necessary to organize the non-union Philadelphia area in order to protect the organized workers in New York. He pointed out that the decrees were intended to prohibit among other things the bringing about of "strikes by peaceful persuasion." The opinion ended with the following statement:

I conclude that the procuring of strikes by the defendants in the complainants' factories under the circumstances of this case and with the intention here manifest constituted violations of the Sherman Act, and as such may be restrained.[6]

This case presents admirably the problems discussed in the present section. By the end of September, 1929, the campaign of the union had resulted in the organization of the Philadelphia market. Even some of the firms which had sought the injunctions had by that time agreed to deal with the union. By March, 1930, all of the complainants except the Alco-Zander Company had signed agreements with the organization.[7] The use of the Sherman Act in this instance did not, therefore, result in any great damage to the organizing campaign. Regardless of that fact, however, it was intended by the court to have such an effect, and, if it had been issued earlier, might have done so.

The courts should recognize that it is impossible to conduct an organization campaign in a wide area without materially affecting interstate commerce. It is impossible to build up a strong national union which collective bargaining in such an industry as coal requires without securing nation-wide recognition of the union. The courts admit unions to be lawful and they have often regarded them as necessary for the welfare of the workers. It is not, therefore, reasonable to interpret the Sherman Law in such a way as to prevent them from securing that nation-wide recognition which is often essential if they are to protect adequately the workers' interests.

Railway Strikes.—It is clear that every railway strike of importance, whether confined to a single system or affect-

[6] Alco-Zander Co. et al. v. Amalgamated Clothing Workers et al., 35 F (2) 203 (1929); *Daily News Record*, New York, October 9, 1929; *Congressional Record*, Vol. 71, p. 3784, September 16, 1929.

[7] *Advance*, Vol. XVI, No. 11, March 14, 1930.

ing the entire country, would bring about a direct and substantial restraint of interstate commerce. Are such strikes, when they are carried on to aid the strikers themselves, so harmful that the courts should consider them illegal under the Sherman Act?

There would be some disagreement among economists as to the answer. Many of them would be opposed to the view that railway strikes should be considered unlawful. Many proposals have been made to the effect that strikes of railway workers should be prohibited, and that all railway labor disputes should be submitted to compulsory arbitration. Despite the widespread publicity given to such proposals Congress has refused to enact them.[8] It is perhaps fair to assume that this refusal to prohibit railway strikes indicates a belief on the part of most citizens that such a procedure would be socially undesirable. The courts, however, have, by means of the Anti-trust Act, accomplished by indirection what Congress has refused to do directly.

The belief that such a use of the statute has not been desirable is strengthened by the consideration that railway workers, after unsuccessfully trying amicable methods of securing what they consider their just demands, may find a strike to be the only way open. Until some other method of securing an approach to fair treatment is developed it does not seem just to deprive them of this weapon as a last resort. Their quitting of work may seem to be productive of great social hardship, yet the responsibility for it may rest upon the refusal of the railway companies to adopt reasonable labor policies. The Sherman Act has never been used

[8] The state of Kansas, in 1920, enacted a law which had for one of its purposes compulsory arbitration and the prohibition of strikes in the transportation industry. By 1927 the law had been practically discarded.

to punish railway employers when the responsibility for causing a strike may be properly assigned to them.

In any event the establishment of satisfactory machinery for settling railway labor disputes, which now appears to have been secured, may bring with it the desired absence of railway strikes. Those, however, who believe that such strikes should be made illegal, should attempt to secure legislation directly accomplishing this result, instead of depending upon the Sherman Act.

Sympathetic Strikes and the Refusal to Work on Non-Union Materials.—The courts have often considered these activities illegal when they have affected interstate commerce. In some instances a proper consideration of the facts would have shown the actual restraint upon interstate commerce to be so slight as to be of trifling importance. In others, however, the effect on sales was sufficient to have warranted raising the question of social justifiability.

Before passing judgment upon such activities it would be desirable to consider whether the workers involved have a sufficiently close interest in the dispute to justify them in carrying it on. If the interest of a particular group of workers is closely connected with the favorable settlement of a dispute, their activities, though they involve incidental injury to others, might properly be considered permissible. If, on the other hand, their interest in such a favorable settlement is remote, if they would stand to gain little or nothing thereby, the injury to others attendant upon their engaging in the dispute would not be merely incidental, and a court might properly hinder them from carrying on the quarrel. The application of this criterion of proximity of interest will be clear if it is considered in connection with certain labor cases decided under the Sherman Act.

In the great railway strike of 1894 the members of the

American Railway Union, by refusing to work on trains hauling Pullman cars, brought about a great and destructive strike. They engaged in a sympathetic strike. Their refusal to work was not directed toward the settlement of their own grievances. They were interested in helping the employees in the Pullman shops to win a dispute, and they chose a railway strike (or boycott of Pullman cars) to accomplish their purpose. The winning of the dispute at the car shops was not of such direct and outstanding importance to the railway workers as to have justified the great social harm for which their strike was so largely responsible. The identity of interest which bound them to the Pullman workers was limited to the fact that they belonged to the same union and that the work of both groups was related to the transportation industry. If such a sympathetic railway strike should again occur it seems clear that the application of a developed rule of reason would properly result in the use of the Sherman Act against it.

The railway strike of 1894 is not the only instance of a sympathetic strike which has come to the attention of the courts in cases brought under the Sherman Act. The numerous refusals of unionists to work on non-union materials may also be regarded as sympathetic strikes. Unionists may refuse to work on such materials because they are not made by the members of their own organization. Their purpose is obviously to aid their fellow members in winning a dispute. Is their legitimate interest in the settlement of the dispute so great as to justify them in taking part in it, even at the cost of injuring their own employer, against whom they have no original grievance? The workers engaged in the dispute at its origin and the workers who strike in sympathy with them (i. e., refuse to work on non-union materials while the dispute continues) are members of the same union. Does this give the two groups a sufficient community of interest to justify a sympathetic strike on the part of the second group?

The answer to this question depends upon the nature of the work done by the two groups, and upon the economic and social conditions affecting the situation. It has been indicated that common membership of train service workers and of car-manufacturing workers in the American Railway Union was not thought sufficient to justify the former in bringing about a great railway strike in order to aid the latter. In other circumstances, however, common membership in a union might be considered adequate justification.

The amount of injury caused by the railway strike of 1894 was much greater than that involved in a case coming into the courts in which sheet metal workers refused to install furnaces not made by unionists.[9] There is a difference between the possible danger which may threaten organized railway conductors and engineers because of the competition of unorganized car manufacturing workers, and that which may threaten organized sheet metal workers installing furnaces because of the competition of unorganized sheet metal workers manufacturing them. The Pullman Company's employees were engaged in work which had no closer relationship to that done by railway conductors or firemen than the fact that both kinds of work had to do with the transportation industry. On the other hand, sheet metal workers in the building industry were doing work

[9] Columbus Heating and Ventilating Co. v. Pittsburgh Building Trades Council et al., 17 F (2) 806 (1927). See Appendix C, Case 79. Only that phase of this case which involves the sympathetic strike of the sheet metal workers is here considered. It is assumed for the moment that a substantial restraint of trade resulted.

very similar, as regards the nature of the training and skill required, to that done by sheet metal workers in the furnace industry. The interest which the sheet metal workers in the former industry had in the strength of those in the latter was direct. If either group were left unorganized the other group would be weakened, since it would be in constant danger of being underbid by unorganized workers seeking and capable of filling jobs in its own industry. Hence the efforts of the national union to organize both groups. Hence also the readiness of one group to protect the wages and the bargaining power of the others. In view of the foregoing considerations one is led to the conclusion that the refusal of a skilled group to work upon materials made by non-union workers who possess the same type of skill is a justifiable attempt to protect their own interests and those of their fellow members.

Similar considerations are applicable to the situation presented to the courts in the Bedford Stone case.[10] The Supreme Court declared that the refusal of members of the Journeyman Stone Cutters' Union employed in the building industry to work on stone produced at Bedford, Ind., by non-union stone cutters was an unlawful conspiracy in violation of the Sherman Act. The dissenting opinion of Justice Brandeis in that case is believed to be in many respects an admirable application of the rule of reason.[11] This belief is borne out by considering the factor of proximity of interest in connection with the issue in the case.

The members of the national union were skilled stone cutters, whose skill was the result of a long period of training. The work of cutting stone at the Bedford quarries,

[10] Bedford Stone v. Journeyman Stone Cutters, 47 Sup. Ct. Rep. 522 (1927).
[11] See above, pp. 175-178.

though not identical with, was nevertheless similar to and required the same type of skill as the work of trimming the stone at the places where buildings were being erected. The stone cutters at the quarries and those in the building industry, working at the same materials, possessing very similar skills, and to a certain extent working with the same tools, possessed such a high degree of community of interest that they were united in the same national union. The strength of that national union of only 5,000 stone cutters was a matter of first importance to both groups. One indication of this is the fact that the dues which the stone cutters on buildings paid to the union were used to pay strike benefits to the quarry workers. Its loss of control over the workers in either industry would inevitably result in a large reduction in membership, a diminishing treasury, the danger of competition from unorganized stone cutters, and the consequent loss of bargaining power for the group still organized.

When the stone companies entered upon a policy of refusing to deal with the union the economic status of all the organized stone cutters in the country was threatened. Since their own strength as unionists depended upon the strength of the national union, they all had a direct interest in defeating the policy of the companies, regardless of whether they were quarry workers or building workers. When the strike at the quarries was lost the companies brought in complete new forces of non-union men. It is very probable that the displaced unionists tried to find jobs in the building industry in more or less direct competition with their own fellow members. Under the circumstances the only weapon of importance open to the national union was to invoke the aid of the members working on buildings and to advise them to refuse to install Bedford stone. This, it is true, resulted in a sympathetic strike, but it was a sympathetic strike justified not only by the importance of collective bargaining at the quarries, for the maintenance of which it was instituted, but also by the high degree of importance which the maintenance of such collective bargaining had for the building workers themselves.

If collective bargaining is reasonable, an act like this of the stone cutters should not have been considered unreasonable. It may be objected that even though one grants the desirability of collective bargaining one is justified in refusing to approve all methods of securing it. In the present instance, it may be said, the union policy brought unjustifiable hardship to the stone companies and perhaps to the building contractors. The answer to this objection is that the employers' refusal to employ union stone cutters had the effect of weakening the union and injuring the status of its members. If the employers were justified in refusing to deal with union men the latter were justified in refusing to work on stone produced against their own interests. If such a refusal was a justifiable means of protecting the workers' interests, the Sherman Act should not have been used to prohibit it. Even if one assumes that the contractors were injured by the refusal of the stone cutters to install non-union stone, it still seems reasonable to conclude that collective bargaining was sufficiently important socially to justify the imposition of such an incidental injury.

If the refusal of union men to work on materials not made by their fellow unionists, resulting from the enforcement of a rule of the union, as in the case of the sheet metal workers and the stone cutters, is justifiable, so also is a trade agreement which embodies a similar rule, such as that between union carpenters, millwork manufacturers, and building contractors, which the Supreme Court declared unlawful in the Brims case.[12] The provision contained in the agreement to the effect that carpenters in the building industry would install only union-made millwork was one in which the carpenters had the greatest interest. It was directly intended to aid their fellow unionists in the millwork industry. Since the carpenters in both industries had the same kind of skill and were potential competitors the maintenance of collective bargaining and of good wages in each group was of the first importance to both. The community of interest involved was substantial enough to justify the agreement in question, despite the fact that by means of it manufacturers of non-union millwork were injured. In the last analysis the justifiability of collective bargaining for carpenters in both building and millwork industries determined the justifiability of the agreement.

The question of proximity of interest has a close relation to the issues presented to the Supreme Court in the Duplex case.[13] For the purposes of analysis the boycott activities in the fight of the machinists' union against the Duplex Company may be divided into two groups: (1) those activities carried on by the members of the union, and (2) those carried on by members of other unions in aid of the machinists.

As part of the boycott members of the machinists' union in New York were persuaded not to repair or to install Duplex presses manufactured by non-union machinists in the company's plant in Michigan. It is important to point out that unless the machinists' union was successful in organizing the Duplex Company's employees, it was in danger of losing control of the machinists employed by the concerns competing with the company. Those concerns had threatened that they would refuse to deal with the union unless the

[12] U. S. v. Brims, 272 U. S. 549 (1926).
[13] Duplex v. Deering, 254 U. S. 443 (1921).

Duplex Company's employees were organized. Facing the possibility of a loss in membership and the destruction of collective bargaining in the press manufacturing industry the union called a strike of the Duplex Company's machinists, a strike so unsuccessful that only eleven men left the plant. Having failed in this direct attempt the national union had before it the possibility that it could induce the firm to deal with it with the aid of the union machinists employed in repairing and installing the presses. Was it justified in seeking their help? Did the machinists in New York have a sufficiently close interest in the organization of the Duplex machinists to justify them in taking part in the boycott?

The case is not entirely analogous to the stone cutters', sheet metal workers' and carpenters' cases. The members of the machinists' union are not all engaged in similar work, at similar machines, using the same tools. Neither are they all possessed of the same high degree of skill. The general nature of their work is to a considerable extent the same, but this is not true to such a degree as in the case of the other crafts. It is nevertheless a fact, however, that a skilled machinist is capable of doing the large variety of tasks at which machinists are usually employed. Machinists are as a class potential competitors with each other. They therefore have a direct interest in each other's wages and working conditions, and in enhancing the bargaining power of the group as a whole.

It is worth observing that the National Association of Machinists is not among the strongest of American unions. It does not have control over such a large number of machinists that it can demand collective bargaining for them and secure it with ease. It is a relatively weak union in an industry in which the employers are themselves powerful and well organized. (The National Metal Trades Association is an example.) Is not such a union justified in securing the cooperation of all its members when it engages in a struggle for organization? And do not all of its members have a direct interest in increasing the strength of the national union upon which they depend? These questions, it is believed, deserve an affirmative answer. The conclusion indicated is that the Duplex boycott, to the extent that it resulted in sympathetic strikes of the machinists themselves, should have been considered reasonable by the courts.

The boycott was not confined, however, to the refusal of machinists to install and repair the presses. The machinists' union secured the cooperation of truckmen, who refused to haul the presses, and it threatened to bring about sympathetic strikes of other workers if the employers of these workers purchased or exhibited Duplex presses. It is obvious that these boycott activities were not in the same class as those confined to the machinists themselves. The New York machinists possessed a high degree of interest in the organization of the Duplex employees. The union truck drivers and the employees of an exposition company obviously did not have such a significant interest at stake. They did not belong to the national union of the machinists. They were not employed in the same industry. They did not use the same tools, or possess similar skill. They had a very slight connection indeed with the machinists.

It may be asserted that every union man has a legitimate interest in the success of unionism in general. The assertion is clearly true. The issue is not, however, the mere presence of a general interest. It is the determination of the extent of a community of interest which justifies activities which, however helpful they may be to the union engaged in the original dispute, results in material injuries to others. In this instance the legitimate interest which the truck drivers, for example, had in the machinists' dispute with the Duplex Company was not great enough to counterbalance the injury caused when they entered upon a sympathetic strike against the firm's presses, nor was the machinists' union justified in inducing them to strike. These parts of the boycott might reasonably have been hindered, as they actually were, by the courts.

It is not possible to draw clear-cut conclusions as a result of the foregoing considerations. One can say no more than that the justifiability of sympathetic strikes, the refusal to work on non-union materials, and the more indirect forms of the boycott, activities which are often identical with each other, depend upon such factors as the extent of a common interest among the affected groups, the nature of the benefits to be secured by the activities in question, and the extent of the injury to others which may accompany such activities.

Secondary Boycotts.—In Loewe v. Lawlor[14] the Supreme Court took the position that widespread secondary boycotts were illegal under the Anti-trust Act. The restraint upon interstate commerce imposed in this instance was material and significant. Would the application of an advanced rule of reason by the Supreme Court have resulted in a decision similar to that actually rendered?[15]

One who believes in collective bargaining finds it difficult to understand why secondary boycotts should be considered

[14] 208 U. S. 274 (1908).

[15] It should be noted that despite the view of the Supreme Court that secondary boycotts are unlawful under the common law, they are not always so regarded. Though most state courts so consider them, courts in Arizona, California, Montana, and New York have held them justifiable and lawful. Commons and Andrews, *Principles of Labor Legislation*, New York, 1927, 3rd Edition, p. 117.

unlawful. Fundamentally a secondary boycott resembles a strike. By means of strikes workers seek to bring pressure to bear directly upon their employers in order to secure their demands. In the case of a secondary boycott of commodities, such as that in the Danbury Hatters' case, workers seek to bring pressure to bear upon their employers by persuading their friends and fellows to withhold patronage. The coercion upon employers in both cases is intended to secure, and if successful will secure, similar concessions.

A century ago strikes were regarded as illegal because of their coercive nature. Today they are in nearly all cases regarded as legal if carried on for the purpose of benefiting the strikers. The boycott, which is still regarded as coercive, and is often held to be carried on for the purpose of injuring innocent third parties, is as a matter of fact inherently no more coercive than strikes, and is nearly always carried on for the purpose of benefiting the boycotters. If it is said that unionists, in conducting a boycott, are trying to influence innocent third parties, it may be answered that the press and the mails are also open to the employer, and he has the right to attempt to counteract that influence. If it be said that a secondary boycott brings pressure to bear upon the merchants, disinterested third parties, it may be answered that such pressure may be a justifiable method of securing collective bargaining. The disinterested parties who may be injured by a boycott may also be injured by an ordinary strike, since they may be unable to secure products which they regard as necessary because of it. Such an injury is not regarded as a reason for considering ordinary strikes illegal. A similar injury should not be regarded as rendering boycotts illegal.

The acts of an employer who refuses employment to union men and enters anti-union campaigns, in which, as in the

Industrial Association case,[16] pressure is exerted to induce other employers to sever their relations with the unions, is regarded by the courts as permissible. Why should not the same attitude be adopted by the courts with respect to the acts of trade unionists in urging their fellows and their sympathizers to join them in a campaign against anti-union employers? An employers' campaign against unionists is no more justifiable socially than a union campaign against employers. The labor boycott is a campaign of the latter type.

If collective bargaining is desirable and strikes are reasonable means of securing and defending it, so also are secondary boycotts. The rule of reason requires that they should not be considered illegal under the Sherman Act.

Acts of Violence.—The Sherman Act, as we have seen, has been invoked in numerous instances in which violent acts have taken place. Assaults, the dynamiting of railway tracks, the firing of railway cars, and the disabling of locomotives have been punished under its terms. What does the application of the rule of reason require in these cases?

One may assume that some of the violence and sabotage under discussion resulted in substantial interferences with interstate commerce. Would one therefore be justified in punishing these activities under the Act of 1890? Since the offenders have in these cases engaged in deeds which are unquestionably anti-social no serious objection can be raised to punishing them by some means. It may be asked, however, whether the Anti-trust Law is the proper measure to invoke. Every state has laws which are intended to punish acts of violence and the destruction of property. According to the District Court in United States v. Hency,[17] "The Sher-

[16] Industrial Association v. U. S., 268 U. S. 64 (1925).
[17] 286 Fed. 165, 171 (1923).

man law punishes those who combine in restraint of trade
and not for sabotage." So long as there are adequate means
other than that statute available for the punishment of
violence, it would probably be wiser to refrain from applying
it in such cases.

In discussing the application of the rule of reason to strikes
and boycotts in the preceding sections no mention was made
of the fact that these activities are often accompanied by
violence and intimidation. In cases where such conduct is
common should not the Anti-trust Act be used to prohibit
it? It will be recalled that frequently the courts, though declaring such an activity as a strike an unlawful restraint of
trade, have issued injunctions prohibiting only such practices as violence and intimidation. They have in these cases
used the statute as a means of securing jurisdiction over
labor disputes. If, however, strikers are guilty of violence
and intimidation, or of other illegal acts, state courts and
statutes are available to prevent or punish their conduct. If
diversity of citizenship exists such labor disputes may be
properly brought to the federal courts. It is not justifiable
to invoke the Sherman Law merely to secure jurisdiction
over cases of violence.

The objection will probably be raised that such an application of the rule of reason as that made in the present chapter
would have operated to prevent the Sherman Act from being used against trade unions in most of the labor cases
which have arisen under it in the past. Such a result would
not necessarily be undesirable, however, in view of the fact,
demonstrated in Part I, that Congress never intended that
the Act of 1890 should be applied to labor unions. If the
rule of reason is to reach back to the purpose of the law it

would result in the complete abandonment of its use in labor cases.

In the present chapter an attempt has been made to decide, upon the basis of the social and economic facts, which labor activities are justifiable and which are not. Undoubtedly these conclusions have been affected by a particular social philosophy. Undoubtedly, also, another person with a different social philosophy would reach somewhat different conclusions. It is not likely, for example, that the courts will in the near future apply the rule of reason in such a way as to relieve labor of most of the burden of the statute. Nevertheless the conscious application of a rule based upon considerations of social welfare would in time do much to improve the position of labor under the law.

CHAPTER XIV

LABOR, THE SHERMAN ACT, AND THE FUTURE

We have seen how a law originally intended to prevent the anti-social activities of business combinations has become an important weapon against trade unions.

This development, naturally offensive to unionists, has been gratifying to many employers, especially those represented by the League for Industrial Rights. The League, known prior to 1919 as the American Anti-Boycott Association, was formally organized in 1903. It has actively supported employers in such important proceedings against trade unions as the Danbury Hatters', Bucks' Stove, Duplex, Coronado, and Bedford Stone cases.[1]

In a pamphlet published by the League in 1926 the anti-trust laws are praised as "liberty laws." The fact that the Sherman Act has been successfully used against trade union activities is an important factor in the League's approval of it, as the following statement shows:

Whatever other people may tell you, remember that as the laws now stand labor and labor combinations are not exempt from the Anti-Trust laws, and that these laws are one of the great bulwarks of the open shop and of the right of the independent employer and non-union man to have their products flow freely through the channels of interstate commerce to the

[1] See the League's pamphlet, *History of the League for Industrial Rights*, by Walter Gordon Merritt, New York, 1925.

markets of the nation, where every consumer may exercise his right of commercial suffrage.[2]

The attitude of the trade unions, on the other hand, is shown by the fact that the American Federation of Labor, in 1924, urged the passage of "an act repealing the Sherman Anti-Trust Law, which was intended by Congress to prevent illegal combinations in restraint of trade, commonly known as 'trusts,' but through judicial misinterpretation and perversion has been repeatedly and mainly invoked to deprive the toiling masses of their natural and normal rights."[3] Later conventions of the Federation have heard vigorous criticisms of the statute and a demand for its repeal, often accompanied by the suggestion that an anti-monopoly law be enacted to take its place.[4]

The repeal of the Act of 1890 has been suggested not only

[2] Merritt, *Liberty Laws*, p. 16. The League has, since 1919, published a monthly, *Law and Labor*, which has been a valuable source of information, especially concerning labor cases under the Sherman Act which have not been officially reported.

[3] *Report of the Proceedings of the Forty-Fourth Annual Convention of the American Federation of Labor*, 1924, p. 40.

[4] See, for example, *Report of the Proceedings of the Forty-Seventh Annual Convention of the American Federation of Labor,* 1927, pp. 154, 314-316. As early as 1913, and as late as 1927, labor secured the adoption of riders to the federal appropriation acts providing that none of the funds so appropriated should be used to prosecute labor organizations under the anti-trust laws. These provisions have proved ineffective, probably because they contained a clause to the effect that such funds should not be used to prosecute labor organizations for an act "not in itself unlawful." Thornton, *Combinations in Restraint of Trade,* Cincinnati, 1928, pp. 843, 1435. Since the courts would consider various activities in restraint of trade unlawful under the Sherman Act these riders would naturally have slight consequences.

by labor, but also by various groups of business men who resent its restrictions. Though the adoption of such a proposal would relieve labor it would at the same time leave business monopolies free to carry on activities which might be generally considered harmful. On that account alone labor should hesitate to advocate the repeal of the law, unless it be accompanied by the passage of another measure better suited to protect society against monopolies and anti-social business practices.

A second way out of the present undesirable situation lies in the passage of a measure clearly and unmistakably exempting labor organizations from the operation of the Sherman Act. The enactment of such a statute might, however, require a degree of political power which American labor does not appear to possess. It does not seem likely that it could have been secured from the conservative Congresses which have been in session since the war.

A third possibility, accomplishing the same result as that secured by the passage of an act exempting labor, is the reversal by the courts of the position they have taken in the past. It will be recalled that in the early labor cases they declared that Congress intended that labor unions should be reached by the provisions of the act. Assuming that Part I of this volume demonstrates conclusively that Congress had no such intention, and that the courts accept this demonstration, would they not be justified in changing their position? Such a reversal, considering the fact that there are precedents of thirty-seven years (1893 to date) behind them, and that their attitude toward trade unionism is generally conservative, is not likely to occur.

There remains the possibility that the courts, in enforcing the Sherman Act, will apply the rule of reason in such a way as to permit numerous socially justifiable labor activities which have in the past been considered unlawful. In view of the fact that the rule of reason has already been applied in business cases it would be both just and consistent to apply it to labor activities. The study by the courts of the economic and social facts concerning each case which the use of the rule of reason requires, would in time produce a more progressive judicial attitude. Such a result would be hastened if lawyers for labor emphasized in their briefs the nature of the economic and social conditions giving rise to litigation.

No change which substantially relieves labor from the burdens of the Sherman Act is likely to be secured with ease in the near future. Changing the attitude of the courts would be at least as difficult as securing political power sufficient to obtain the passage of the necessary legislation. The possibility of bringing about the desired change depends in the end upon the extent to which the public, the politicians, and the courts can be educated toward an attitude in line with modern economic conditions. The process of education may be slow, but it is productive of results. It requires a labor movement which is aware of the need for obtaining political power and influence, and which attempts to keep the public fully informed concerning labor conditions. Such a movement need not lose hope of securing the alleviation of a political and economic injustice which every citizen should deplore.

APPENDICES

THE SHERMAN ANTI-TRUST ACT

Act of July 2, 1890 (26 Stat., 209).

An act to protect trade and commerce against unlawful restraints and monopolies.

Be it enacted by the Senate and the House of Representatives of the United States of America in Congress assembled,

SECTION 1. Every contract, combination in the form of trust or otherwise, or conspiracy, in restraint of trade or commerce among the several States, or with foreign nations, is hereby declared to be illegal. Every person who shall make any such contract or engage in any such combination or conspiracy shall be deemed guilty of a misdemeanor, and, on conviction thereof, shall be punished by fine not exceeding five thousand dollars, or by imprisonment not exceeding one year, or by both said punishments, in the discretion of the court.

SECTION 2. Every person who shall monopolize, or attempt to monopolize, or combine or conspire with any other person or persons, to monopolize any part of the trade or commerce among the several States, or with foreign nations, shall be deemed guilty of a misdemeanor, and, on conviction thereof, shall be punished by fine not exceeding five thousand dollars, or by imprisonment not exceeding one year, or by both said punishments, in the discretion of the court.

SECTION 3. Every contract, combination in the form of trust or otherwise, or conspiracy, in restraint of trade or commerce in any Territory of the United States or of the District of Columbia, or in restraint of trade or commerce between any such Territory and another, and between any such Territory or

Territories and any State or States or the District of Columbia, or with foreign nations, or between the District of Columbia and any State or States or foreign nations, is hereby declared illegal. Every person who shall make any such contract or engage in any such combination or conspiracy shall be deemed guilty of a misdemeanor, and, on conviction thereof, shall be punished by fine not exceeding five thousand dollars, or by imprisonment not exceeding one year, or by both said punishments, in the discretion of the court.

SECTION 4. The several circuit courts of the United States are hereby invested with jurisdiction to prevent and restrain violations of this Act; and it shall be the duty of the several district attorneys of the United States, in their respective districts, under the direction of the Attorney General, to institute proceedings in equity to prevent and restrain such violations. Such proceedings may be by way of petition setting forth the case and praying that such violation shall be enjoined or otherwise prohibited. When the parties complained of shall have been duly notified of such petition the court shall proceed, as soon as may be, to the hearing and determination of the case; and pending such petition and before final decree, the court may at any time make such temporary restraining order or prohibition as shall be deemed just in the premises.

SECTION 5. Whenever it shall appear to the court before which any proceeding under section four of this Act may be pending that the ends of justice require that other parties should be brought before the court, the court may cause them to be summoned, whether they reside in the district in which the court is held or not; and subpœnas to that end may be served in any district by the marshal thereof.

SECTION 6. Any property owned under any contract or by any combination, or pursuant to any conspiracy (and being the subject thereof) mentioned in section one of this Act, and being in the course of transportation from one State to another, or to a foreign country, shall be forfeited to the United States, and may be seized and condemned by like proceedings as those provided by law for the forfeiture, seizure, and condemnation of property imported into the United States contrary to law.

SECTION 7. Any person who shall be injured in his business or property by any other person or corporation, by reason of anything forbidden or declared to be unlawful by this Act, may sue therefor in any circuit court of the United States in the district in which the defendant resides or is found, without respect to the amount in controversy, and shall recover threefold the damages by him sustained, and the costs of suit, including a reasonable attorney's fee.

SECTION 8. That the word "person," or "persons," wherever used in this Act, shall be deemed to include corporations and associations existing under or authorized by the laws of either the United States, the laws of any of the Territories, the laws of any State, or the laws of any foreign country.

TABLE I

Table of Cases in which Labor Unions, their Officers, or their Members have been Defendants under the Sherman Anti-trust Act.

NOTE. Where there is no record of a case in the official judicial reports the best other source is cited. B. B. refers to Blue Book, i. e., the volume published November 30, 1928, by the United States Department of Justice under the title, *The Federal Antitrust Laws with Amendments*. The volume contains a list of cases instituted by the federal authorities under the anti-trust laws. The final number after each citation, contained in parentheses, and following the date of the case, refers to the brief description of cases in Appendix C.

Aeolian v. Fischer, 27 F (2) 560 (1928).

   29 F (2) 679 (1928).

   35 F (2) (1929). (83)

Alco-Zander Co. et al. v. Amalgamated Clothing Workers et al., 35 F (2) 203 (1929). (85)

Amalgamated Council v. U. S., 57 Fed. 85 (1893). (1)

Barker v. Painters, 23 F (2) 743 (1927). (82)

Bedford Stone Co. v. Journeyman Stone Cutters, 9 F (2) 40 (1925).

   274 U. S. 37, 47 Sup. Ct. Rep. 522 (1927). (77)

Blindell v. Hagan, 54 Fed. 40 (1893). (45)

Borderland Coal Corporation v. United Mine Workers, 275 Fed. 871 (1921). (69)

Boyle v. U. S., 259 Fed. 803 (1919). (21)

Brims v. U. S., 6 F (2) 98 (1925).
 21 F (2) 889 (1927). (23)
Buyer v. Guillan, 271 Fed. 65 (1921). (55)
Chesapeake and Ohio Railway v. Railway Clerks, 290 Fed. 214
 (1922).
 290 Fed. 906 (1923). (73)
Christian v. Machinists, 7 F (2) 481 (1925). (44)
Clements v. U. S., 297 Fed. 206 (1924). (29)
Columbus Heating Co. v. Building Trades Council, 17 F (2)
 806 (1927). (79)
Coronado Coal v. United Mine Workers, 268 U. S. 295, 45 Sup.
 Ct. Rep. 551 (1925). (42)
Curran v. Allied Printing Council, 5 Law and Labor 91 (1923).
 (75)
Dail-Overland v. Willys-Overland, 263 Fed. 171 (1919). (52)
Danville Brick Workers v. Brick Co., 283 Fed. 909 (1922). (70)
Decorative Stone Co. v. Building Trades Council, 18 F (2) 333
 (1927). (80)
Dowd v. United Mine Workers, 235 Fed. 1 (1916). (42)
Duplex Printing Press Co. v. Deering, 247 Fed. 192 (1917).
 252 Fed. 722 (1918).
 254 U. S. 443, 41 Sup. Ct. Rep. 172 (1921). (50)
Dwyer v. Alpha Pocahontas Co., 282 Fed. 270 (1922). (57-68)
Finley v. United Mine Workers, 300 Fed. 972 (1924). (42)
Gable v. Vonnegut, 274 Fed. 66 (1921). (56)
Gasaway v. Borderland Coal Corp., 278 Fed. 56 (1921). (69)
Great Northern v. Machinists, 283 Fed. 557 (1922). (71)
Great Northern v. Perkins, 4 Law and Labor 253 (1922). (72)
Herkert and Meisel v. United Leatherworkers, 268 Fed. 662
 (1920). (54)
Hitchman Coal & Coke Co. v. Mitchell, 172 Fed. 963 (1909).
 202 Fed. 512 (1912).
 245 U. S. 229, 38 Sup. Ct. Rep. 65 (1917). (47)
In re Charge to Grand Jury, 62 Fed. 828 (1894). (11)
In re Debs, 158 U. S. 564, 15 Sup. Ct. Rep. 900 (1895). (2)

In re National Association of Window Glass Manufacturers, 287 Fed. 219 (1923). (8)

International Brotherhood of Electrical Workers v. Western Union, 6 F (2) 444 (1925). (76)

Irving v. Neal, 209 Fed. 471 (1913). (48)

Jewel Tea Co. v. Teamsters, *Law and Labor,* July, 1919, p. 11. (1919). (53)

Journeyman Stone Cutters v. United States, 73 L. ed. 179, 49 Sup. Ct. Rep. 78 (1928). (9)

Keeney v. Borderland Coal Corp., 282 Fed. 269 (1922). (57-68)

Lawlor v. Loewe, 187 Fed. 522 (1911).

   209 Fed. 721 (1913).

   235 U. S. 522, 35 Sup. Ct. Rep. 170 (1915). (41)

Loewe v. Lawlor, 130 Fed. 63 (1903).

   142 Fed. 216 (1905).

   148 Fed. 924 (1906).

   208 U. S. 274, 28 Sup. Ct. Rep. 301 (1908). (41)

Mitchell v. Hitchman Coal & Coke Co., 214 Fed. 685 (1914). (47)

National Association of Window Glass Manufacturers v. U. S., 263 U. S. 403, 44 Sup. Ct. Rep. 148 (1923). (8)

National Fireproofing Co. v. Mason Builders' Association, 169 Fed. 259 (1909). (46)

O'Brien v. U .S., 290 Fed. 185 (1923). (27)

Paine v. Neal, 212 Fed. 259 (1913).

   214 Fed. 82 (1914).

   244 U. S. 459, 37 Sup. Ct. Rep. 718 (1917). (49)

Pennsylvania Mining Co. v. United Mine Workers, 28 F (2) 851 (1928). (43)

Pittsburgh Terminal Coal Co. v. United Mine Workers, 22 F (2) 559 (1927). (81)

Rockwood Corporation v. Bricklayers' Union, 33 F (2) 25 (1929). (84)

Silverstein v. Journeyman Tailors, 284 Fed. 833 (1922). (74)

Taliaferro v. U. S., 290 Fed. 906 (1923). (73)

Toledo Transfer Co. v. Teamsters, 7 *Law and Labor* 33 (1925). (78)

United Leather Workers v. Herkert and Meisel, 284 Fed. 446 (1922).

265 U. S. 457, 44 Sup. Ct. Rep. 623 (1924). (54)

United Mine Workers v. Carbon Fuel Co., 288 Fed. 1020 (1923). (57-68)

United Mine Workers v. Coronado Coal Co., 258 Fed. 829.

259 U. S. 344, 42 Sup. Ct. Rep. 570 (1922). (42)

United Mine Workers v. Leevale Coal Co., 285 Fed. 32 (1922). (57-68)

United Mine Workers v. Pennsylvania Mining Co., 300 Fed. 965 (1924). (43)

United Mine Workers v. Red Jacket Consolidated Coal Co., 18 F (2) 839 (1927).

72 L. ed. 112, 48 Sup. Ct. Rep. 31 (1927). (57-68)

U. S. v. Agler, 62 Fed. 824 (1894). (3 or 4)

U. S. v. Amalgamated Council, 54 Fed. 994 (1893). (1)

U. S. v. American Window Glass Co., B. B. 173 (1922). (32)

U. S. v. Andrews Lumber and Mill Co., B. B. 160, 165 (1921). (23)

U. S. v. Artery, B. B. 136 (1915). (20)

U. S. v. Biegler, B. B. 165 (1921). (26)

U. S. v. Boyle, B. B. 137 (1915). (21)

U. S. v. Bricklayers, 4 *Law and Labor* 95 (1922). (6)

U. S. v. Brims, 272 U. S. 549, 71 L. ed. 403 (1926). (23)

U. S. v. Cassidy, 67 Fed. 698 (1895). (12)

U. S. v. Clements, B. B. 177 (1922). (29)

U. S. v. Cotton, B. B. 114 (1912). (14)

U. S. v. Debs, 64 Fed. 724 (1894). (2)

U. S. v. Debs, B. B. 87 (1894). (3)

U. S. v. Debs, 63 Fed. 436 (1894). (11)

U. S. v. Dryllic, 6 *Law and Labor* 69 (1924). (36)

U. S. v. Elliott, 62 Fed. 801 (1894).

64 Fed. 27 (1894). (4)

U. S. v. Feeney, B. B. 137 (1915). (22)

U. S. v. Fitzgerald, B. B. 181 (1925). (37)

U. S. v. Haines, B. B. 115 (1911). (15)

U. S. v. Harvel, B. B. 179 (1922). (33)

U. S. v. Hayes, B. B. 131 (1913). (18)

U. S. v. Hency, 286 Fed. 165 (1923). (35)

U. S. v. Electrical Workers, B. B. 125 (1913). (5)

U. S. v. Johnston Brokerage Co., B. B. 170 (1921). (28)

U. S. v. Jones, . B. 162 (1921). (24)

U. S. v. Journeyman Stone Cutters, 9 *Law and Labor* 263 (1927). 10 *Law and Labor* 265 (1928). (9)

U. S. v. Master Steam Fitters Association, B. B. 165 (1921). (25)

U. S. v. Meyers, B. B. 211 (1928). (40)

U. S. v. Mitchell, B. B. 200 (1926). (38)

U. S. v. National Association of Window Glass Manufacturers, 287 Fed. 228 (1923). (8)

U. S. v. Norris, 255 Fed. 423 (1918). (19)

U. S. v. O'Brien, B. B. 175 (1922). (27)

U. S. v. Painters, B. B. 212 (1928). (10)

U. S. v. Powell, B. B. 178 (1922). (31)

U. S. v. Railway Employees' Department, 283 Fed. 479 (1922). 286 Fed. 228 (1923). 290 Fed. 978 (1923). (7)

U. S. v. Ray, B. B. 101, 102 (1908). (13)

U. S. v. Reilly, B. B. 180 (1923). (34)

U. S. v. Taliaferro, 290 Fed. 214 (1922). (73)

U. S. v. Wallace, B. B. 209 (1928). (39)

U. S. v. White, B. B. 128 (1913). (16)

U. S. v. White, B. B. 131 (1913). (17)

U. S. v. Williams, B. B. 177 (1922). (30)

Vandell v. U. S., 6 F (2) 188 (1925). (34)

Wagner v. Machinists, 252 Fed. 597 (1918). (51)

Western Union v. Electrical Workers, 2 F (2) 993 (1924). (76)

Williams v. U. S., 295 Fed. 302 (1924). (30)

TABLE II

Table of Cases Referred to Other than Those in Which Labor was Defendant under the Sherman Act.

Addyston Pipe and Steel Co. v. U. S., 175 U. S. 211, 20 Sup. Ct. Rep. 96 (1899).

Aikens v. Wisconsin, 195 U. S. 194, 25 Sup. Ct. Rep. 3 (1904).

American Column and Lumber Co. v. U. S., 257 U. S. 377, 42 Sup. Ct. Rep. 114 (1921).

American Steel Foundries v. Tri-City Central Trades Council, 257 U. S. 184, 42 Sup. Ct. Rep. 72, (1921).

American Tobacco Co. v. U. S., 221 U. S. 106, 31 Sup. Ct. Rep. 632 (1911).

Anderson v. Shipowners' Association, 10 F (2) 96 (1926).
272 U. S. 359, 47 Sup. Ct. Rep. 125 (1926).
27 F (2) 163 (1928).
31 F (2) 539 (1929).

Anderson v. U. S., 171 U. S. 604, 19 Sup. Ct. Rep. 50 (1898).

Belfi v. U. S., 259 Fed. 822 (1919).

Callan v. Wilson, 127 U. S. 540, 8 Sup. Ct. Rep. 1301 (1888).

Cement Manufacturers' Protective Association v. U. S., 268 U. S. 588, 45 Sup. Ct. Rep. 586 (1925).

Chicago Board of Trade v. U. S., 246 U. S. 231, 38 Sup. Ct. Rep. 242 (1918).

County of Mobile v. Kimball, 102 U. S. 691, 26 L. ed. 238 (1881).

Eastern States Retail Lumber Association v. U. S., 234 U. S. 600, 34 Sup. Ct. Rep. 951 (1914).

Ellis v. Inman, Poulsen and Co., 131 Fed. 182 (1904).

Gompers v. Bucks Stove and Range Co., 221 U. S. 418, 31 Sup. Ct. Rep. 492 (1911).

Hopkins v. U. S., 171 U. S. 578, 19 Sup. Ct. Rep. 40 (1898).

Industrial Association v. U. S., 268 U. S. 64, 45 Sup. Ct. Rep. 403 (1925).

Kidd v. Pearson, 128 U. S. 1, 9 Sup. Ct. Rep. 6 (1888).

Lamar v. U. S., 260 Fed. 561 (1919).

Maple Flooring Association v. U. S., 268 U. S. 563, 45 Sup. Ct. Rep. 578 (1925).

Michaelson et al. v. U. S., 266 U. S. 42, 45 Sup. Ct. Rep. 18 (1924).

Montague and Co. v. Lowry, 193 U. S. 38, 24 Sup. Ct. Rep. 307 (1904).

Nash v. U. S., 229 U. S. 373, 33 Sup. Ct. Rep. 780 (1913).

Northern Securities Co. v. U. S., 193 U. S. 197, 24 Sup. Ct. Rep. 436 (1904).

People v. Fisher, 14 Wendell 9 (1835).

Post v. Bucks Stove and Range Co. et al., 200 Fed. 918 (1912).

Standard Oil Co. v. U. S., 221 U. S. 1, 31 Sup. Ct. Rep. 502 (1911).

Standard Sanitary Manufacturing Co. v. U. S., 226 U. S. 20, 33 Sup. Ct. Rep. 9 (1912).

Steers v. U. S., 192 Fed. 1 (1911).

Swift and Co. v. U. S., 196 U. S. 375, 25 Sup. Ct. Rep. 276 (1905).

Thomas v. Cincinnati—In re Phelan, 62 Fed. 803 (1894).

Truax v. Corrigan, 257 U. S. 312, 42 Sup. Ct. Rep. 124 (1921).

U. S. v. E. C. Knight Co., 156 U. S. 1, 15 Sup. Ct. Rep. 249 (1895).

U. S. v. Industrial Association, 293 Fed. 925 (1923).

U. S. v. International Harvester Co., 214 Fed. 987 (1914).

U. S. v. Jellico Mountain Coal Co., 43 Fed. 898 (1890). 46 Fed. 432 (1891).

U. S. v. Joint Traffic Association, 171 U. S. 505, 19 Sup. Ct. Rep. 25 (1898).

U. S. v. Patterson, 55 Fed. 605 (1893).

U. S. v. Rintelen, 233 Fed. 793 (1916).

U. S. v. Terminal Railroad Association, 224 U. S. 383, 32 Sup. Ct. Rep. 507 (1912).

U. S. v. Trans-Missouri Freight Association, 166 U. S. 290, 17 Sup. Ct. Rep. 540 (1897).

U. S. v. Trenton Potteries Co., 273 U. S. 392, 47 Sup. Ct. Rep. 377 (1927).

U. S. v. United Shoe Machinery Co., 247 U. S. 32, 38 Sup. Ct. Rep. 473 (1918).

U. S. v. U. S. Steel Corporation, 223 Fed. 55 (1915). 251 U. S. 417, 40 Sup. Ct. Rep. 293 (1920).

Wabash Railway Co. v. Hannahan et al., 121 Fed. 563 (1903).

Waterhouse v. Comer, 55 Fed. 149 (1893).

APPENDIX C

Brief Histories of the Cases in which a Labor Union, its Officers,
or its Members have been Defendants under the
Sherman Act.

Note. B. B. refers to Blue Book, i. e., the volume entitled, *The Federal Antitrust Laws with Amendments,* published on November 30, 1928, by the United States Department of Justice.

I. GOVERNMENT SUITS FOR INJUNCTIONS.

1. United States v. Workingmen's Amalgamated Council of New Orleans et al. In November, 1893, a dispute between the draymen and the warehousemen of New Orleans and their employees resulted in a strike, which soon spread to other workers who walked out in sympathy. As a result the business of the city was greatly handicapped, and the transit of goods through the city from state to state and to foreign countries "was totally interrupted." The attorneys for the United States sought an injunction against the unions on the ground that the strike was a conspiracy in restraint of interstate and foreign commerce and a violation of the Sherman Act. The petition was filed on March 25, 1893, in the Circuit Court for the Eastern District of Louisiana, and the injunction was granted. The court concluded that Congress had meant the act to apply to combinations of labor as well as of capital. 54 Fed. 994. The injunction decree was affirmed by the Circuit Court of Appeals for the Fifth Circuit, on June 13, 1893. Workingmen's Amalgamated Council of New Orleans v. United States, 57 Fed. 85 (B. B. 85).

2. United States v. Debs et al. In June, 1894, the American Railway Union asked its members not to work on railway trains to which Pullman cars were attached. The order was issued to help members of the union who worked at the shops of the Pullman Company win their strike. In a few days the strike was so extensive as to tie up railway traffic throughout the central and western sections of the country. On July 2, 1894, attorneys representing the United States filed a petition for an injunction in the Circuit Court, Northern District of Illinois, restraining Eugene V. Debs, president of the union, and all others, from carrying on activity which obstructed the mails or interfered with interstate commerce. It was held that the strike was a conspiracy in restraint of trade in violation of the Sherman Act. A temporary injunction was granted on the same day, July 2. On July 17 government attorneys filed information with the court charging Debs and others with contempt for violating the injunction. Later in the month the court postponed the hearing of the contempt charges. (Appendix to *Report of the Attorney General*, 1896, pp. 87, 90-93.) Finally, on December 14, 1894, the court found Debs and his associates guilty of contempt and sentenced them to jail for terms varying from three to six months. United States v. Debs et al., 64 Fed. 724. On January 14, 1895, the defendants appealed to the Supreme Court for writs of error and of habeas corpus. The first writ was at once denied. After hearings, the court, on May 27, 1895, denied the writ of habeas corpus. It upheld the injunction, but found other grounds for it than the Sherman Act. In re Debs, 158 U. S. 564. The original petition for the injunction was finally dismissed on July 28, 1899, at the instance of the government. (B. B. 88.)

3. *United States v. Debs et al.* In connection with the Pullman strike, United States attorneys, on July 3, 1894, asked for an injunction similar to the one described above, in the Circuit Court, District of Indiana. The order was directed at the American Railway Union and 49 individual defendants. It was issued on the same grounds as the Chicago injunction on July 3, and was continued in force until September 19, 1898, when the case was dismissed at the instance of the government. (B. B. 87.)

4. United States v. Elliott et al. Preliminary injunctions to restrain Elliott, Debs, and 293 other defendants were granted at the request of government attorneys on July 6 and October 24, 1894, in the Circuit Court, Eastern District of Missouri. The occasion and the grounds for the injunctions were the same as in the two injunctions above. On April 6, 1896, a final decree was entered and the injunction made permanent. 62 Fed. 801, 64 Fed. 27. (B. B. 87.)

(*Note.* U. S. v. Agler. Information was filed in the Circuit Court, District of Indiana, on July 12, 1894, charging Agler and others with contempt of court for violating one of the injunctions issued in the Pullman strike. Agler was adjudged guilty of contempt on the same day, July 12, 1894, the court asserting that the Act of 1890 was intended to prevent interference with railway transportation by labor. Sentence was suspended during good behavior. 62 Fed. 824. [B. B. 87.])

5. United States v. International Brotherhood of Electrical Workers, Local Unions Nos. 9 and 134, et al. This was a petition filed on February 24, 1913, in the District Court, Northern District of Illinois, seeking to enjoin electrical workers from interfering with the interstate business of the Postal Telegraph-Cable Company. A temporary injunction was granted at once and was made permanent by a final decree entered on February 27, 1914. (B. B. 125.)

6. United States v. Bricklayers', Masons', and Plasterers' International Union of America et al. This was a petition filed February 28, 1922, in the District Court, Southern District of New York, charging the international union, its officers, and the representatives of numerous local unions with combining and conspiring to restrain interstate trade and commerce in marble, cut stone, brick, and other commodities used in the construction of buildings. The unions were charged with agreeing with employers not to work on non-union materials, and with having adopted rules whereby the output of each worker was restricted. At the same time the petition was filed a consent decree was entered against all the defendants except the representatives of three New York locals, against whom the case was still pending in November, 1928. The decree enjoined the restrictive rules and the refusal to work on non-union materials. (4 *Law and Labor* 95, April, 1922.) (B. B. 172.)

7. *United States v. Railway Employees' Department of the American Federation of Labor et al.* The railway shopmen all over the country went on strike during the summer of 1922 in protest against a decision cutting wages which was handed down by the United States Railroad Labor Board. On the ground, among others, that the strike, which hampered transportation, was a conspiracy in restraint of trade and thus a violation of the Sherman Act, the Attorney-General, on September 1, 1922, secured a temporary restraining order from the District Court for the Northern District of Illinois. The order restrained almost every act the effect of which would be to aid in continuing the strike. The first preliminary injunction was granted on September 25, and the second on October 5, 1922. 283 Fed. 479. The defendants filed motions to dissolve and dismiss the injunction on the next day. These motions were denied on January 5, 1923. 286 Fed. 228. After a final hearing the court, on July 12, 1923, rendered an opinion in favor of the government and made the injunction permanent. 290 Fed. 978. (B. B. 176.)

8. *United States v. National Association of Window Glass Manufacturers et al.* The manufacturers' association and the union in the handmade window glass industry had entered into an agreement under which one half of the total number of factories operated for one part of each year, after which the remaining factories operated during the other part. Charging that the agreement was a violation of the Sherman Law, the government asked for a restraining order in the District Court for the Northern District of Ohio. A temporary restraining order to prevent further performance of the agreement was granted on January 5, 1923. A trial on the application for a preliminary injunction took place in January, 1923, and on February 2, 1923,

a decision favorable to the government was handed down. 287 Fed. 219. A final decree was entered on April 19, 1923, whereupon the defendants appealed to the Supreme Court. That court rendered a decision reversing the lower court on December 10, 1923. It held that the agreement in question was not in unreasonable restraint of trade. National Association of Window Glass Manufacturers v. United States, 263 U. S. 403. (B. B. 180.)

9. *United States v. Journeyman Stone Cutters' Association of North America et al.* In a petition for an injunction filed by the government on February 28, 1927, in the District Court of the Southern District of New York, the national stone cutters' union, various local unions, and certain individuals, were charged with a conspiracy to restrain interstate commerce by hindering the sale and use of cast stone cut outside the Metropolitan District on buildings in the district. On September 27 the court sustained the government's contention. (*New York Times*, September 28, 1927.) (9 *Law and Labor* 263. October, 1927.) A final decree was entered on October 22, 1928. The defendants were enjoined from doing anything to prevent the transportation of the stone into the district, or to interfere with its sale or use. (10 *Law and Labor* 265, December, 1928.) The national union and its officers appealed to the Supreme Court, which considered the case on October 22, 1928. On November 19, 1928, it dismissed the appeal in a memorandum decision for lack of showing service of summons and severance on those defendants who did not appeal. Journeyman Stone Cutters' Association v. United States, 73 L. ed. 179. See case 38, this appendix.

10. *United States v. Painters' District No. 14 of Chicago, et al.* This is a petition filed August 22, 1928, in the District Court, Northern District of Illinois, against the council above named, numerous painters' and glaziers' unions, and their officers, all connected with the Brotherhood of Painters, Decorators and Paper Hangers of America. The government set forth a conspiracy in restraint of interstate trade and commerce in finished "built-in" kitchen cabinets, carried out by demanding that the

cabinets delivered in Chicago and vicinity have only a single coat of paint on them, and calling or threatening to call strikes to enforce the demand, causing buyers to cancel their orders; and fining one company for installing cabinets with more than one coat of paint. At the end of November, 1928, the petition was still pending on a motion to dismiss. (Chicago *Tribune*, April 19, 1928.) (B. B. 212.) See case 39, this appendix.

II. INDICTMENTS BROUGHT AT THE INSTANCE OF THE GOVERNMENT.

11. United States v. Debs et al. On July 10, 1894, United States attorneys secured indictments from the District Court in Chicago charging the officers of the American Railway Union with obstructing the mails and with a conspiracy in restraint of interstate commerce. On July 19 the Grand Jury returned more than twenty indictments versus Debs and others on the same charges. When the trial of the defendants on these charges began, early the next winter, the government attorneys had the case dismissed. In re Grand Jury, 62 Fed. 828; United States v. Debs et al., 63 Fed. 436. (Cleveland, *The Government in the Chicago Strike of 1894,* p. 34.) (*Appendix to the Report of the Attorney General, 1896,* pp. 90-93.) (*Report of the Commission on Industrial Relations,* Vol. XI, 1916, p. 10771.)

12. United States v. Cassidy et al. This was an indictment returned in July, 1894, in the District Court, Northern District of California, charging the defendants with conspiracy to obstruct the mails and restrain interstate commerce in connection with the Pullman strike. The trial started at the beginning of April, 1895, and ended with a disagreement of the jury on April 6. On July 1, 1895, a nolle prosequi was entered. 67 Fed. 698. (B. B. 88.)

13. United States v. E. J. Ray et al. An indictment was returned February 14, 1908, in the Circuit Court, Eastern District of Louisiana, against 72 laborers, charging them with conspiracy in restraint of foreign trade and commerce. On the next day another indictment was returned against the same defendants, who were this time charged with conspiracy in restraint of interstate trade or commerce. The two indictments were consolidated for trial on January 26, 1911. A verdict of guilty was returned as to three defendants, and fines aggregating $110 were imposed. This judgment was later affirmed by the Circuit Court of Appeals. (B. B. 101, 102.)

14. United States v. Joe Cotton et al. An indictment was returned November 15, 1911, in the District Court of the Southern District of Mississippi, charging the defendants with conspiring to restrain interstate commerce during the course of a strike on the Illinois Central Railroad. Since the strike had terminated, no further action was taken, and the case was remanded to the files November 15, 1912. (B. B. 114.)

15. United States v. A. Haines et al. On December 16, 1911, four indictments were returned in the District Court of the Southern District of Florida against members of a longshoremen's union. Two of the indictments charged the defendants with conspiring to interfere with the interstate operations of the Mason Forwarding Company, which had declined to recognize one of the defendants who was the business agent. The other indictments charged that the regulations and requirements of the union with reference to the employment of workmen to load vessels with lumber interfered with interstate shipment. The indictments were consolidated for trial. The defendants entered pleas of guilty, and each was sentenced to four hours' confinement. (B. B. 115.)

16. United States v. White et al. On June 7, 1913, an indictment was returned in the District Court, Southern District of West Virginia, against 19 members of the United Mine Workers, charging a conspiracy to interfere with interstate commerce in coal mined in West Virginia. The case was noll prossed on June 20, 1914. (B. B. 128.)

17. United States v. John P. White et al. On December 1, 1913, an indictment was returned in the District Court, District of

Colorado, against officials and members of the United Mine Workers, charging them with monopolizing all coal diggers and mine laborers and with restraining interstate commerce in coal. The case was noll prossed on January 8, 1916. (B. B. 131.)

18. United States v. Frank J. Hayes et al. On December 1, 1913, an indictment was returned in the District Court, District of Colorado, against members of the miners' union, charging them with conspiring to interfere with the mining of coal in Colorado and with its transportation to and sale in other states. The case was noll prossed on January 8, 1916. (B. B. 131.)

19. United States v. Norris et al. The defendants were found guilty, on an indictment filed January 26, 1915, charging a conspiracy to violate the Sherman Act, of attempting to force an employer to pay them blackmail by calling strikes. Thus hauling of sand and the unloading of sand from railroad cars were prevented, and other cars were diverted to the wrong parties. The defendants moved to arrest judgment, and in a decision entered on December 16, 1918, the court denied the motion. The case was tried in the District Court, Northern District of Illinois, Eastern Division. 255 Fed. 423. (*Law and Labor,* June, 1919, p. 14.)

20. United States v. Michael Artery et al. Eight indictments were returned in January and April, 1915, in the District Court, Northern District of Illinois, against certain business agents of trade unions in Chicago. They were charged with combining to prevent the unloading in Chicago of goods shipped from other states. Demurrers to the indictments were overruled. The trial of three of the defendants under one of the indictments resulted in a verdict of guilty. On December 20, 1918, fines aggregating $2,500 were imposed. On March 8, 1919, the defendants under the other indictments pleaded guilty and fines aggregating $2,000 were imposed. A nolle prosequi was entered as to one indictment. (B. B. 136.)

21. United States v. Michael Boyle et al. Two indictments, one against Boyle et al., and one against Feeney et al., were returned April 27, 1915, in the District Court, Northern District of Illinois, Eastern Division, charging a conspiracy in violation of the Sherman Act among labor unions and certain manufacturers in Chicago to prevent the installation of electrical appliances, such as switchboards and panels manufactured elsewhere, the purpose being to eliminate competition from that source. Demurrers to the indictments were overruled. In the course of the trial of the Boyle case it was made clear that the union had agreed not to install appliances unless they were union-made. The trial resulted in a verdict of guilty. Sentences of 60 days and one year in jail were imposed upon two defendants, and these and eleven others were fined an aggregate of $15,500. The Seventh Circuit Court of Appeals affirmed the judgment on April 4, 1919. 259 Fed. 803. An application for a rehearing was denied. Boyle's sentence was commuted to four months. A nolle prosequi or dismissal was entered as to eight defendants. (B. B. 137.)

22. *United States v. Boyle et al.* (*The Feeney Indictment.*) The facts charged in this indictment were the same as those in the Boyle case. The trial of the Feeney case was postponed until the Boyle case was concluded. On October 31, 1923, motions to dismiss were denied and the case was set for trial on December 3, 1923. In November, 1923, three of the principal individual defendants and five of the principal corporate defendants entered pleas of guilty. They were fined amounts aggregating $6,000. The case was dismissed as to the remaining defendants. (B. B. 137.)

23. *United States v. Andrews Lumber and Mill Company et al. United States v. Brims.* On January 21, 1921, an indictment was returned at Chicago charging 68 defendants, constituting substantially all of the manufacturers in Chicago of sash, doors, and interior finish, a number of building contractors, and members of the United Brotherhood of Carpenters and Joiners of America, with restraining interstate commerce in sash, doors, and interior finish in violation of the Sherman Act. The indict-

ments charged that the defendants were enabled to monopolize the trade in Chicago by agreeing that the manufacturers would not employ persons not members of the union and that members of the union would not install material made by manufacturers in other states. On March 12, 1921, all the defendants filed demurrers and motions to quash. Because it was thought that objection might be entered to the foregoing indictment on the question of the authority of the Grand Jury, United States attorneys thought it advisable to secure another indictment on similar grounds against the same defendants. This was done on September 2, 1921, in the District Court for the Northern District of Illinois, Eastern Division. Trial was begun June 12, 1923. The case was dismissed as to a number of defendants, and fines aggregating $58,300 were imposed. A number of defendants paid their fines and the remainder appealed to the Circuit Court of Appeals, Seventh Circuit. On June 4, 1925, that court held that the trial had proved only that the union had agreed not to work on non-union millwork, whether made in or out of Illinois, and that the Sherman Act was not violated. It reversed the judgment of the lower court and remanded the cause for further proceedings. Brims et al. v. United States, 6 F (2) 98. The government appealed to the Supreme Court on a writ of certiorari. On November 23, 1926, that court reversed the judgment of the Circuit Court of Appeals and remanded the cause for further proceedings. United States v. W. F. Brims et al., 71 L. ed. 403. On October 22, 1927, the Circuit Court of Appeals affirmed the judgment of conviction by the District Court. Brims et al. v. United States, 21 F (2) 889. (B. B. 160, 167.)

24. *United States v. Jones et al.* On February 25, 1921, an indictment was filed in the District Court at Indianapolis charging operators of bituminous mines and officials of the miners' union with conspiracy to restrain interstate trade and commerce. The indictment charged that the defendants had agreed to create shortages, to limit production and distribution, to establish a uniform accounting system, and to act in concert to increase

wages and the price of coal. The indictment was dismissed upon motion of the government on June 28, 1923. (B. B. 162.)

25. *United States v. Chicago Master Steam Fitters' Association et al.* On April 30, 1921, an indictment was returned in the District Court at Chicago against 19 corporations and 24 individual defendants, including the business manager of the union called the Chicago Steam Fitters' Protective Association. The defendants were charged with monopolizing and restraining interstate commerce in furnishing and installing heating apparatus in Chicago. Demurrers were overruled on October 17, 1921. After a thorough investigation the case was noll prossed on May 28, 1926. (B. B. 165.)

26. *United States v. Louis Biegler Company et al.* On April 30, 1921, an indictment was returned in the District Court at Chicago against 11 corporations and 18 individuals, including representatives of the Amalgamated Sheet Metal Workers' Union, charging monopolization and restraint of interstate trade in furnishing and installing heating apparatus in Chicago. Demurrers were overruled on October 17, 1921. After a thorough investigation the case was noll prossed on May 28, 1926. (B. B. 165.)

27. *United States v. James O'Brien et al.* In April, 1922, an indictment was returned against O'Brien and four others in the District Court of the Eastern District of Kentucky. The defendants, acting as pickets, had, by telling a truck driver that he could not proceed with his load, interfered with the delivery of a steel billet across the state boundary. They were charged with violating the Sherman Act and were tried and convicted at the same term of court. Four were sentenced to jail terms of eight months each and one to a term of 30 days. Four of them appealed to the Circuit Court of Appeals for the Sixth Circuit. The decision of the lower court was affirmed on June 5, 1923. O'Brien v. United States, 290 Fed. 185. The court denied a petition for a rehearing on July 18, 1923. (B. B. 175.)

28. *United States v. Johnston Brokerage Company et al.* On November 28, 1921, an indictment was returned in the District

Court, Southern District of New York, charging the defendants, among whom were 53 firms producing handmade window glass, and the president of the National Window Glass Workers, with a conspiracy to enhance prices and suppress competition in violation of the Sherman Act. The manufacturers were said to produce about two-thirds of all the handmade glass used in the United States. Complaint was made of an agreement whereby the period during which each plant might work was restricted. In February, 1922, a demurrer to the indictment was sustained on the ground that it had not been shown that the alleged conspiracy was formulated in the Southern District of New York. Nolle prosequi was filed as to all the defendants on August 29, 1927. (B. B. 170.) (Information partly secured from a Ph.D. thesis at the University of Wisconsin, written by Alfred W. Briggs and entitled "Labor in the Window Glass Industry.")

29. *United States v. Clements et al.* In August, 1922, during the railway shopmen's strike, the defendants induced certain employees of the Atchison, Topeka, and Santa Fé Railway Company to go on strike and to abandon the trains they were operating. Trains were abandoned, to the discomfort of passengers, at Needles, Calif., and at several desert villages. An indictment was returned on September 25, 1922, in the District Court for the Southern District of California, charging conspiracy to obstruct the United States mails and to interfere with interstate commerce in violation of the Sherman Act. A demurrer to this indictment was sustained, and a second indictment was returned on November 8, 1922. The eight defendants were tried and found guilty on December 20, 1922. Fines aggregating $10,000 were imposed. The Circuit Court of Appeals for the Ninth Circuit affirmed the judgment of the lower court on March 17, 1924. It denied a rehearing on May 5, 1924. Clements et al. v. United States, 297 Fed. 206. Petition for a writ of certiorari was denied by the Supreme Court on October 13, 1924. (B. B. 177.)

30. *United States v. Williams, Hanley, et al.* On September

27, 1922, an indictment was returned in the District Court for the Western District of Texas, charging a conspiracy to violate the Sherman Act by interfering with interstate commerce during the shopmen's strike. The defendants were alleged to have put quicksilver in the boilers of locomotives on the Southern Pacific Railroad. The first trial resulted in a mistrial because of the illness of a juror. A second indictment was returned and on retrial five defendants were found guilty. On January 24, 1923, one defendant was acquitted. The case against three defendants was dismissed because of insufficient evidence. On February 3, 1923, the convicted defendants were each sentenced to 10 months' confinement and fined $2,500. This judgment was affirmed by the Circuit Court of Appeals for the Fifth Circuit on December 1, 1923. Williams et al. v. United States, 295 Fed. 302. On June 9, 1924, the Supreme Court denied a petition for a writ of certiorari. (B. B. 177.)

31. United States v. Ed. Powell. On October 18, 1922, an indictment was returned against Powell charging him and other persons, unknown, with a conspiracy to restrain interstate commerce during the shopmen's strike by setting fire to certain carloads of coal. On October 19, 1922, he pleaded guilty and was sentenced to ten days in jail. The other conspirators were never identified. (B. B. 178.)

32. United States v. American Window Glass Company et al. On March 17, 1922, an indictment was returned in the District Court of the Southern District of New York, charging the union and the handmade window glass manufacturers' association with a conspiracy to violate the Sherman Act, carried out by means of price fixing agreements and by an agreement to operate each group of factories only half of each year. The court overruled a demurrer on June 29, 1922. The indictment had not yet gone to trial by November, 1922. The government counsel connected with the New York indictment started a Grand Jury investigation in the District Court of the Northern District of Ohio, Eastern Division. The counsel admitted their intention to use testimony procured from the subpœnaed witnesses in the New York prosecution. These witnesses moved to quash and vacate the subpœnas directing them to appear before the Grand Jury. On November 9, 1922, the court granted the motion and restrained the Grand Jury investigation until such time as a trial had taken place in New York, or until the government should decide to try the expected Ohio indictment first. In re National Window Glass Workers et al., 287 Fed. 219. In view of the Supreme Court's decision in the National Association of Window Glass Manufacturers et al. v. United States, 263 U. S. 403 (1923) (See case 8, this appendix), the government finally noll prossed the case on September 16, 1926. (Information partly secured from a Ph.D. thesis at the University of Wisconsin, written by Alfred W. Briggs and entitled "Labor in the Window Glass Industry.") (B. B. 173.)

33. United States v. A. L. Harvel et al. On December 13, 1922, an indictment was returned in the District Court for the Western District of Louisiana charging a conspiracy to restrain interstate commerce, in pursuance of which an assault was made upon a roadmaster of the Kansas City Southern Railroad about July 2. On December 17, 1923, the case against one defendant was noll prossed, and the two remaining defendants pleaded guilty and were each fined $25. This indictment was a result of activities carried on in connection with the shopmen's strike of 1922. (B. B. 179.)

34. United States v. Francis Reilly et al. On January 5, 1923, two indictments were returned in the District Court, Western District of New York, against 14 defendants, charging a conspiracy in violation of the Sherman Act in connection with the dynamiting of the High-Speed Line of the International Railway on August 17, 1922. On January 7, 1923, a third indictment was returned against 22 defendants. To this indictment four defendants pleaded guilty on January 9, 1924. Sentences were suspended pending the trial of four defendants who pleaded not guilty. The trial resulted in a verdict of guilty on January 21,

1924. Each of those convicted was sentenced to one year in jail. Fines aggregating $13,000 were also imposed. The judgment was confirmed by the Circuit Court of Appeals, Second Circuit, on March 2, 1925. Vandell et al. v. United States, 6 F (2) 188. Nolle prosequi was entered June 14, 1926, as to all but four of the remaining defendants, certain of whom were made parties to the indictment described in case 37 below. The cases against those not so made parties were noll prossed on November 23, 1926. (B. B. 180.)

35. *United States v. Tom Hency et al.* On January 16, 1923, an indictment was returned in the District Court for the Northern District of Texas, alleging a conspiracy to interfere with interstate commerce in violation of the Sherman Act by disabling locomotives through introducing quicksilver and other chemicals into their boilers. It was shown only that the defendants had these chemicals in their possession, not that they had actually used them. The court sustained a demurrer to the indictment on February 10, 1893, asserting that the Sherman Act was not intended to prevent sabotage. The case grew out of the shopmen's strike. 286 Fed. 165. (B. B. 181.)

36. *United States v. Dryllic et al.* On January 16, 1924, seven members of the railway shop craft unions pleaded guilty in a District Court in Ohio to a violation of the Sherman Act by committing sabotage during the shopmen's strike of 1922. Among the acts of which they were guilty were the following: placing a large nut so that it would fall into the cylinder of an engine when it started; placing quicksilver and emery dust in locomotive boilers; and placing lye in the shoes of a railway employee. (6 *Law and Labor* 69, March, 1924.)

37. *United States v. William B. Fitzgerald et al.* On May 20, 1925, an indictment was returned in the District Court, Western District of New York, against 25 officials and members of railway unions, including certain defendants indicted in case 34, described above. The indictment charged violation of the Sherman Act in connection with the dynamiting of the High-Speed

Line of the International Railway. The case went to trial as to ten defendants on January 14, 1926. The indictment was dismissed as to six defendants and on January 21 the jury returned a verdict of not guilty as to the other four. The case against the remaining defendants was noll prossed in June, 1926. (B. B. 181.)

38. United States v. Michael W. Mitchell et al. On July 7, 1926, an indictment was returned in the District Court, Southern District of New York, charging five officers of trade unions having to do with stone cutting with a conspiracy to prevent the usc of cast stone within the Metropolitan District which had been manufactured outside that district. The government's demurrers to special pleas in bar were argued, and were sustained on July 5, 1927. No further advance in the case had occurred by the end of November, 1928. (B. B. 200.) See above, case 9.

39. United States v. Arthur W. Wallace et al. On April 18, 1928, an indictment was returned in the District Court, Northern District of Illinois, against 12 officers and business agents of the Painter's District Council No. 14 of Chicago, charging a conspiracy to restrain interstate trade and commerce in violation of the Sherman Act. The defendants were alleged to have carried out their conspiracy by demanding that "built-in" kitchen cabinets delivered in Chicago and vicinity have only a single coat of paint on them, by calling or threatening to call strikes to enforce this demand, thus causing buyers to cancel orders, and by fining one company for installing cabinets with more than one coat of paint. Demurrers were overruled on August 17, 1928. The case was awaiting trial at the end of November, 1928. (B. B. 209.) See above, case 10. (Chicago *Tribune,* April 19, 1928.)

40. United States v. George H. Meyers et al. On June 28, 1928, an indictment was returned in the District Court, Northern District of Illinois, against four officers and employees of the Glaziers' Local Union No. 27, and against Benjamin Beris, president of the American Glass Company. The defendants were charged with a conspiracy to restrain interstate commerce in glazed bathroom cabinets and other glazed products, the principal means used to accomplish the restraint being strikes or threats to declare strikes. The case had not yet gone to trial in November, 1928. (B. B. 211.)

III. Damage Suits.

41. Loewe et al. v. Lawlor et al. In 1902, as a result of a dispute between the hat manufacturers of Danbury, Conn., and the hatters' union, the latter initiated a nation-wide secondary boycott against the products of the firms. On August 31, 1903, the manufacturers brought suit for damages against the officers and members of the union, charging a conspiracy in restraint of interstate trade and commerce in violation of the Sherman Act, as a consequence of which it had suffered financial losses of some $80,000. The complaint was entered in the Circuit Court for the District of Connecticut. The defendants entered a demurrer to a plea of abatement and were sustained. 130 Fed. 63. They later entered a plea that the complaint against them was insufficient. The court held the complaint to be sufficient. Loewe v. Lawlor, 142 Fed. 216. December 13, 1905. The defendants thereafter filed a demurrer to the entire complaint of the manufacturers. The court rendered a decision on this demurrer on December 7, 1906. It asserted that none of the acts of the hatters, taken by themselves, could be considered interstate commerce, and that it was very uncertain what the Supreme Court would say if it were to consider the acts as a whole. In view of the great delay and expense involved if the suit should go to trial, and in view of the uncertainty of the Supreme Court's position, the court considered it best to dismiss the complaint of the manufacturers. Loewe v. Lawlor, 148 Fed. 924. The complainants thereupon appealed and secured a writ of certiorari, which was issued to the Circuit Court of Appeals for the Second Circuit. On February 3, 1908, the Supreme Court handed down a decision reversing the judgment of the lower court and remanding the cause with directions to proceed accordingly. The

Supreme Court held that the combination described in the manufacturers' complaint was a conspiracy in restraint of trade which violated the Sherman Act. Loewe v. Lawlor, 208 U. S. 274. The case thereupon went back to the Circuit Court, and the suit for damages was tried. The trial lasted from October 13, 1909, until February 4, 1910, when the case went to the jury, which assessed the damages at $74,000. This amount was trebled by the court in accordance with Section 7 of the Sherman Act. The judgment in favor of Loewe, which included costs, amounted to $232,240.12. The hatters thereupon appealed on a writ of error to the Circuit Court of Appeals, Second Circuit, and asked for a reversal of judgment. That court, on April 10, 1911, reversed the judgment of the court below. It asserted that the court had erred in practically directing the jury to return a verdict against the hatters, leaving only the amount of damages to the consideration of the jury. It held that the question as to whether the evidence showed that individual members of the union should be held liable for the acts of their agents was a question for the jury, not the judge. On May 8, 1911, the court denied a petition for a rehearing, reasserting the position above stated, and stating its expectation that the suit would proceed to a new trial. Lawlor v. Loewe, 187 Fed. 522. The second trial occurred in the lower court, now known as the District Court for the District of Connecticut, from August 26 to October 11, 1912. The jury rendered a verdict for the full amount demanded by the complainants. On November 15, 1912, judgment was entered for $252,130. The hatters appealed from this judgment to the Circuit Court of Appeals, Second Circuit. The question before the court was whether the evidence proved the Sherman Act violated and whether it was sufficient to hold the individual members of the union responsible for the acts of their officers in carrying out the boycott. The court held the evidence sufficient and affirmed the judgment with costs. Lawlor v. Loewe, 209 Fed. 721. December 18, 1913. The defendants thereupon appealed on a writ of error to the Supreme Court. On January 5, 1915, that body affirmed the judgment of the court below. Lawlor v. Loewe, 235 U. S. 522. The plaintiffs were not able to collect the damages awarded them until 1917. (Merritt, *History of the League for Industrial Rights,* New York, 1925, pp. 28-29.)

42. *Dowd v. United Mine Workers of America et al. (The Coronado Case.)* In September, 1914, the Coronado Coal Company, through Dowd, its receiver, filed a suit for damages against the international union of the miners, the Arkansas union, and others, in the District Court for the Western District of Arkansas. The company complained of losses incurred through the destruction of property in a strike, and asserted that the events were part of an illegal conspiracy to restrain interstate commerce in coal. The suit was accordingly brought under the Sherman Act. The defendants asserted first, that they, being unincorporated associations, could not be sued, and second, that they had not violated the Sherman Act. The District Court sustained the demurrer of the unions. Dowd thereupon appealed to the Circuit Court of Appeals, Eighth Circuit, on a writ of error. On July 21, 1916, that court reversed the judgment of the court below and ordered the trial to proceed. The court ruled against the unions on both points in their demurrer. Dowd v. United Mine Workers of America et al., 235 Fed. 1. The trial of the suit in the lower courts resulted in a verdict of $200,000 for the plaintiffs. This amount was trebled by the court and a counsel fee of $25,000 plus interest was added. The unions then appealed on error to the Circuit Court of Appeals, asserting again that as unincorporated associations they were not suable and that they had not engaged in a conspiracy to restrain interstate commerce. The court ruled against them on both points, reversed the judgment of the District Court as to interest, but affirmed it in other respects. United Mine Workers of America et al. v. Coronado Coal Company, 258 Fed. 829. Thereupon the defendants appealed on a writ of error to the Supreme Court. In a decision rendered June 5, 1922, the court reversed the judgment and remanded the case to the District Court for further proceedings.

It held (1) that there was no evidence to show that the international union was officially responsible for the strike, (2) that that affair was purely a local issue, and (3) that the restraint of trade occurring as a result of it was relatively unimportant, and did not justify the conclusion that the Sherman Act was violated. It also held that a union might sue or be sued just as though it were a corporation. United Mine Workers of America et al. v. Coronado Coal Company, 259 U. S. 344. In October, 1923, the new trial resulted in a verdict for the unions. On appeal, brought by C. H. Finley, receiver for the company at the time, the Circuit Court of Appeals, on July 12, 1924, affirmed the judgment of the trial court. Finley based his appeal on alleged new evidence, but the Circuit Court, reviewing the new facts, found nothing justifying a change from the position stated by the Supreme Court. Finley et al. v. United Mine Workers of America et al., 300 Fed. 972. Finley then carried his appeal to the Supreme Court, which rendered a decision on May 25, 1925. The court again declared that there was no evidence to hold the international union responsible for the damages incurred by the company. It asserted, however, that the Arkansas unions were guilty of violating the Sherman Act and should have been held for damages. This view of the court was based upon new evidence which showed that the Arkansas officers of the union intended to affect interstate commerce when they called the strike, and that the production of the company was much greater and thus much more important in its effect upon interstate commerce than had been supposed. The court ordered the judgment in favor of all the defendants except the international union reversed, and remanded the case for a new trial. Coronado Coal Company v. United Mine Workers of America et al., 268 U. S. 295. On October 17, 1927, the case was dismissed by order of the District Court after an adjustment had been made between the parties whereby the union paid the plaintiffs $27,500, the costs of the trial scheduled for the next month. (*Monthly Labor Review,* Vol. 25, p. 1291, December, 1927.) (9 *Law and Labor* 295.) (*Monthly Report,* American Civil Liberties Union, September-October, 1927, p. 2.)

43. *Pennsylvania Mining Company v. United Mine Workers of America et al.* The company brought suit for damages in the District Court for the Western District of Arkansas. It complained that it had suffered losses from the attempt of the miners to organize its plant in 1915, and from violence occurring as a result. It asserted that if its operations had not been interfered with it could have mined 500 tons of coal a day, and maintained that the acts of the unions were part of a conspiracy to restrain interstate commerce in violation of the Sherman Act. The jury returned a verdict of $100,000 for the company. This judgment was trebled by the court. The defendants then appealed on a writ of error to the Circuit Court of Appeals for the Eighth Circuit. That court, on July 12, 1924, rendered a decision reversing the judgment of the court below and ordered a new trial. It asserted, on the basis of the first Supreme Court decision in the Coronado case, that the international union was not responsible for the damages incurred, and that the acts of the defendants were so indirectly related to interstate commerce as not to be embraced by the Sherman Act. United Mine Workers of America et al. v. Pennsylvania Mining Company, 300 Fed. 965. As a result of the new trial in the District Court the trial judge instructed a verdict for the international union, J. P. White, its former president, and several others. The case as to the Arkansas union and the remaining defendants was submitted to the jury, which failed to agree. The company appealed to the Circuit Court of Appeals, asserting that the trial court had erred in its instructions to the jury. The Circuit Court of Appeals considered the additional evidence against White and the international union insufficient, and affirmed the judgment of the court below. Pennsylvania Mining Company v. United Mine Workers of America et al. 28 F (2) 851. October 13, 1928.

44. *Christian v. International Association of Machinists et al.* Christian, who was a car foreman on the Chesapeake and Ohio

Railroad in the summer of 1922, brought suit for damages against various unions connected with the railway strike, alleging that he had lost his position because of the conspiracy of the defendants in restraint of interstate commerce and in violation of the Sherman Act. The case was brought in the District Court for the Eastern District of Kentucky. The defendants moved to quash service of process. The court, in a decision rendered April 1, 1925, refused to quash service as to System Federation 41, but did so as to the local officers of the international unions, asserting that they were not agents of their internationals. 7 F (2) 481. The case was finally dismissed on motion of the plaintiff at his own cost. (Letter of May 7, 1929, from Clerk of United States District Court, Covington, Ky.)

IV. PRIVATE SUITS FOR INJUNCTIONS.

45. Blindell et al. v. Hagan et al. In December, 1892, the crew of a British steamer in port at New Orleans walked off the ship just before it it was due to sail. On the ground that this constituted a conspiracy in restraint of interstate and foreign commerce in violation of the Sherman Act the agents sought an injunction against the crew in the Circuit Court of the Eastern District of Louisiana. The court, on February 9, 1893, ruled that private parties could not sue for an injunction under the Sherman Act. The plaintiffs had also asked for an injunction on general equity grounds, and the court granted the petition on that basis. This is the first reported instance of an attempt to invoke the Sherman Act against labor. 54 Fed. 40. Affirmed in 56 Fed. 696.

(45 a. *Wabash Railway Company v. Hannahan et al.*, 121 Fed. 563. In March, 1903, the locomotive fireman's and the railway trainmen's unions were planning a strike for higher wages against the Wabash Railway. The company brought suit for an injunction against the union officers to restrain them from calling the strike. The bill of complaint asserted that the unions' purpose was to secure a closed shop by means of an unlawful conspiracy to interfere with the operation of trains in violation

of the Interstate Commerce Act of 1887 and of the Sherman Act. The Circuit Court for the Eastern District of Missouri, Eastern Division, issued a temporary restraining order forbidding the calling of the strike. On April 1, 1903, after argument, it rendered a decision vacating the restraining order and denying a preliminary injunction, holding that the defendants had a right to call the strike. The court did not discuss the Act of 1890, remarking that "counsel have not by proof or argument drawn the federal anti-trust act of July 2, 1890, into consideration in this case." 121 Fed. 563, 567, [Since it appears that the complainant's argument before the court when the restraining order was granted was not concerned, except by brief mention in the bill of complaint, with the Sherman Act, and since that measure was not considered in the later proceeding, this case is not covered by the data in the text concerning the number and nature of the various proceedings against labor under the act.])

46. *National Fireproofing Company v. Mason Builders' Association et al.* The plaintiff company sued for an injunction under the Anti-trust Law in the Circuit Court of the Southern District of New York. It complained that the builders' association and various bricklayers' unions, the defendants, were operating under an agreement which contained two rules injuring its own interests. The first of these rules provided that the employers must include in their contracts not only bricklaying, but much work connected with it, such as the setting of fireproofing arches and slabs. The second rule provided that bricklayers would work only for those complying with the agreement. The plaintiff found itself unable to get subcontracts for fireproofing because of this agreement. The court dismissed the complaint and the plaintiff appealed to the Circuit Court of Appeals, Second Circuit. That court affirmed the decision of the lower court on March 26, 1909. It asserted that since the agreement did not affect interstate commerce it was not reached by the Sherman Act, and that even if it did come under the

statute, private parties were not entitled to an injunction under it. 169 Fed. 259.

47. *Hitchman Coal and Coke Company v. Mitchell*. As a result of a suit in equity begun October 24, 1907, the Circuit Court of the Northern District of West Virginia had issued a preliminary injunction restraining the attempts of the United Mine Workers to organize the employees of the Hitchman Company. On September 21, 1909, the court refused to modify or dissolve the injunction. One of the charges against the union was that it was an attempt to monopolize labor in violation of the Sherman Law. The court did not consider this charge at the time. 172 Fed. 963. On December 23, 1912, the same court, now known as the District Court, rendered a decision after a final hearing. It declared that the United Mine Workers was an unlawful organization under the statute, because it attempted to create a monopoly of mine labor, and because it had joined a conspiracy with the operators from other states to restrain the coal trade of West Virginia. The court therefore concluded that the union, an unlawful organization, had no right to induce the plaintiff's employees to join it. The injunction was also upheld on general equity grounds, and was made perpetual. Hitchman Coal and Coke Company v. Mitchell, 202 Fed. 512. The defendants appealed to the Circuit Court of Appeals, Fourth Circuit, which reversed the judgment of the court below on May 28, 1914. That court denied that the United Mine Workers was an unlawful organization, declared that the Sherman Act could not be a basis for an injunction sought by a private party, and asserted that the union's attempt to organize the company's employees, despite the fact that they had signed an anti-union contract, was not unlawful. Mitchell v. Hitchman Coal and Coke Company, 214 Fed. 685. The company appealed to the Supreme Court, which, in a majority opinion rendered on December 10, 1917, reversed the judgment of the Circuit Court. It made no mention of the Sherman Act, though it did assert that the union's purpose was unlawful. It declared that the union's attempt to

organize was equivalent to inducing breach of contract, and was thus unlawful. Justice Brandeis, with whom Justices Holmes and Clarke concurred, wrote a dissenting opinion approving the position of the Circuit Court of Appeals. Hitchman Coal and Coke Company v. Mitchell, 245 U. S. 229.

(*47a. Post v. Bucks Stove and Range Company et al.* 200 Fed. 918. While appeals from the decision granting an injunction against the American Federation of Labor and others in the Bucks Stove boycott were pending before the United States Supreme Court, the firm and the unions arrived at an amicable settlement. Under one of its provisions the company waived its right to sue the unions for damages because of past controversies. C. W. Post, a stockholder of the company, displeased with the settlement, brought suit in the Circuit Court for the Eastern District of Missouri to enforce for the company a cause of action against the unions for triple damages under the Sherman Act. Post asserted that the boycott had violated the Sherman Act, that the loss to the firm was $250,000, that its agreement to waive the right to sue was without consideration, and that it was illegal and void. The Circuit Court decided against him and he appealed to the Circuit Court of Appeals for the Eighth Circuit. On November 22, 1912, that court affirmed the judgment of the court below. 200 Fed. 918. [Although this case is concerned with a suit for damages under the Act of 1890, the real issue raised was the legality of the settlement between the unions and the firm. On that account the case is not covered by the data in the text concerning the number and nature of the proceedings against labor under the act.])

48. Irving et al. v. Neal et al. The plaintiffs were a firm of trim manufacturers who operated a non-union mill in Massachusetts. The defendants were officers of the carpenters' unions in New York who had carried out their district and national rules not to work on non-union trim by distributing "fair lists," by a system of fines on members, and by threatening a strike. A restraining order and a preliminary injunction against interference with the firm's business had already been issued in the District Court of the Southern District of New York. After a final hearing the court rendered an opinion on November 6, 1913. It declared that the combination was in illegal restraint of trade and a violation of the Sherman Act, but pointed out that no private party could obtain an injunction under the statute. It issued an injunction, however, on the basis of a New York statute making it a misdemeanor to conspire to commit an act "injurious to trade or commerce." 209 Fed. 471.

49. *Paine Lumber Company et al v. Neal et al.* The plaintiffs were trim manufacturers with plants outside of New York who sought an injunction against officers of various carpenters' unions, an association of union trim manufacturers, and the members of an association of master carpenters. The defendants were accused of carrying out an agreement whereby union men would work only on union-made trim and employers would hire only union men. The plaintiffs alleged that this was a conspiracy in restraint of interstate commerce. The District Court of the Southern District of New York, in November, 1913, refused to grant an injunction against the agreement. It agreed that the Sherman Law was being violated, but pointed out that no acts were shown to have been directed against the plaintiffs personally, and that private parties were not entitled to an injunction under the act. 212 Fed. 259. This decree was affirmed by the Circuit Court of Appeals. 214 Fed. 82. An appeal to the Supreme Court resulted in an opinion, rendered by a majority of the court, on June 11, 1917, upholding the opinion of the lower courts. The minority asserted that a private party was not precluded from obtaining an injunction by the Sherman Act, and that in any case injunctions to private parties were permitted by the Clayton Act of 1914. 244 U. S. 459.

50. *Duplex Printing Press Company v. Deering et al.* The machinists' union, in its attempt to organize the Duplex Company's plant in Michigan, instituted a secondary boycott designed to prevent the purchase and use of Duplex presses in New York

City. They induced truckmen to refuse to haul the presses, hindered their being installed and repaired, and appealed to the public not to buy them. The firm brought suit for an injunction in the District Court of the Southern District of New York. The court, on April 23, 1917, refused to grant the decree, asserting that the conduct of the union had been peaceful, lawful, and within its rights, and that, under the Clayton Act, no injunction might be issued. 247 Fed. 192. The complainant appealed to the Circuit Court of Appeals, Second Circuit. That court, on May 25, 1918, handed down a decision affirming the opinion of the lower court. Each of the three judges agreed that the boycott was a violation of the Sherman Act. Two of them, however, believed that the Clayton Act had changed the situation and had legalized the secondary boycott. The third judge thought an injunction should have been granted. 252 Fed. 722. The issue was then appealed to the Supreme Court, which, on January 3, 1921, rendered a majority opinion reversing the lower courts and directing that an injunction restraining the acts of the defendants be issued. The majority, asserting that the boycott was clearly a violation of the Sherman Act, declared that such an act had not been made lawful by the Clayton Law. Justice Brandeis dissented, with the concurrence of Justices Holmes and Clarke, and asserted his belief that the secondary boycott had been legalized. 254 U. S. 443.

51. *Wagner Electric Manufacturing Company v. District Lodge, No. 9, International Association of Machinists et al.* The Wagner Company was in 1918 manufacturing goods, both in its private capacity and under contract for the government, most of which went into interstate commerce. The union had called a strike for the eight-hour day and a closed shop. The company asked for an injunction to prevent the interference with its interstate commerce caused by the strike. The District Court of the Eastern District of Missouri, on June 6, 1918, rendered a decision on the defendants' motion to dismiss. The court ruled against the union, declaring that the company was entitled to an

injunction under the Sherman Act, and declining to dismiss the suit. 252 Fed. 597.

52. *Dail-Overland Company v. Willys-Overland, Inc. et al.* In May, 1919, the Toledo local of machinists called a strike at the plant of the Willys-Overland Company. As a result production of automobiles stopped and considerable violence occurred. The Dail-Overland Company, which had the Willys-Overland agency in North Carolina and had contracts under which cars were to be delivered by the manufacturers' sales organization, brought suit for an injunction on June 5, 1919, in the District Court for the Northern District of Ohio, Western Division, against the manufacturing company, its sales organization, and the machinists' union. The complainant asserted that it was being injured because it could not deliver cars, and asked for an order compelling the company to resume manufacturing and the strikers to cease interference. It complained also that there was a conspiracy to interfere with interstate commerce in violation of the Sherman Act. The court issued a restraining order and an injunction in June, ordering the company to open the plant and setting regulations for picketing. The strikers failed to appear at the hearings. Later there was a hearing on the question as to whether the injunction should be made permanent. The strikers now appeared and asserted that all the companies should have been joined, and that the Willys-Overland Co. was really on the side of the plaintiffs. They declared that the companies had been separated only so that diversity of citizenship might bring the case into the federal court. The court denied the validity of this position. It declared further that jurisdiction also existed because of the violation of the Sherman Act which the defendants admitted by default when they failed to appear and answer the charge that they were illegally interfering with interstate commerce. 263 Fed. 171. The injunction was made permanent on December 27, 1919. (2 *Law and Labor* 33, February, 1920.)

53. *Jewel Tea Company v. International Brotherhood of Teamsters et al.* The teamsters' union, in an attempt to organize the

drivers employed by the Jewel Tea Company in St. Louis, carried on active picketing against them. On the plea that it was engaged in receiving and selling goods in interstate commerce the company obtained a restraining order from the District Court for the Eastern District of Missouri, Eastern Division, on May 22, 1919. The defendants were enjoined from interfering with the company's employees by force, threats or intimidation. A preliminary injunction was issued on June 14, 1919, the court declaring that the defendants were guilty of a combination in violation of the Sherman Act. (*Law and Labor*, July, 1919, p. 11.)

54. *Herkert and Meisel Trunk Company et al. v. United Leatherworkers' International Union et al.* In April, 1920, the union began a strike against five companies, which resulted in the shutting down of the plants. About 90 per cent of the companies' contracts involved interstate business. When the strike took place the companies had unfilled orders of the value of $327,000. The only basis under which the case could come into the federal court was the Sherman Act. The companies charged a conspiracy in restraint of interstate trade and sought an injunction to restrain interference by the picketers in the District Court for the Eastern District of Missouri. The court declared that the Sherman Act was being violated, and, on November 26, 1920, ordered a permanent injunction granted. 268 Fed. 662. The union appealed to the Circuit Court of Appeals, Eighth Circuit. In a decision rendered on October 19, 1922, a majority of the three judges affirmed the decree of the lower court. The third judge dissented. He declared that the Sherman Act did not reach manufacturing within a state, and asserted that the consequence of the majority's decision would be to render every strike illegal if the entry of any appreciable amount of goods into interstate commerce were affected. United Leather Workers v. Herkert and Meisel Trunk Co., 284 Fed. 446. The union then appealed to the Supreme Court. On June 9, 1924, a majority of the court rendered an opinion reversing the judgment of the lower courts, and declaring that the obstruction to interstate

commerce involved in the strike was too indirect and remote to be considered a violation of the Sherman Act. Justices McKenna, Van Devanter, and Butler dissented. United Leather Workers v. Herkert and Meisel Trunk Company, 265 U. S. 457.

55. *Buyer v. Guillan et al.* The plaintiff, who was engaged in the notion business, had twice taken goods for shipment to the Old Dominion Line, but had had the goods refused because they came on trucks operated by non-union men. Affidavits showed that various unions of teamsters, longshoremen, etc., had agreed not to handle merchandise transported by companies refusing to recognize the unions. A restraining order against the Old Dominion Line, its agents, and the unions, had been granted in the District Court for the Southern District of New York. This order was later vacated in the same court. The plaintiff appealed to the Circuit Court of Appeals, Second Circuit. On February 2, 1921, that court declared that, in view of the Supreme Court decision in the Duplex case, the combination must be held a conspiracy in violation of the Sherman Act. It directed the court below to issue a preliminary injunction. 271 Fed. 65.

56. *Gable et al. v. Vonnegut Machinery Company et al.* A strike was called at the plant of the Toledo Machine and Tool Company for the purpose of preventing open shop operation. The Toledo Company was an Ohio corporation. The Vonnegut Company, an Indiana corporation, complained that the strike interfered with the production of goods which the Toledo Company was under contract to deliver to it, and was thus a conspiracy in violation of the Sherman Act. It secured an injunction against the union and the Toledo Company in the District Court, restraining interference with production. The union appealed to the Circuit Court of Appeals, Sixth Circuit, asserting that the Toledo Company was wrongly made a defendant in order to secure the diversity of citizenship necessary to bring the case into the federal court. The court, on July 19, 1921, declared that the companies should not have been separated, and that the District Court had no jurisdiction by reason of diverse citizenship. It

held also that the strike interfered with interstate commerce so incidentally and indirectly that the Sherman Act was not involved. The decree of the lower court was reversed. 274 Fed. 66.

57-68. Red Jacket Consolidated Coal and Coke Company v. United Mine Workers et al. (The Red Jacket Cases.) On September 30, 1920, the Red Jacket Company sought an injunction against the United Mine Workers in the District Court of the Southern District of West Virginia, charging that the union was engaged in a conspiracy, illegal under the Sherman Act, to restrain interstate commerce in West Virginia coal (Case 57). Similar suits were brought in the same court on September 26, 1921, by the Borderland Coal Corporation (Case 58); on April 8, 1922, by the Alpha Pocahontas Coal Company and 57 other companies (Case 59); on April 4, 1922, by the Aetnae Sewell Smokeless Coal Company and 76 other companies (Case 60); on April 15, 1922, by the Dry Branch Coal Company and 14 other companies (Case 61); on April 24, 1922, by the Nelson Fuel Company and five other companies (Case 62); on May 22, 1922, by the Leevale Coal Company and one other company (Case 63); on June 1, 1922, by the Seng Creek Coal Company and one other company (Case 64); on June 3, 1922, by the Raleigh Wyoming Coal Company and two other companies (Case 65); on June 19, 1922, by the Anchor Coal Company and 67 other companies (Case 66); and on July 4, 1922, by the Southern States Coal Company and seven other companies (Case 67). In all these cases temporary injunctions were issued, which were slightly modified by the Circuit Court of Appeals for the Fourth Circuit. (7 *Law and Labor* 276, November, 1925.) As thus modified the injunctions enjoined the miners from interfering by threats, molestation, or violence with those seeking employment; from trespassing; and from persuading employees to sever their contracts of employment. Keeney v. Borderland Coal Corporation, 282 Fed. 269, June 8, 1922; Dwyer v. Alpha Pocahontas Company and four other cases, 282 Fed. 270, July 19, 1922; United Mine Workers v. Leevale Coal Company, 285

Fed. 32, December 6, 1922. On September 18, 1922, the Carbon Fuel Company and 22 other companies (Case 68) asked for an injunction against the miners and certain operators who had signed agreements, charging a conspiracy in restraint of trade in coal. The court granted the injunction, which restrained the operation of the check-off system. On March 20, 1922, the court also enjoined the union from sending money into West Virginia for the purpose of organization. On March 24, 1922, Judge Waddill of the Circuit Court of Appeals suspended the injunction orders against the check-off and organization. (5 *Law and Labor* 150, June, 1923.) On May 7, 1923, the Court of Appeals directed that an injunction similar to those in the previous cases be issued to the Carbon Fuel Company. In addition the union was to be restrained from keeping strikers in company houses unlawfully. United Mine Workers v. Carbon Fuel Company, 288 Fed. 1020. In May, 1923, the 12 suits here described were consolidated and tried. The District Court rendered a decision on October 16, 1925, holding the union to have conspired to restrain interstate commerce in coal. Separate injunction decrees were issued, the terms of which were those approved by the Circuit Court of Appeals in the Carbon Fuel Company case. The cases were appealed to the higher court, which, on April 18, 1927, rendered a decision affirming the injunctions and approving nearly all of the findings of the District Court. United Mine Workers v. Red Jacket Consolidated Coal and Coke Company and 11 other cases, 18 F. (2) 839. (7 *Law and Labor* 276, November, 1925.) On October 17, 1927, the Supreme Court denied a petition to appeal the case on a writ of certiorari. 72 L. ed. 112.

69. *Borderland Coal Corporation v. United Mine Workers et al.* The company, operating in West Virginia, sought an injunction in September, 1921, against the union and the operators of the Central Competitive Field to restrain the latter from checking-off miners' dues, and the former from using any of its funds to organize the non-union mines in Mingo County, West Virginia, and Pike County, Kentucky. On October 31,

1921, the District Court of Indiana granted a temporary injunction to this effect. The court declared that there was clear evidence of the existence of an unlawful conspiracy between the miners and the union operators to destroy competition in the sale of coal, and that such a conspiracy violated the Sherman Act. 275 Fed. 871. The union thereupon appealed to the Circuit Court of Appeals, Seventh Circuit, which rendered an opinion on December 15, 1921. The court held that the check-off and peaceful attempts to organize were lawful, that an injunction might properly be issued in the present case to prevent injury to property, but that it should restrain only the unlawful acts of the miners. Gasaway v. Borderland Coal Corporation, 278 Fed. 56.

70. *Danville Brick Company v. Danville Local, United Brick and Clay Workers, et al.* As a result of a strike of brick workers in 1921, the company sought and obtained a preliminary injunction in the District Court, Eastern District of Illinois, on June 7, 1921, against certain of the strikers' activities. The sole ground for jurisdiction was the alleged violation of the Sherman Act. The union appealed to the Circuit Court of Appeals, Seventh Circuit, which reversed the decree on July 27, 1922. The court declared that since the strikers had not interfered with transportation, the restraint upon interstate commerce, despite the fact that most of the product was destined to be shipped out of the state, was too insignificant to be covered by the Sherman Act. Danville Local Union, United Brick and Clay Workers v. Danville Brick Company, 283 Fed. 909.

71. *Great Northern Railway Company v. Great Falls Local, International Association of Machinists, et al.* In the course of the shopmen's strike the railroad sought an injunction against the acts, both violent and peaceful, of the strikers, claiming that since the strike was an unlawful interference with interstate commerce in violation of the Sherman Law, all acts done to carry it on were unlawful. The District Court of the District of Montana, in decisions rendered on July 27, 1922, and September 8,

1922, asserted that the interference with interstate transportation was an unintended consequence, and confined the injunction to threats and acts of violence. The court refused to enjoin peaceful persuasion. 283 Fed. 557.

72. *Great Northern Railway Company v. Perkins.* On July 19, 1922, the Great Northern Railway Company brought suit for an injunction in the District Court of the Western District of Washington, against the striking railway shopmen. The defendants were charged, among other things, with a conspiracy in restraint of interstate commerce in violation of the Sherman Act. On July 31, 1922, the court issued a preliminary injunction restraining interference with the company's employees by means of force, threats, suggestion of danger, etc. Loitering and trespassing were also forbidden, and picketing was limited to one representative of the strikers at each entrance to or exit from the company's property. (4 *Law and Labor* 253, September, 1922.)

73. *Chesapeake and Ohio Railway v. Brotherhood of Railway and Steamship Clerks.* During a strike of the railway clerks the railway company, about August 5, 1922, obtained several injunctions in the District Court of the Western District of Virginia. The injunctions were issued on the assumption that the strike violated the Sherman Act. The unionists and all persons "associated with them" were enjoined from "abusing, intimidating, molesting, annoying, insulting, and interfering" with persons seeking employment with, or in the employ of, the company. Thereafter the strikers asked Taliaferro, a barber whose shop was near the freight house, to post a placard in his shop window. This was done. The placard was inscribed, "No scabs wanted in here." Taliaferro was soon after charged with violating the terms of the injunction, and after trial for contempt was fined $200. The court declared that the act of exhibiting the placard tended to restrict interstate transportation. United States v. Taliaferro, 290 Fed. 214. October 2, 1922. Taliaferro appealed to the Circuit Court of Appeals, Fourth Circuit, which, on May 21, 1923, affirmed the judgment of the court below. Though the court did

not mention the Sherman Act it upheld the District Court. Taliaferro v. United States, 290 Fed. 906.

74. *Silverstein v. Local No. 280, Journeyman Tailors' Union.* Silverstein, an employing tailor, sought an injunction against his striking employees on the ground that some of the product normally entered interstate commerce. He charged a conspiracy to violate the Sherman Act. The District Court of the Eastern District of Missouri refused to grant the injunction and the plaintiff appealed to the Circuit Court of Appeals, Eighth Circuit. On October 19, 1922, that court affirmed the lower court's judgment. It asserted that there was no evidence to show that the strikers intended to restrain interstate commerce, and that the strike's effect was not direct or substantial enough to indicate such an intent. 284 Fed. 833.

75. *Curran Printing Company v. Allied Printing Council et al.* A strike took place at the plant of the company, which did a nation-wide business in the printing of railroad tickets. The strike was part of a national campaign of the Typographical Union for a 44-hour week. The company, whose plant was being picketed, applied for an injunction on the ground that the defendants were engaged in a conspiracy in restraint of interstate trade. On March 7, 1923, the District Court in St. Louis rendered an oral opinion in favor of the plaintiff. The court declared that the interference with the company's interstate commerce was appreciable and that the strike, which was one of many then being carried on by the International Typographical Union, was part of a nation-wide combination in violation of the Anti-trust Act. (5 *Law and Labor* 91, April, 1923.)

76. *Western Union Telegraph Company v. International Brotherhood of Electrical Workers, Local Union 134 et al.* This was a suit for an injunction under the Sherman Act against the electricians' union. The company, which operated open shop, employed men who installed call boxes and other devices in buildings under construction. In order to prevent the employment of these non-union men the union threatened to call strikes. The

District Court in Chicago, on July 16, 1924, granted an injunction against the union, on the ground that its activities, by hindering the installation of equipment for the sending of messages, constituted a conspiracy in restraint of interstate commerce. Since diversity of citizenship existed, the court held the injunction desired might be issued to prevent the unlawful boycott as well. The union was ordered not to call strikes or to interfere with the business of the company. 2 F (2) 993. (6 *Law and Labor* 208, August, 1924.) The union appealed to the Circuit Court of Appeals, Seventh Circuit, which rendered a decision on June 1, 1925. That court, making no reference to the allegation with respect to interstate commerce, affirmed the injunction on the basis of the law respecting secondary boycotts. International Brotherhood of Electrical Workers v. Western Union Telegraph Company, 6 F (2) 444.)

77. *Bedford Cut Stone Company et al. v. Journeyman Stone Cutters' Association of North America et al.* Before 1921 the stone cutters' union had operated under agreements with the stone companies about Bedford, Ind. Thereafter it was unable to get the firms to deal with it. In accordance with its rules the union instructed its members not to work on any stone cut under non-union conditions. These instructions were carried out in different parts of the country. The firms, asserting that the union was guilty of a conspiracy in violation of the Sherman Act, asked for a temporary injunction in the District Court of Indiana. The injunction was denied and the plaintiffs appealed to the Circuit Court of Appeals, Seventh Circuit. That court, in a decision rendered on October 28, 1925, affirmed the judgment of the court below. It held that no intention to interfere with interstate commerce appeared, and that the union was within its rights in trying to induce the membership not to handle non-union stone. Though the act might in some degree tend to restrain interstate commerce the appellees had not resorted to unlawful means to accomplish their lawful purpose. 9 F (2) 40. The firms thereupon appealed to the Supreme Court, which, on April 11, 1927,

reversed the judgment of the lower courts. The majority asserted that the union had intended to restrain interstate commerce in the plaintiffs' product, that it had carried on a secondary boycott which violated the Sherman Act, and that it should have been enjoined. Although Justices Stone and Sanford concurred, they did so only because they considered the decision in Duplex v. Deering, 254 U. S. 443, controlling. Justice Brandeis, with whom Justice Holmes concurred, dissented. He declared that the acts of the union did not impose an unreasonable restraint upon interstate commerce and that the case was different from that in Duplex v. Deering. Bedford Cut Stone Company et al. v. Journeyman Stone Cutters' Association et al., 47 Sup. Ct. Rep. 522. An injunction in line with the majority decision was issued by the District Court on October 8, 1927. (9 *Law and Labor* 297, November, 1927.)

78. *Toledo Transfer Company v. International Brotherhood of Teamsters.* The company operated taxicabs in Toledo, Ohio, and had contracts with various railroads to carry passengers from one station to another on through tickets in interstate transportation. The company's drivers struck, picketed the stations and the company's office, and prevented it from carrying on its business. The firm brought suit for an injunction against the union on the ground that the latter was unlawfully restraining interstate commerce. The District Court issued a restraining order, and later a temporary injunction. The court found the existence of an unlawful conspiracy in restraint of interstate commerce. The defendants were enjoined from violent, threatening, and annoying picketing, from loitering, and from interfering with the plaintiff's business. (7 *Law and Labor* 33, February, 1925.)

79. *Columbus Heating and Ventilating Company v. Pittsburgh Building Trades Council et al.* The defendant unions, in order to aid the sheet metal workers in organizing the company's plant in Columbus, Ohio, ordered the employees of the company, a furnace manufacturer, not to work for the firm in Pittsburgh,

and threatened to call a general strike of the building trades if the company continued to carry out its contracts to install furnaces. The District Court of the Western District of Pennsylvania, on February 1, 1927, granted a preliminary injunction against the unions on the ground that their acts constituted a violation of the Sherman Act. They were enjoined from causing sympathetic strikes and from ordering their members not to install the company's furnaces. 17 F (2) 806. (9 *Law and Labor* 52, March, 1927.)

80. Decorative Stone Company v. Building Trades Council of Westchester County et al. The machine stone workers' union, the members of which worked in New York City, refused to work on machine-cut stone if any such stone not manufactured by themselves was also being used on buildings in the city. In order to compel builders to use machine-cut stone only when made by union men in New York it had secured the cooperation of other organizations whose members were actually engaged in construction. The company sued for an injunction and damages under the Sherman Act in the District Court of the Southern District of New York. On March 26, 1927, the court granted an injunction. It asserted that since the purpose of the combination was to exclude stone cut outside the Metropolitan District from that district, there was a clear violation of the Sherman Act. The court denied the request for damages. 18 F (2) 333. The company appealed from this decision to the Circuit Court of Appeals, which, on January 9, 1928, affirmed the opinion of the lower court. It held that the anti-trust laws made no provision for damages in an action for an injunction. (10 *Law and Labor* 54, March, 1928.)

81. Pittsburgh Terminal Coal Corporation v. United Mine Workers et al. The company, in connection with the bituminous coal strike of 1927, sought an injunction which would restrain the union from interfering with its attempt to operate and from aiding the strikers occupying company houses to continue to do so. The company, whose normal output was 12,000,000 tons per year, 70 per cent of which entered interstate commerce, declared that the strike was a conspiracy in violation of the Sherman Law. The District Court, Western District of Pennsylvania, in a decision rendered on September 30, 1927, approved this position, and, assuming jurisdiction under the Sherman Act, issued a preliminary injunction prohibiting further attempts to maintain the strikers' families in company houses, and restricting the strikers' activities to closely regulated peaceful picketing. 22 F (2) 559.

82. *Barker Painting Company v. Brotherhood of Painters', Decorators and Paperhangers.* The Barker company did a painting and decorating business in New York and other states. The union rules required that contractors doing such business must in all places pay the highest wages and operate the fewest hours which were in effect in any of the various places in which they did business; in other words, the most favorable conditions should be in effect wherever the work was done. They were also required to employ workers at least 50 per cent of whom were local residents. The company, while doing work in Washington, obtained a temporary restraining order in the Supreme Court of the District of Columbia against these rules. This injunction was later dismissed and an appeal was taken to the Court of Appeals of the District of Columbia. The plaintiffs claimed that the enforcement of the union rules under penalty constituted a conspiracy in violation of the Anti-trust Law. The court, in a decision rendered November 7, 1927, affirmed the dismissal of the injunction by the lower court, and declared that since the union was lawfully carrying out its legitimate objects, it could not be held to be violating the Sherman Act. 23 F (2) 743.

83. *Aeolian Company et al. v. Fischer et al.* In 1925 the Organ Workers' Union in New York was defeated in a strike for the purpose of organizing the men employed by the organ companies to install organs. The union induced the building trades to refuse to work on buildings in which non-union men installed organs. The companies, asserting that they had plants outside of the state, asked for an injunction on the ground that there was

a conspiracy in restraint of interstate trade and commerce in violation of the Sherman Act. The District Court, Southern District of New York, in a decision rendered on May 15, 1928, refused an injunction, asserting that the defendants' acts, being interferences with the local installation of organs for a purely local purpose, were not reached by the Sherman Act. 27 F (2) 560. The companies appealed to the Circuit Court of Appeals, Second Circuit, which, on December 10, 1928, rendered a majority opinion affirming the decision below. In a dissenting opinion Judge Manton expressed the belief that the acts of the defendants constituted a secondary boycott affecting the interstate sale of organs and constituting a violation of the Anti-trust Act. 29 F (2) 679. After a final hearing the District Court, on October 8, 1929, handed down a decision reaffirming its earlier decision. 35 F (2) 34.

Note. The following cases, coming into the courts after the year 1928, are included here in order that the record may be as complete as possible. They are not covered by the data concerning the number and nature of the various proceedings against labor under the act.

84. Rockwood Corporation of St. Louis v. Bricklayers' Local Union No. 1, 33 F (2) 25. The plaintiff, with a plant at East St. Louis, Ill., manufactured out of gypsum a fire-proof building material which it called Rockwood lumber. Although bricklayers ordinarily installed gypsum blocks this material was made of long slabs, with tongues and grooves, and with joints to be closed plastically. Carpenters began to install the material and as a result a jurisdictional dispute arose between them and the bricklayers. In 1927 a bricklayers' business agent in St. Louis ordered his men off a job if the carpenters continued to install Rockwood lumber. The bricklayers quit work for a short time, after which the carpenters withdrew and the bricklayers went back to work. Though the bricklayers' agent did not request it the plaintiff's material was removed. Thereafter architects, contractors, and builders in St. Louis ceased specifying Rockwood lumber for fear of labor trouble. The company brought a suit for damages and an injunction under the Sherman Act against the bricklayers' union. The District Court of the Eastern District of Missouri refused to uphold the suit on the grounds that the business agent alone was responsible for what happened, that a single person could not be guilty of a conspiracy, and that hence the Sherman Act, which prohibited conspiracies in restraint of interstate commerce, had not been violated. The plaintiff appealed to the Circuit Court of Appeals, Eighth Circuit. On May 13, 1929, that court handed down a decision affirming the judgment of the lower court. 33 F (2) 25. It declared that even if the existence of a conspiracy had been proved it could not be considered a violation of the Act of 1890, since it had no such purpose and since its effect upon interstate commerce was indirect and remote.

85. *Alco-Zander Company et al. v. Amalgamated Clothing Workers of America et al*, 35 F (2) 203. In the summer of 1929 the Amalgamated Clothing Workers brought to a culmination its campaign to organize the Philadelphia clothing market with a series of strikes. On September 4 the complainants, eight firms manufacturing men's clothing in Philadelphia whose employees had gone on strike, filed two bills in equity in the United States District Court of the Eastern District of Pennsylvania against the union and its officers. One of the bills was based on an alleged violation of the Sherman Act, and the other on an alleged violation of the common law. On September 9 the court issued temporary restraining orders substantially as prayed for, which were modified on September 16 to prevent misunderstanding as to their scope. They were intended to prevent various activities carried on in connection with strikes and were especially worded so as to prevent peaceful persuasion. On September 20 it was stipulated that the orders should be deemed preliminary injunctions. The union appealed from the judgment. Thereafter, on October 8, 1929, Judge Kirkpatrick of the District Court handed down a written opinion so that the records might show the rea-

sons for the issuance of the injunctions. 35 F (2) 203. The court, relying principally upon the Supreme Court decision in Hitchman v. Mitchell, asserted that the defendants' acts were in violation of the common law, since they had the unlawful purpose of preventing production in Philadelphia except upon a union basis. Basing its conclusions upon the second Coronado decision, the court declared that the defendants had also violated the Sherman Act. The court had held that the strikes were carried on primarily to prevent non-union clothing manufactured in Philadelphia from competing in interstate commerce with that produced in the union centers. One of the results of the injunctions was the introduction in the United States Senate, by Senator LaFollette, on September 16, 1929, of a resolution authorizing an investigation of the case by the Committee on the Judiciary or a subcommittee thereof. (*Congressional Record*, Vol. 71, p. 3784.) (Such an investigation had not yet taken place in April, 1930.) In March, 1930, it was reported that the eight complainant firms had applied to the courts to dismiss the injunctions against the defendants. It was asserted that all of these firms except the Alco-Zander Company had entered into agreements with the union. As a result Judge Buffington, of the Circuit Court of Appeals, directed that the record of the case be returned to the District Court and the petition for dismissal of the suit be disposed of there. (*Advance*, Vol. XVI, No. 11, March 14, 1930.)

INDEX

Industrial Association of San Francisco, 164, 170

Ingalls, Senator, 21

Ingalls amendment, 21, 22, 25, 40

Injunctions, extent of use of, 218, 219; government suits for, 284; in Bedford Case, 178; in Pullman strike, 66, 69, 70; in shopmen's strike, 141, 144; private suits for, 305

Intent, doctrine of, 197, 199, 200, 202, 226, 235, 236; of Congress in passing Sherman Act, Chaps. I, II, and III, 203, 265, 269

International Railway Co., 186

Interstate commerce, definition of, 194; when illegally restrained, 197, 202

Irving v. Neal, 190, 308

Jewel Tea v. Teamsters, 311

Journeyman Stonecutters' Association, 170, 171, 177, 256

Judiciary Committee, 19, 22, 23, 27, 29, 30, 37, 38, 39, 40, 41, 43, 45, 84, 226

Judiciary Committee bill 28, 29, 31, 32, 34, 37, 38, 39, 42, 51, 84

Jurisdiction of federal courts, 160, 210

Kansas City Southern R. R., 186

Keeney v. Borderland, 133, 314

Kid v. Pearsons, 195

Kirkpatrick, Judge, 250

Knights of Labor, 16, 17

Labor cases, number of, under Sherman Act, 4

Labor exemption provisos, 21, 35, 36, 38, 39, 40, 49, 50, 51, 82, 84

Lamar, 111, 112

Lamar, Justice, 89

Lamar v. U. S., 111, 201

Law and Labor, 213

Lawlor v. Loewe, 87, 102, 301

League for Industrial Rights, 267

Lennon, Commissioner, 5

Lewis, John L., 132

Loewe and Co., 77

Loewe v. Lawlor, 8, 53, 70, 77, 107, 110, 125, 128, 179, 189, 193, 196, 197, 213, 215, 221, 239, 262, 267, 300

Machinists' union, 103, 260

Manton, Judge, 105

Maple Flooring Association v. U. S., 231, 234, 244

Martin, 111, 112

Mason, A. T., 41, 42, 43, 44, 45, 46 n.

McKenna, Justice, 158

McReynolds, Justice, 162

Millwork manufacturers, 161

Mitchell, John, 88, 89

Mitchell v. Hitchman, 307

Montague v. Lowry, 74, 122, 184

Morgan, Senator, 20, 30, 36, 39

Morrison, Frank, 88, 89

Morrow, Judge, 68

Motive, as distinguished from intent, 236

Nash v. U. S., 112, 201

National Association of Window Glass Manufacturers v. U. S., 149, 152, 233, 234, 244, 288

National Fireproofing v. Mason Builders, 306

National Metal Trades Association, 261

New York Central R. R., 144

Non-union goods, refusal to handle or work on, 48, 104, 161, 164, 171, 187, 189, 190, 191, 193, 253, 256, 258, 259

Northern Pacific Railway, 74

Northern Securities v. U. S., 74, 183

O'Brien v. U. S., 147, 186, 187, 294

Olney, Attorney-General, 65

Organization campaigns, 130, 138, 139, 187, 203, 207, 235, 249, 250, 251

Paine v. Neal, 190, 309

Parker, Judge, 136

Peckham, Justice, 80

Pennsylvania Mining Co. v. United Mine Workers, 216, 304